Max Weber's
Comparative-Historical
Sociology

For Claudia

Max Weber's Comparative-Historical Sociology

Stephen Kalberg

The University of Chicago Press

STEPHEN KALBERG is assistant professor of sociology at Boston University

The University of Chicago Press, Chicago 60637
Polity Press, Cambridge, United Kingdom

03 02 01 00 99 98 97 96 95 94   1 2 3 4 5
ISBN: 0-226-42302-6 (cloth); 0-226-42303-4 (paper)

Library of Congress Cataloging-in-Publication Data
Kalberg, Stephen.
  Max Weber's comparative-historical sociology
  Stephen Kalberg
  p. cm.
  Includes bibliographical references and index.
  1. Weber. Max. 1864–1920.   2. Sociology – Germany – History.
I. Title.
HM22.G32W435   1994
302'.0943 – dc 20   93-10012
                                                              CIP

This book is printed on acid-free paper.

Contents

Acknowledgments   viii
List of abbreviations   ix

Introduction   1
  Comparative-Historical Sociology Today: Dilemmas and Problems   3
    World systems theory   4
    The interpretive historical approach   5
    The causal analytic approach   7
  Dilemmas, Problems, and Weber's Contributions   9
    The agency–structure linkage   9
    Multicausality   10
    The level of analysis: theory vs. delineated problems   11
    Model building   12
    The mode of causal analysis   12
  The Secondary Literature: the Weber Renascence   15

Part I Foundational Strategies and Procedures   21

1 The Agency–Structure Linkage: the Pluralism of Motives and
  Weber's Structuralism   23
  The Foundational Components: Methodological Individualism,
    Verstehen, Four Types of Action, and a Pluralism of Motives   24
  Agency and Structure: the Modes of Patterning Action   30
    Orders and legitimate orders   32
    The contextual sociology: sociologial loci for action   39
  The Agency–Structure Linkage   46

2 Weber's Multicausality   50
  The Principled Commitment to Multicausality   52

Social Carriers   58
The Variable Intensity of Action: the Opposition
    to Rational Choice Theory   62
Historical Events, Technology, and Geography   68
Power, Conflict, and Competition   71
    Conflict and competition   75

Part II   The Causal Sociology: Strategies and Procedures   79

3   The Level of Analysis: the Ideal Type   81
    The Aim of Causal Analysis   81
    The Ideal Type   84
        Formation and major features   84
        The yardstick usage: the definition of empirical cases   87

4   Ideal Types as Hypothesis-Forming Models: *Economy
    and Society*   92
    Ideal Types as Dynamic Models   95
        Bureaucracy   95
        Patrimonialism   96
    Ideal-typical Contextual Models   98
    Affinity and Antagonism Models   102
        Intra-domain models of antagonistic relationships   106
        Inter-domain models of affinities and antagonism   108
    Developmental Models   117
        *The closure of social relationships and the routinization of
            charisma models*   120
        Formal and theoretical rationalization models   127

5   The Mode of Causal Analysis Reconstructed:
    Causal Methodology and Theoretical Framework   143
    The Mode of Causal Analysis: an Overview and Comparison
        to Recent Schools   144
        The causal methodology   145
        The theoretical framework   149
    The Mode of Causal Analysis Reconstructed:
        Causal Methodology and Theoretical Framework   151
        Degrees of causality: facilitating and necessary action-orientations   152
        Synchronic and diachronic interactions of action   155
        Conjunctural interactions and the context of patterned action   168

An Illustration; the Dominance of the Caste System in India   177
   Degrees of causal centrality   179
   Synchronic and diachronic interactions of action   186
   Conjunctural interactions of action   190
Conclusion   Max Weber's Comparative-Historical Sociology
           and Recent Schools   193
   An Overview   194
   Setting the Agenda   202

References   206
Index   216

Acknowledgments

This book, a long time in the making, would not have assumed its present form without the assistance of a number of friends and colleagues. I have benefited enormously over the years from their suggestions and owe to all a very deep debt of gratitude. It is a pleasure now to acknowledge these debts.

I am particularly indebted to Robert J. Antonio, who commented in depth upon several earlier and later versions of this study, and to Lewis A. Coser, Anthony Giddens, Constans Seyfarth, Neil Smelser, Hartmann Tyrell, and especially Ira J. Cohen; all read the entire study and offered invaluable suggestions. I am deeply grateful as well to friends who commented upon various chapters, above all Caesar Mavratsas, Guy Oakes, Joachim Savelsberg, Ilana Friedrich Silber, and Willfried Spohn. Josef Chytry offered generous and enduring support. Without the continuous encouragement given by my wife, Claudia Wies Kalberg, this study would never have been completed. It is to her that I owe my deepest debt.

Abbreviations

(All references to Weber's texts give the English translation first, followed by the page numbers of the original German.)

AG   1976. *The Agrarian Sociology of Ancient Civilizations.* Translated by R. I. Frank. London: NLB. Originally: 1924 (1988). Pp. 1–288 in *Gesammelte Aufsätze zur Sozial- und Wirtschaftsgeschichte. Tübingen: Mohr/UTB.*

"AI"   1930 (1958). "Author's Introduction." Pp. 13–31 in *The Protestant Ethic and the Spirit of Capitalism.* Translated by Talcott Parsons. New York: Scribner's. Originally: (1920) 1972. Pp. 1–16 in *Gesammelte Aufsätze zur Religionssoziologie*, vol. I. Tübingen: Mohr.

AJ   1952. *Ancient Judaism.* Translated and edited by Hans H. Gerth and Don Martindale. New York: Free Press. Originally: (1920) 1972. *Gesammelte Aufsätze zur Religionssoziologie*, vol. III. Tübingen: Mohr.

EEWR   *The Economic Ethics of the World Religions.* This is the general title given to the investigations that include "I," "IR," *RofC, RofI*, and *AJ.*

"EK"   (1922) 1973. "Über einige Kategorien der verstehenden Soziologie." Pp. 427–74 in *Gesammelte Aufsätze zur Wissenschaftslehre*, ed. Johannes Winckelmann. Tübingen: Mohr. A partial translation appears in *E&S*, pp. 1375–80.

"EN"   1949. "The Meaning of 'Ethical Neutrality' in Sociology and Economics." Pp. 1–49 in *The Methodology of the Social Sciences.* Translated and edited by Edward A. Shils and Henry A. Finch. New York: Free Press. Originally: (1922) 1973. Pp. 489–540 in *Gesammelte Aufsätze zur Wissenschaftslehre*, ed. Johannes Winckelmann. Tübingen: Mohr.

E&S   1968. *Economy and Society*, ed. Guenther Roth and Claus

Wittich. New York: Bedminster. Originally: (1921) 1976. *Wirtschaft und Gesellschaft*, ed. by Johannes Winckelmann. Tübingen: Mohr.

GAzSW   1924 (1988). *Gesammelte Aufsätze zur Sozial- und Wirtschaftsgeschichte*. Tübingen: Mohr/UTB.

GEH   1927. *General Economic History*. Translated by Frank H. Knight. Glencoe, Il: Free Press. Originally: 1923. *Wirtschaftsgeschichte*, ed. S. Hellman and M. Palyi. München: Duncker & Humblot.

"I"   (1946) 1958. "Introduction" (translated as "The Social Psychology of the World Religions"). Pp. 267–301 in *From Max Weber: Essays in Sociology*, ed. and translated by Hans H. Gerth and C. Wright Mills. New York: Oxford University Press. Originally: (1920) 1972. Pp. 237–68 in *Gesammelte Aufsätze zur Religionsgeschichte*, vol. I. Tübingen: Mohr.

"IR"   (1946) 1958. "Intermediate Reflections" (translated as "Religious Rejections of the World and Their Directions"). Pp. 323–58 in *From Max Weber: Essays in Sociology*, ed. and translated by Hans H. Gerth and C. Wright Mills. New York: Oxford University Press. Originally: (1920) 1972. Pp. 207–36 in *Gesammelte Aufsätze zur Religionsgeschichte*, vol. I. Tübingen: Mohr.

"Logic"   1949. "Critical Studies in the Logic of the Cultural Sciences." Pp. 113–88 in *The Methodology of the Social Sciences*. Translated and edited by Edward A. Shils and Henry A. Finch. New York: Free Press. Originally: (1922) 1973. Pp. 215–90 in *Gesammelte Aufsätze zur Wissenschaftslehre*, ed. Johannes Winckelmann. Tübingen: Mohr.

"Obj"   1949. "'Objectivity' in Social Science and Social Policy." Pp. 50–112 in *The Methodology of the Social Sciences*. Translated and edited by Edward A. Shils and Henry A. Finch. New York: Free Press. Originally: (1922) 1973. Pp. 146–214 in *Gesammelte Aufsätze zur Wissenschaftslehre*, ed. Johannes Winckelmann. Tübingen: Mohr.

PE   1930 (1958). *The Protestant Ethic and the Spirit of Capitalism*. Translated by Talcott Parsons. New York: Scribner's. Originally: (1920) 1972. Pp. 1–206 in *Gesammelte Aufsätze zur Religionsgeschichte*, vol. I. Tübingen: Mohr.

PE II   1907–10 (1972). *Die Protestantische Ethik II: Kritiken und Antikritiken*. Hamburg: Siebenstern.

"PV"   (1946) 1958. "Politics as a Vocation." Pp. 77–128 in *From Max Weber: Essays in Sociology*, ed. and translated by Hans H. Gerth and C. Wright Mills. New York: Oxford University Press. Originally: (1958) 1971. Pp. 505–60 in *Gesammelte Politische Schriften*. Tübingen: Mohr.

RofC   1951. *The Religion of China*. Translated and edited by Hans H. Gerth. New York: Free Press. Originally: (1920) 1972. Pp. 276–536 in *Gesammelte Aufsätze zur Religionssoziologie*, vol. I. Tübingen: Mohr.

RofI   1958. *The Religion of India*. Translated and edited by Hans H. Gerth and Don Martindale. New York: Free Press. Originally: (1920) 1972. *Gesammelte Aufsätze zur Religionssoziologie*, vol. II. Tübingen: Mohr.

R&K   1975. *Roscher and Knies*. New York: Free Press. Originally: (1922) 1973. Pp. 1–145 in *Gesammelte Aufsätze zur Wissenschaftslehre*, ed. Johannes Winckelmann. Tübingen: Mohr.

"Sects"   (1946) 1958. "The Protestant Sects and the Spirit of Capitalism." Pp. 302–22 in *From Max Weber: Essays in Sociology*, ed. and translated by Hans H. Gerth and C. Wright Mills. New York: Oxford University Press. Originally: (1920) 1972. Pp. 207–36 in *Gesammelte Aufsätze zur Religionssoziologie*, vol. I. Tübingen: Mohr.

"SV"   (1946) 1958. "Science as a Vocation." Pp. 129–56 in *From Max Weber: Essays in Sociology*, ed. and translated by Hans H. Gerth and C. Wright Mills. New York: Oxford University Press. Originally: (1922) 1973. Pp. 582–613 in *Gesammelte Aufsätze zur Wissenschaftlehre*, ed. by Johannes Winckelmann. Tübingen: Mohr.

Additional reference to Weber's texts are in the References section.

Introduction

The revival of comparative-historical sociology in recent decades has been influenced only indirectly by Max Weber, even though he created an empirically-based, comparative, and historical sociology of universal breadth and depth. Since his death in 1920, Weber's reputation as the seminal sociologist of our time has continued to grow. In recent years, a worldwide renascence of interest in his writings has called forth a veritable flood of literature on all aspects of his sociology. Nonetheless, even Reinhard Bendix, the author of a distinguished series of empirical investigations that utilize important aspects of Weber (see 1974, 1977, 1978), has been overshadowed by comparative-historical sociologists more indebted to Marxism, such as Barrington Moore and Theda Skocpol, and to Braudellian social history, such as Charles Tilly. Immanuel Wallerstein, who has founded a tremendously influential school, has been influenced by both the Marxian and Braudellian traditions.

To a certain extent, Weber's modest influence upon comparative-historical sociology today can be easily explained. The many accolades that have greeted his works have been unremittingly accompanied by reservation and critique. While acclaimed as unrivaled in breadth and of such grandeur as to dwarf those of many of sociology's other founders, his comparative-historical texts often appear to be spread randomly across the discipline's entire terrain. They span the spectrum from the case study and the emphasis upon values in *The Protestant Ethic and the Spirit of Capitalism* (*PE*) to the universal comparisons and orientation to economic, legal, and rulership variables in *Economy and Society* (*E&S*), *General Economic History* (*GEH*), *The Agrarian Sociology of Ancient Civilizations* (*AG*), and *The Economic Ethics of the World Religions* (*EEWR*).[1]

---

1 The synonymous terms "substantive texts," "empirical works," and "comparative-historical writings" will refer to these works.

Repeatedly, these studies have been judged incomplete and frag-mented,[2] not to mention obtuse and contradictory (Alexander, 1983). This lack of clarity has erected formidable obstacles to their full utilization and contributed to the unusually diffuse character of the Weber reception. Many sociologists today view his comparative-historical sociology in the global terms of "irresistible bureaucratization," "universal rationalization," and the alternation of the "revolutionary force" of charisma with the rou-tine of daily life; others dismiss his substantive texts as incapable of yielding more than a vast inventory of important ideal types (see, for example, Ragin and Zaret, 1983; Skocpol and Somers, 1980). Some commentators place him at the "idealist" end of the spectrum while others locate him firmly at the "materialist" and even "instrumentalist" poles. The unfinished character of his empirical works and their labyrinthine presentation,[3] as well as the delimited aims and purposes each was designed to fulfill at the time of its writing (see Tenbruck, 1975, 1977, 1980, 1986, 1989; Roth, 1979; Schluchter, 1979, pp. 59–64; 1989, pp. 411–72; Winckelmann, 1980, 1986), have as well effectively obscured their contours.

Despite these obstacles, a detailed scrutiny of Weber's comparative-historical writings is now required. These texts offer much more than a series of ideal types or demarcated and problem-based case studies on discrete themes,[4] such as charismatic leadership, power, status honor, mod-ern bureaucracy, and the relationship between religion and the rise of capitalism. Even a focus upon the central theme in his substantive texts – the rise of Western rationalism (see Tenbruck, 1980; Schluchter, 1981; Lash and Whimster, 1987) – does not unveil the basic orientations that undergird these texts: Weber's sociologically rigorous procedures and practiced strat-egies of research.

To systematize and, in some respects, to reconstruct these delimited procedures and strategies constitutes the task of this study. A synthetic reading that unceasingly cross-cuts *PE*, *EEWR*, *E&S*, *GEH*, and *AG* will be necessary. Because these procedures and strategies have never been scruti-

2   To Talcott Parsons, Weber's "work was . . . not a rounded system" (1937, p. 502) and his "social theory remained at his death far more a beginning than an end" (1963, p. xxiv). According to Guenther Roth, "Weber rendered no systematic account of his strategy of comparative study. . . . His works are longish problem-centered research papers" (1968, pp. xxxiii, ci). S. N. Eisenstadt, in noting that Weber's *Ancient Judaism* "did not present an orderly, systematic analytic exposition," comments that this is the case for "almost all of his works" (1981, p. 6).
3   As well as an encumbered writing style and unwieldly mode of presentation. Because translations have been fragmentary and uneven in quality the reader without access to the German texts confronts an additional significant obstacle.
4   Weber's oeuvre is still frequently dealt with as merely a lexicon of useful concepts, few of which are seen as relating to one another. This view pictures Weber as a man endowed with an enormous capacity to classify, conceptualize and systematize – and a desire to do so for itself. Such an explanation of his corpus provides the underlying legitimation for the common procedure of dissecting its separate chapters while leaving the issue of overriding aims, inter-ests, pivotal guideposts, procedures, research strategies, and thematic orientations aside.

nized in detail,[5] this investigation seeks to cast a new light upon his oeuvre.

It has, however, a further aim. This study attempts as well to examine Weber's empirical works in a manner that clarifies their present-day utility to comparative-historical sociologists. Despite their broad appeal and capacity to generate innovative research, contemporary approaches to comparative-historical sociology have been unable to surmount a series of fundamental dilemmas and problems. If the full analytic power of Weber's substantive writings is rendered in an accessible form, it will be seen to offer a much needed and distinct contribution to comparative-historical sociology today. In doing so, it promises to strengthen this sub-discipline of sociology. Thus, on the basis of a detailed analysis of the procedures and research strategies Weber actually employs in his substantive texts, this study aims to address dilemmas and problems widespread in comparative-historical sociology today. What are Weber's contributions? In many ways his works provide perspectives neglected by contemporary approaches; in other ways they suggest trenchant criticisms. In what ways can the procedures and research strategies suggested by Weber's empirical writings be utilized profitably now?[6] The major contours of prominent approaches in comparative-historical sociology today, including the dilemmas and problems each confronts, must be examined briefly at the outset.

Comparative-Historical Sociology Today: Dilemmas and Problems

Structural functional theories of political development constituted the dominant macro paradigm in American sociology of the fifties and sixties (see, for example, Hoselitz, 1960; Hoselitz and Moore, 1963; Parsons, 1966, 1971; Levy, 1966; Almond and Coleman, 1960; Almond and Powell, 1966). The Parsonsian foundation of these theories oriented "modernization studies" toward assessment of empirical movement in various nations along pathways demarcated by a set of dichotomous "pattern variables" (particularism/universalism, ascription/achievement, diffuseness/specificity, and affect/affect neutrality). All retained a strongly evolutionary emphasis and a concern with "integration," "strain," and "differentiaton." The Parsonsian legacy is highly visible in two of the most celebrated studies of this period. Eisenstadt's *The Political Systems of Empires* (1963) argues for the power of a structural-functionalist model to explain the origin, rise, and fall of a number of centralized and bureaucratically-organized historical

---

5 For a commentary upon the secondary literature on Weber see pp. 15–19 in this chapter. This literature is addressed throughout this study also in the notes.

6 This focus upon the present-day utility of Weber's empirical works and their contributions to comparative-historical sociology does not imply that Weber's weaknesses will be neglected. They, as well as the fact that his definition of the task of sociology diverges sharply from the positivist definition that reigns today, will be noted.

empires; Smelser's *Social Change in the Industrial Revolution* (1959) deduces a theory of working-class protest from Parsons's theory of action and seeks its confirmation through empirical evidence that reveals structural change in the family and the organization of the British cotton industry.

Characteristic of all modernization studies was an abstract level of analysis on the one hand and hypothesis-testing of a pre-formulated theory on the other hand. All became the subject of a sustained critique during the late sixties. The global models of overriding societal differentiation, economic growth, and modernization they formulated were roundly condemned as too ahistorical and static (see, for example, Bendix, 1968, 1977b; Collins, 1968). By the mid-seventies, numerous critics had themselves begun to produce an entire body of more historically-informed studies that stood explicitly in opposition to structural functionalism's stage models. To this day, the revival of the "generally historical" remains strong in comparative-historical sociology (Tilly, 1984, p. 79), as does a protest against the "dogma of universality" (Skocpol, 1984, p. 376) and all advocates of "differentiation as a progressive master process" (see Tilly, 1984, pp. 43–50).

Yet the broad discontent failed to congeal into a single current, even as a renewed interest in comparative-historical work continued to spread in the seventies and eighties across the discipline. Although comparative-historical sociologists today avoid treating social change simply by reference to a series of stages and aim to "give history its due," no new consensus has crystallized. Three competing approaches stand opposed to one another.[7]

World systems theory

World systems theory has been prominent since the early seventies (see, for example, Wallerstein, 1974, 1979, 1980, 1984, 1989; Bergesen, 1983; Hopkins, 1982; Goldfrank, 1979; Hopkins and Wallerstein, 1980; Rubinson, 1981). Having derived the existence of a "world economy" logically rather than empirically (see Wallerstein, 1974, pp. 8, 346–57), Wallerstein explains particular historical developments by reference to the structural variables of his world systems model; for example, urbanization, capital accumulation, and political stability. The divergent fates of entire geographical regions are then explained in terms of their location and functional relationship to the single and cohesive international marketplace. Once the location of the particular country in the "core," "periphery" or "semi-periphery" of the world system has been established, the key to an understanding of its major characteristics has been discovered. In other words, because the particular histories, cultures, and social organization of single countries merely "illustrate the general features of the world system" (Ragin and Chirot, 1984, pp. 304–5), the connections and relationships of

7 I will be using the terms "approaches," "perspectives," and "schools" synonymously. See Skocpol and Somers, 1980; Bonnell, 1980; Skocpol, 1984a, 1984b; Tilly, 1984.

each to the world system comprise the primary subject of investigation. The operation and laws of the world system constitute the theoretical model in reference to which particular cases are to be surveyed and their defining features explained.

The examination of history through the lens of a particular conceptual scheme constitutes the foremost concern of all who utilize the world systems approach. A demonstration of a model's validity is sought. Many problem-oriented comparative-historical sociologists today contest this use of the empirical material. Their strong reaction follows directly from a polar opposite aim: they seek to provide an historically-grounded causal analysis of specific cases. The confirmation of a theory's explanatory power, however contextual the empirical research may be, fails to constitute for them a causal explanation; rather, a detailed accounting of specific historical cases, developments, and problems is preferred. Uniqueness, historical circumstances, and well-defined processes are emphasized.

Thus, the critics prefer to chart the complexities of a small number of distinct cases and to carry out careful comparisons in order to isolate particularity. Whenever sociologists gather data by reference to a pre-formulated theory, a neglect of that which is most important to these comparative-historical sociologists occurs: the specific cultural, political, and economic forces within which social phenomena are situated and endowed with significance. However, and despite their common focus upon delineated problems and opposition to all theory-centered strategies to establish causality, the critics divide into two distinct camps: the *interpretive historical* and *causal analytic* schools.[8]

The interpretive historical approach

The particular case itself – its integrity, complexity, historical development, and social context – constitutes the focus of the interpretive historical approach. Delimited concepts closely bound to empirical events are constructed. Having examined each irreducible case carefully in reference to a guiding concept, question, or theme, historical interpretation seeks, rather than the formation of cross-case causal relationships, to compare and contrast cases one with another. This method of "contrasting concepts" (Bendix and Berger, 1970; Bendix, 1976) yields an accurate isolation of the unique aspects and multiple lines of causality of *each* case. In the process, its embeddedness in particular contextual forces is illuminated. Particularity is highlighted.

Thus, rather than the testing of hypotheses or the formation of theoretical statements or causal models, the interpretive historical school focusses upon the accurate construction of concepts and reconstruction of cases. Causal statements, it is argued, must apply only to the development of the

8   These terms are from Skocpol (1984a).

case itself; they are formulated from the fullness of the historical detail and chronology of events provided rather than by reference to a rigorous causal methodology and the testing of alternative hypotheses. Proponents of the interpretive historical approach refuse to construct, on the basis of the cases studied, general causal statements and propositions.

In *Kings or Peoples*, Bendix (1978) takes authority as his central concept and, through detailed examinations of its manifestations in the English, French, German, Japanese, and Russian cases, articulates clear definitions. Utilizing the concept as an orienting device that enables assessments of the significance of discrete historical events, he then traces the specific fate of authority in various countries, some of which experienced a transformation from rulership by kings to rulership by people. Orienting questions are asked in respect to each nation, yet no assumptions are made regarding outcomes. By proceeding in this comparative manner, Bendix seeks to define the distinguishing characteristics of the several countries that successfully implemented parliamentary government, yet he also allows for the possibility of, and freely expects to find, divergent pathways (see also Bendix, 1974, 1977a, 1984).

As Charles Tilly notes, Bendix's comparisons serve the purpose of "individualizing" the case focussed upon, rendering it more "visible" and preserving its historical particularity (Tilly, 1984, p. 82; see also Bendix, 1977a, pp. 16–17; 1974, 1984). Indeed, because he refuses to approach his subject from the vantage point of broad postulates, he argues that no clear set of conditions in the "rule by kings" epoch foreordained a successful transition to the "rule by people" era (see Bendix, 1976, p. 247). On the contrary, he takes pains to stress that, when examined in depth, a great variety of patterns characterizes authority in the name both of people and of kings (1978, p. 5). However, once such comparative studies have elucidated detailed contexts and the major features and boundaries of each case, causal inferences, *for these cases*, can be drawn.

Tilly is also a distinguished proponent of the interpretive historical approach and opponent of all generalizing strategies. Indeed, he calls for an even more "concrete," historically-grounded level of analysis than that typical in Bendix's research (see Tilly, 1984, pp. 82–96). Not an orientation to elite status groups, forms of rulership, and beliefs characterizes his investigations, as for Bendix, but a focus upon, for example, taxation, strikes and collective violence, military service, war-making, the accumulation of capital, and the mobilization of "ordinary people" in respect to beliefs (see 1984, pp. 60–5, 142–3). Tilly searches continuously for covariation, yet, for him as for Bendix, such relationships can result only from the empirical material. Cross-national comparisons serve, in his investigations, to render concepts more precise and to isolate case-specific causal relationships (see also, for example, Tilly, Tilly, and Tilly, 1975). The first task is "to get the history right" in respect to the small number of cases focussed upon (see 1984, pp. 76–7, 79, 143). The Tillys' *Rebellious Century* (1975), for example, investigates fluctuations in popular collective violence in reference to the development of the state and capitalism in three countries: Italy, France, and Germany. Charles Tilly in particular emphasizes the importance of focussing upon a small number of cases and carrying out historically-grounded comparisons regarding quite tangible factors.

Bonnell and Mann also undertake studies that utilize the interpretive historical approach. In an effort to assess the degree of worker organization among urban workers in pre-revolutionary Russia, Bonnell (1983) examines primary sources and makes delimited comparisons to workers in Western Europe. Michael Mann (1986), in a sweeping analysis that begins with Neolithic times, addresses the character of power and its sources. Among more recent comparative-historical sociologists, Bendix, Tilly, Bonnell, and Mann seem to pay the highest respect to history.[9]

The causal analytic approach

Although both the interpretive historical and causal analytic schools stand opposed to the theorizing of the world systems approach, adherents of the causal analytic school are less cautious regarding causal statements than their interpretive historical colleagues. Whereas Bendix, Tilly, and other interpretive historical practitioners wish mainly to isolate the uniqueness of each case through comparisons and contrasts, and do so by utilizing a guiding theme, concept, or question alone as a theoretical framework, causal analytic practitioners take as their aim the construction of explanatory theories. In doing so, however, they abjure a move to the other end of the spectrum and the formulation of invariant causal laws; rather, the detailed examination of empirical cases serves as the foundation for their theories. Moreover, and again unlike adherents of the interpretive historical approach, their construction of causal arguments is guided by explicit research designs that aim to demarcate sources of variation and to produce valid inferences despite small numbers of cases. Through the utilization of the causal methodology provided by Mill's methods of "difference" and "agreement" (Mill, 1843), or combinations of both, attempts at controlled comparisons are undertaken in order to establish likely causes and to formulate theoretical conclusions. Barrington Moore (1966) and Theda Skocpol (1979; Skocpol and Weir, 1984) are prominent practitioners of this school.

Moore attempts to identify the determinants of long-term developmental paths toward three political outcomes: democracy, fascism, or communism. He takes as his focus the question of whether the landed classes – peasants as well as lords – reacted to changes in the organization of agricul-

9 See also e.g. Starr (1982), Schwartz (1976), Aminzade (1981), and Traugott (1985). Thompson (1966) and Geertz (1971) are also distinguished proponents of the interpretive historical approach.

ture in a manner that facilitated mass participation in political decision-making processes. Systematic comparisons, each undertaken in order to isolate specificity and expose differences in the historical experiences of eight nation-states, are carried out. Throughout, historical narrative and contextual comparisons across cases serve a larger purpose: to delineate the causes for the varying outcomes. Diverse models of the extent of the commercialization of agriculture, the strength of the bourgeoisie, and the relationship of peasants to landlords and landlords to the bourgeoisie are formulated, and these are examined in relation to the development of the three political routes. By investigating each route, Moore erects a causal thesis and argues, in reference to two or three specific cases, for its superior explanatory power. Plausible alternative explanatory hypotheses are continuously addressed as he assembles the historical material, yet reference to differences among the cases allows their dismissal. Causal theories for the separate developmental paths are then constructed. Comparisons of cases across the three routes serve to illuminate the particular features of the divergent developmental routes and to provide evidence for the causal argument. To Moore, such procedures "may lead to new historical generalizations" (1966, p. xiii) and provide a "hope of discerning general causes" (1966, p. xiv).

On the basis of in-depth comparisons and contrasts of successful (France, China, and Russia, 1917) and failed social revolutions, Skocpol (1979) seeks to isolate features common to the successful cases. In doing so, she aims to provide a causal theory.

By identifying conditions favorable to social revolutions, she investigates on the one hand crises in the relationships of states to the landed upper classes and/or the agrarian economy (contrasts drawn to the Meiji Restoration and reform movements in Prussia), and on the other hand the extent to which certain types of agrarian structures and peasant uprisings appear (contrasts drawn to the English revolution and the 1848 German revolution). Comparisons across those societies that underwent revolutionary crises are undertaken in order to identify, despite clear differences, causal similarities (Mill's method of agreement). The uniqueness of the successful cases is isolated further first by specific contrasts between China, France, and Russia in 1917 and then through repeated contrasts to those countries that, despite significant structural similarities, did not experience successful social revolutions (Mill's method of difference). Contrasts drawn to the unsuccessful control cases assist her as well to verify an overall causal hypothesis: namely, that the state – national politics and its capacity to coerce – must be viewed as a viable and independent actor in such revolutions. Indeed, Skocpol aims to define necessary and even sufficient causes, and thereby to establish "valid, complete explanations of [social] revolutions" (1979, p. 5).[10]

10   For measured critiques, see e.g. Tilly (1984, pp. 109–15), Sewell (1985), Nichols (1986), and Burawoy (1989).

Thus, both Moore and Skocpol, as well as other adherents of the causal analytic approach,[11] utilize research design procedures in order to attain their aim of testing causal hypotheses and generating new explanatory generalizations. This aim, and their causal methodology, separate them from the interpretive historical school, which conveys causality through a detailed chronicle of events and limits causal explorations to statements about the case. Citing the impossibility of controlled comparisons, proponents of the interpretive historical school renounce the formulation of even limited causal generalizations as well as a research design methodology. Themes, concepts, and questions alone provide a framework for their investigations.

The world systems, interpretive historical, and causal analytic schools are now the dominant approaches in comparative-historical sociology.[12] However, and despite their widely acknowledged contributions, these schools leave unsolved a number of dilemmas and problems. In many ways, the procedures and practiced strategies of research that underlie Weber's substantive texts contribute to their resolution. What are these dilemmas and problems? If Weber's capacity to address these dilemmas and problems is demonstrated, his utility to present-day comparative-historical sociologists will become apparent.

Dilemmas, Problems, and Weber's Contributions

The agency–structure linkage

Proponents of the world systems, interpretive historical, and causal analytic approaches never articulate explicit mechanisms to link agency and structure. Micro–macro linkages of any sort do not characterize their investigations. Subjective meaning and the variable intensity of social action play no part in their analyses.

For Weber, a clear analysis of the linkage between individual action and social structure constitutes a central task of an historically-informed sociology. He provides explicit procedures, concepts, and strategies in this regard; they are turned to in chapter 1. Separate sections examine foundational components of Weber's sociology: his "methodological individualism," "four types of social action," notion of *Verstehen*, and emphasis upon a pluralism of motives. This chapter then addresses the three "modes of patterning action" that, for him, tie agency to structure: "orders," "legiti-

11   Walton (1984) studies the causes of national revolts in the developing countries; Calhoun (1982) investigates "populist" movements in late eighteenth and early nineteenth century England and their stance in respect to the emerging industrial society; and Hamilton (1977) provides a comparative analysis of the resistance of the Chinese in the nineteenth century to foreign goods. See also Goldstone (1983, 1987, 1991), Downing (1988), and Brenner (1976).
12   Further major features of these schools will be discussed in each chapter below.

mate orders," and "sociological loci for action." Comparisons between these aspects of Weber's comparative-historical sociology and recent schools are undertaken throughout this chapter.

Multicausality

Proponents of the interpretive historical approach alone, among contemporary comparative-historical sociologists, advocate a broad multicausal approach. These practitioners, and especially Charles Tilly, establish causality from a detailed richness of description. While Weber also strongly upholds a radically multicausal mode of procedure, his axiom of "value-relevance," understanding of social reality as inexhaustible, and utilization of ideal types lead him to oppose in principle the establishment of causality in this fashion.

Neither the world systems nor the causal analytic approaches adheres to a broadly multicausal methodology. World systems theorists stress the causal priority of a single variable: the international economy. Different constraints are placed upon a nation's development depending upon whether it is located in the core, periphery, or semi-periphery, and these constraints are viewed as decisive for industrial development. In testing alternative hypotheses, and even though not constrained by their Millian research design methodology to downplay multiple causes, adherents of the causal analytic school invariably fail in practice to uphold broadly multicausal procedures. Structural forces, primarily class relations and the state, are emphasized. Moore's structuralism emphasizes classes, changes in class structures, and the interests of ruling classes; he pays little attention to the family, religious beliefs, or culture in general. Similarly, in focussing upon national politics and in seeking to provide a structural analysis of the ways in which states act independently, Skocpol downplays these same factors.[13] Characteristic of the causal analytic school is the assumption that a particular institution, such as the state or the economy, can be accorded in general a position of causal priority.

Weber's sociology, on the other hand, insists upon a principled and radical multicausality. Cultural forces, in particular, are awarded equal weight. The investigation, for example, of all enduring forms of rulership and economic organization must include, he argues, reference to the beliefs and values that legitimate these "structures." Indeed, an array of forces are accorded, in Weber's substantive analyses, causal status, including, for example, laws, religions, rulership (*Herrschaft*),[14] status groups, historical

13 Skocpol has, on occasion and in respect to particular cases only, acknowledged the importance of culture. See, for example, her examination of the Iranian Revolution (1982).
14 This translation of *Herrschaft*, suggested by Benjamin Nelson, is preferred throughout over "authority" or "domination."

events, technological innovations, geography, power, conflict, and competition.The elevation of any particular factor to a position of general causal priority is adamently rejected. Moreover, unlike contemporary approaches, Weber explicitly argues that patterned action-orientations may vary in intensity; he presents "the Protestant ethic thesis" as an example of the manner in which just such variation may have significant sociological consequences. Weber also insists upon the centrality of "social carriers." His broad multicausality and its contribution to contemporary approaches constitutes the subject of chapter 2.

The level of analysis: theory vs. delineated problems

In directly reacting against the overly abstract and ahistorical character of earlier structural–functional schools of modernization and political development, proponents of the causal analytic and interpretive historical approaches have moved far in the direction of an historically-informed level of analysis. Their studies focus upon specific problems and investigate a small number of cases in a detailed fashion. A great sensitivity to time, place, and context is typical, as is an attempt to view cases as discrete and to acquire concrete knowledge of them. No preference reigns to see cases as derivatives or exemplars of an overarching developmental tendency. Accordingly, the complex historical development of each case, as well as its contextual embeddedness in the unique features of its particular epoch and setting, can be emphasized. The world systems school, on the other hand, constructs a pre-formulated theory. The many detailed and highly historical case studies carried out by proponents of this approach serve the purpose of substantiating its basic tenets regarding the character of the world economy and the constraints it places upon nations.

Weber rejects in principle this either/or alternative: the focus of the causal analytic and interpretive historical approaches upon delineated problems and the world systems school upon a theory. Although his empirical sociology shares with all recent approaches an appreciation for historically-informed studies and a preference to explore discrete problems, it articulates a level of analysis distinct from all three schools. It is demarcated, throughout his comparative-historical texts, by his major heuristic tool: the ideal type. Chapter 3 examines the formation, major features, and most fundamental usage of the ideal type: to define clearly empirical cases. Weber provides specific procedures and strategies to do so. Indeed, his three-volume analytic treatise, *E&S*, constructs a range of ideal types to assist the precise definition, clear conceptualization, and causal analysis of sociologically-significant cases. A detailed discussion of the methodological questions surrounding the definition of empirical cases is neglected by the world systems, interpretive historical, and causal analytic schools.

Model building

Hypothesis-forming models, as an integral aspect of comparative-historical research strategies, are downplayed by all contemporary schools. Mechanisms to establish the analytic location of cases and developments or to provide a rigorous theoretical framing of empirical questions and problems are never articulated by the world systems, interpretive historical, and causal analytic approaches. Weber, on the other hand, in *E&S* proclaims model building to be an indispensable and pivotal component of the comparative-historical enterprise.

The models of *E&S* seek to orient comparative-historical research away from the establishment of causality solely through the detailed, historical studies of the interpretive historical and causal analytic schools. As ideal types, they stand as well opposed to the pre-formulated theory of the world systems approach. The definition, conceptual framing, and empirical investigation of cases, relationships, and developments is not facilitated, in these approaches, by "working tools" comparable to the models of *E&S*. By offering "limited analytic generalizations" and formulating delineated, empirically-testable causal hypotheses, Weber's models further define comparative-historical sociology as separate from all problem-focussed approaches on the one hand and theory-centered approaches on the other hand. Each model is designed to *engage*, even constrain, comparative-historical researchers in a perpetual back and forth movement between the empirical case, relationship, or development under investigation and a conceptual framework. As such, each injects a theoretical dimension that hinders deep immersion in empirical realities.

Chapter 4 scrutinizes the extensive model building capacity of *E&S*. "Dynamic," "contextual," "elective affinity," "antagonism," and "developmental" models are systematized from this treatise and, in some cases, reconstructed. Among the latter, the "routinization of charisma" and formal rationalization models are perhaps best known.

The mode of causal analysis

Among contemporary approaches, only the causal analytic school provides a clear causal methodology. For interpretive historical practitioners, concepts, general questions, and themes alone guide research; a detailed and rich narrative offers causal explanations. Explicit causal procedures are neglected. Proponents of the world systems approach also fail, owing to their reliance upon a pre-formulated theory, to formulate a causal methodology. The focus of their studies – the development of the capitalist economy – is investigated by reference to a pre-defined world economy. Causal forces are assumed to emanate from this economy.

Conversely, the causal analytic school forcefully articulates procedures and strategies in respect to the issue of causality. The formation of causal hypotheses guides its investigations. The testing of hypotheses, the controlling of variables, and the construction of explanatory theories capture its attention. A rigorous comparative mode of analysis in the form of experimental design procedures and an entire vocabulary of causality stand at the forefront, as well as the goal of formulating, from separate cases, generalizable conclusions.

While Weber would view the omission of an explicit causal methodology by the interpretive historical and world systems schools as a serious problem, he also opposes vehemently the causal analytic approach. He would welcome its rigorous methodology and attention to contexts and even conjunctural interactions, yet criticize its insufficiently multicausal character. On the basis of his conceptualization of societies as only loosely held together, as fragmented along myriad fault lines, and as comprised of endlessly intermingling and ceaselessly jockeying patterns of action, Weber argues that *hosts of* interactive influences are very often effective causal factors. A given effect in principle may result from a variety of action-orientations. Not only must multivocal synchronic (within the present) and diachronic (between past and present) interactions be acknowledged, as is often done in an unsystematic fashion by practitioners of the causal analytic approach; particular attention must be paid as well to the manner in which precisely the interaction of *multiple* forces itself places an independent causal thrust into motion. Only a causal methodology capable of conceptualizing clearly broad hosts of forces and the conjunctural interaction between them can begin, Weber argues, to justify the complexity of empirical reality. Only then can the intricate interweavings of, for example, values, traditions, interests, power, and rulership in different synchronic and diachronic settings be clearly understood. Moreover, unlike all three contemporary schools, Weber's methodology distinguishes between "facilitating" and "necessary" degrees of causality.

He points also to a further basic weakness in the methodology of the causal analytic school, one already mentioned: it remains, like the interpretive historical approach and despite its utilization of research design procedures, problem-focussed. Weber's mode of causal analysis includes not only ideal types, research design procedures, and a three-stage causal methodology, but also orientational constructs that offer a *theoretical framework*. Yet this frame of reference, which is formulated in *E&S*, diverges drastically from that offered by the world systems approach. It remains, through its ideal types, ultimately anchored in empirical reality and, in emphasizing an *array* of "societal domains" and the causal significance of domain-specific ideal types, precludes the elevation of a single realm, such as the economy, to a level of causal superiority.

Unfortunately, Weber's mode of causal analysis, which stands at the very center of his entire comparative-historical sociology, is never articulated. Although the major aim of his substantive sociology is to provide causal explanations of cases and developments, he failed to expound upon either his multicausal, contextual, and conjunctural procedures and strategies or his domain-based theoretical framework in his methodological essays in a systematic manner. Nor do his empirical writings demonstrate, in this regard, consistency. Moreover, the fragmented character of his substantive texts often conceals their conceptual and empirical precision. Incomplete as now available, the mode of analysis underlying his causal investigations must be reconstructed from a detailed and synthetic reading of his empirical works. This is the task of chapter 5.

This chapter also, in order to illustrate the rigor of his mode of causal analysis, turns to an example from his texts. His analysis of the rise to dominance of the caste system in India is reconstructed by reference to (*a*) the major stages, procedures, and strategies of his practiced causal methodology, (*b*) the theoretical framework provided by the *E&S* societal domains and domain-specific ideal types, and (*c*) historical forces unique to the case under investigation.

In sum, a number of problems and dilemmas confront comparative-historical sociology today. In seeking to render accessible the major procedures and strategies for the conduct of comparative-historical research concealed within Max Weber's convoluted and fragmentary empirical works, this study strives to demarcate the precise ways in which Weber contributes to the resolution of these problems and dilemmas. A systematization – and, in some respects, a reconstruction – of the basic orientations of Weber's substantive texts is undertaken. This study examines his agency–structure linkages and principled multicausality, and the manner in which these texts, through the formation of ideal types and delineated models, overcome the frequent contemporary reliance upon cases and historical narrative. Weber's empirical works as well insist upon the theoretical framing of problems and stress a contextual-conjunctural mode of causal analysis. In many respects the procedures and strategies of research he offers, as a consequence on the one hand of their original tenets and on the other hand of the severe criticisms of contemporary schools of comparative-historical sociology they imply, contribute significantly toward a strengthening of this sub-discipline.

A dialogue between Weber's substantive sociology and recent comparative-historical schools is cultivated in each chapter throughout this study. Even those sections that offer a detailed exegesis aim not simply to render clearly Weber's texts, but to establish securely his contribution to the contemporary comparative-historical endeavor.[15] The concluding chapter compares, in summary fashion, the major procedures and re-

15 The notes, as well as occasionally the text (see chapter 2, pp. 62–8), include Weber's criticisms of rational choice theory.

search strategies of Weber's comparative-historical sociology to those of contemporary approaches. It also recapitulates Weber's uniqueness and contributions.

Weber's comparative-historical sociology diverges from recent schools in a further, as yet unmentioned, fashion: contemporary schools omit a universal dimension. They focus upon political modernization and social movements, and themes such as modern social revolutions, totalitarianism, the power of the nation-state, and the transformations over the last few centuries in the West to capitalism, democracy, and industrial societies.[16] Weber's substantive texts are distinct in moving beyond such themes. He turned his attention in *E&S* and *EEWR* on the one hand back to the Middle Ages and ancient Occidental civilizations and on the other to China and India. In compiling these tomes, as well as *AG* and *GEH*, Weber moved freely, for example, from the early Hindus and the Old Testament prophets to the Confucian literati, from Hellenism to the decline of the Roman empire, from Chinese monarchical rulership (patrimonialism) and Indian feudalism to the Western Middle Ages, from the economic organization of early Near Eastern civilizations to the medieval trading companies, and from the ancient Germanic social structure to the origins of continental law and a comparative analysis of the rise of the modern state. Empirical investigations of such a comparative and historical sweep are unrivalled in contemporary comparative-historical scholarship. Weber's universal range will be noted in numerous illustrations throughout this study.

One final task must be addressed in this introduction. How does this study diverge from previous commentaries upon Weber? It aims, in every chapter, to contribute to the secondary literature. The tenor of recent commentaries on Weber must be briefly sketched.

The Secondary Literature: the Weber Renascence

A summary of Weber's varied empirical works is not undertaken here, nor is this study designed to offer a general introduction to them (see Bendix, 1962; Freund, 1969; Käsler, 1988; Collins, 1986a). It also does not seek to identify a single main theme, as do Hennis (1983, 1987a, 1987b) and Tenbruck (1980), that unifies his diverse writings.[17] Nor does this study aim to argue that a single text can be viewed as Weber's "major work," as does Tenbruck (1977, 1980, 1989). The focus here upon the basic orientations of Weber's empirical work requires an omission as well of his political views (see Salomon, 1935b; Beetham, 1974; Mommsen, 1985, 1989) and his more

16 Only some of the works of Bendix and Moore are more universal in scope.
17 Neither interpretation has, in my view, successfully demonstrated the existence of such a theme (not least because neither has investigated in detail Weber's substantive works; see Kalberg, 1979).

"social philosophical" writings. Thus, for example, his rather bleak pronouncements regarding the fate of Western civilization and the reasons for
his pessimism are not treated. Weber's works are not addressed here as
social philosophy or social theory in general, but exclusively in terms of
their capacity to formulate a rigorous comparative-historical sociology.
This concern requires also an omission of the intellectual background of
Weber's sociology (see, for example, Scaff, 1989; Hughes, 1958; Coser,
1971; Seidman, 1983; Ringer, 1969; Sica, 1988) and discussions of Weber's
intellectual antagonists (see, for example, Tenbruck, 1959; Mommsen and
Osterhammel, 1987; Albrow, 1990, pp. 96–113; Burger, 1976, pp. 3–55;
Oakes, 1989). This study avoids as well a popular theme: Weber's biography
(see, for example, Marianne Weber, 1975; Gerth, 1946; Käsler, 1988) and
his internal tensions (see, for example, Albrow, 1990, pp. 13–94; Green,
1974; Goldman, 1988; Mitzman, 1970; Sica, 1988).

In many ways, Reinhard Bendix's classic book (1962) stands as an inspiration for this study. *Max Weber: an Intellectual Portrait* offers an indispensable treatment of a broad range of subjects in Weber's empirical sociology.
Its summaries in respect to a vast array of issues and problems remain
unsurpassed. Moreover, Bendix's study is guided by an overall question
that stands as well at the foundation of this investigation: the extent to
which, and in what ways, Weber's substantive sociology assists our understanding today (see, for example, pp. 464–5). Bendix, however, also serves
as a foil for this investigation. If scrutinized in reference to the tasks of this
study, certain limitations are revealed. Above all, he views Weber primarily
as an historical sociologist rather than as also a rigorous sociological
theorist. While helpful in many ways, this perspective causes Bendix to
downplay Weber's strategies and procedures for comparative inquiry.
Bendix scarcely mines the theoretical capital of Weber's empirical
works.

Although in some ways illuminating, the recent secondary literature on
Weber has assisted this study only indirectly. The international Weber
renaissance over the last twenty years has only begun to disclose the basic
orientations of Weber's comparative-historical sociology.

On the one hand, the development of the secondary literature in the
United States away from a Parsons-dominated interpretation that focussed
upon norm-oriented action enabled a more well-balanced assessment to
appear, one that includes the previously downplayed means–end rational
type of social action and the power, rulership, and conflict dimensions
prominent in Weber's sociology (see, for example, Collins, 1975, 1986b;
Fulbrook, 1978; Cohen, Hazelrigg, and Pope, 1975; Molloy, 1980; Antonio,
1984; Bendix and Roth, 1971).[18] On the other hand, the predominant con-

18 Although Weber was in part "rediscovered" in Germany in the 1950s as a result of
Parsons's writings and translations, the German reception of Weber has only rarely been
influenced by Parsons. The prominent exceptions are Schluchter (1981, 1989), Münch (1982,
1984, 1986), and Habermas (1984).

cern in the fifties and sixties with discrete segments of Weber's works – for example, status groups, charisma, ideal types, bureaucracy, and "the Protestant ethic thesis" – has been replaced by a series of commentaries that have taken large sections of the corpus and its broader themes as their foci. All have rejected the older notion that Weber's putatively non-cumulative investigations constitute his most valuable contribution. These interpreters have argued instead that several basic themes and procedures penetrate Weber's entire oeuvre. Their comprehension, it is argued, reveals a theorist of far deeper profoundity: one who dared to cast his attention in a systematic manner beyond delimited analyses and toward the far more complex, and risky, level of long-range change across millennia. These proponents of a "new Weber" have also sought to replace the erroneous though persisting notion that Weber remained primarily an "idealist" with an articulation of the severe tension in his texts between "ideal" and "material" factors.

Their commentaries can be divided into two groups. First, those that address broad and underlying themes that run throughout Weber's works. These studies have surveyed his view of historical change (Abramowski, 1966; Mommsen, 1974a, 1989; Nelson, 1981; Collins, 1986b), Western rationalism (Schluchter, 1979, 1981; Habermas, 1984; Brubacker, 1984; Whimster and Lash, 1987), rationalization processes (Bendix, 1965; Tenbruck, 1980; Münch, 1982; Glassman and Murvar, 1983; Levine 1985; Lash and Whimster, 1987) and the notion of a "type of person" (*Menschentyp*) that resides in particular civilizations (Hennis, 1983, 1987a, 1987b). Second, those that seek to identify typological models and rigorous procedures Weber employs in his substantive sociology (Eisenstadt, 1968; Roth 1968, 1971a, 1971b, 1971c, 1979, 1981; Collins, 1981; Smelser, 1976; Warner, 1970, 1972, 1973; Fulbrook, 1978). All of these commentaries have expanded enormously the understanding of his tasks and purposes.

However, and despite their achievements, these investigations have not gone beyond an outlining of the procedures and research strategies of Weber's comparative-historical sociology. This holds true even in respect to Schluchter's ambitious analysis of "the rise of Western rationalism" (1981). This study is of little assistance to more empirically-oriented sociologists seeking to utilize Weber in their own research. In remaining for the most part at the level of typologies and classifications, Schluchter has provided an interesting taxonomy of the basic concepts Weber employs in his examination of the development of the West, yet he largely neglects the more pragmatically sociological Weber that concentrates upon, for example, agency–structure linkages, pluralistic motives for action, multicausal strategies, hypothesis-forming causal models, power, social carriers, synchronic and diachronic interactions of patterned action, and a contextual and conjunctural causal methodology.

In focussing attention upon the global theme of rationalization and the particularity of the West, the most prominent recent studies have distracted commentators from a scrutiny of the rigorous strategies and procedures

Weber utilizes in his comparative-historical texts.[19] It *is* the case that Weber's interest in a broad and overarching theme – the "specific and peculiar 'rationalism' of Western culture" (*PE*, p. 26/12) and its unique origins and development – stands at the center of his sociology. However, in investigating this theme, he refused to conduct his research by reference to sweeping "disenchantment of the world" and "rationalization processes." Rather, he proceeded at a thoroughly empirically-informed level of analysis and, in a series of studies, attempted to establish causality in respect to delimited cases and developments (see Kalberg, 1989).

Thus, for example, far from emphasizing common features in his discussions of modern states, Weber focusses upon discrete themes central to particular nations, such as the conditions for an effective German imperialism, the possibility for bourgeoise democracy in Russia, the sociological preconditions of American democracy, and the obstacles Germany faced to parliamentary government. The three-volume *EEWR* discusses an array of delineated historical developments, such as the rise in China of patrimonialism, Confucianism, and the literati stratum, the origins in India of "other-worldly" mysticism, the Brahmins, an impersonal deity, and the caste system, and the rise in ancient Israel of the Levite priesthood, monotheism, missionary prophecy, and the Pharisees. *E&S* as well addresses demarcated themes, such as the rise of logical formal law on the European continent and Common Law in England, the appearance and unique features of independent cities in the medieval West, the central characteristics of the various paths to salvation and the major types of rulership, and the development of the Catholic Church as an hierocratic organization. *AG* and *GEH* also offer deeply historically-saturated analyses. Nowhere in these texts does Weber seek to demonstrate societal evolution.[20]

Acknowledgment of this level of analysis requires, at the outset of this systematization and reconstruction of the basic orientations of Weber's substantive texts, a rejection of the common interpretation of Weber as having understood history as following simply a monumental development

19   The secondary literature and its continuing debates cannot be dealt with in a sustained and critical manner. This omission results not only from acknowledgment of the difficulties presented by its sheer massiveness (see Seyfarth and Schmidt, 1982; Murvar, 1983); in addition, doing so would too frequently disrupt the major lines of argumentation. Most importantly, the focus here will be upon Weber's texts rather than issues of interpretation prominent in the secondary literature. Only selected aspects of the secondary literature will be addressed, and these discussions will remain confined for the most part to notes and brief asides in the text. (The notes include a running commentary upon Parsons's reading of Weber.) Finally, this study does not rest on the assumption that a systematization or "reconstruction" of Weber's works requires the assistance of later theorists, such as Parsons, Habermas, or Luhmann (see Schluchter, 1981; Münch, 1982; Habermas, 1984).
20   It is indeed ironic that Weber's view of history was understood for such a long period of time in the United States as "idealistic." This resulted mainly from the popularity of *PE*, the lack of a complete translation of *E&S* until 1968, and the Parsons-dominated reception of Weber. Unfortunately, the articles by Salomon were neglected (1934, 1935a, 1935b, 1945; see Kalberg, 1993b).

anchored at one end by charismatic outbursts against rigid tradition and at the other by the formal rationality of the "bureaucratized society." It also requires dismissal of the widespread view that, for Weber, historical change involves predictable cycles in which the "revolutionary force" of charisma alternates with the routine and stability of everyday life (see, for example, Salomon, 1935b, 1945; Mommsen, 1974a, pp. 18–20; 1987, pp. 47–50). Finally, it leads to an unequivocal rejection of a further familiar misinterpretation: Weber can be best understood as fundamentally an "idealist" who saw values as history's major moving force.

A focus upon such global themes, or, indeed, a general discussion of his central themes and modes of treating them, will not yield an appropriation of the full analytic power of Weber's substantive texts.[21] If the strategies and research procedures that constitute their basic orientations are systematized and reconstructed, a unique, rigorous, and methodologically sophisticated comparative-historical sociology will be unveiled, indeed one of universal range. It promises to contribute significantly toward an overcoming of the dilemmas and problems confronted by comparative-historical sociology today. Largely overlooked to this day, it must be rendered accessible and utilizable.

This study is divided into two major parts. Part I, which examines foundational and general aspects of Weber's comparative-historical sociology, comprises two chapters: "The Agency–Structure Linkage" and "Weber's Multicausality." Part II addresses his overriding goal: the causal analysis of cases and developments. It charts the diverse strategies and procedures offered by his empirical works to ascertain causality: his level of analysis and ideal types (chapter 3), hypothesis-forming models (chapter 4), and mode of causal analysis (chapter 5).

---

21 Because it has moved the understanding of Weber away from a consideration of his works as merely fragmented and opaque, the commentaries on the theme of rationalization have rendered an important contribution (see Nelson, 1974; Tenbruck, 1980; Schluchter, 1981; Lash and Whimster, 1987). I do not mean to denigrate this contribution. It must be emphasized at the outset, however, that this study does not seek to contribute to this body of literature. (I have attempted to do so elsewhere; see Kalberg, 1979, 1980, 1983, 1990, forthcoming c).

PART I

Foundational Strategies and Procedures

PART I

Foundational Strategies and
Procedures

1

The Agency–Structure Linkage: the Pluralism of Motives and Weber's Structuralism

Max Weber's most memorable phrases – "irresistible bureaucratization," "disenchantment of the world," and "universal rationalization" – describe overarching and millennia-long developments. On other occasions he discusses historical change by reference to a continuous alternation between the "revolutionary force" of charismatic leadership and the enduring powers of everyday routine, traditional action, and bureaucratic forms of organization.

However intriguing, these themes do not represent the sociological precision characteristic of Weber's substantive writings.[1] This remains the case even though each constitutes a major component in his sociology. Weber clearly, for example, sees epochal movements in history and wishes to investigate the question of the origins of Western "rationalism." Nonetheless, a close reading of his empirical works leads to the conclusion that their strategies and procedures cannot be described in these terms. Weber's texts stay at a far less general level of analysis and depict historical development as far more complex than an evolutionary unfolding of ideas and values or a confrontation of charismatic leaders with stable forces. These texts remain consistently bound to delimited themes, problems, and developments, and far removed even from the global level of "society"; indeed, he scarcely uses the term (see Kalberg, 1989).[2]

1 Notably, rather than appearing in Weber's comparative-historical texts, such phrases are found almost exclusively in three particular contexts: the more social philosophical essays, such as "SV" and "PV," the political writings, and the concluding paragraphs of his substantive writings, such as *PE*.
2 I have found only two usages, both in *E&S*. One concerns stratification (p. 306/180) and the other the relations between the economy and society (p. 356/212). A footnote in *PE* refers to the relations between religion and society (p. 284, n. 119/206, n. 1). Salomon notes "that Weber operates entirely without the concept of society," substituting instead the notion of individual meaning on the one hand and ideal types and societal domains on the other hand (see 1935b, p. 68). See also Albrow (1990, pp. 159, 161–2). Weber's wife provided the title for his analytic treatise, *E&S*. Its original title was *Die Wirtschaft und die gesellschaftlichen Ordnungen und Mächte* (The Economy and the Societal Orders and Powers). See chapter 4, note 18.

Yet Weber takes a further step away from an exclusive focus upon the macro level. For him, an historically-informed sociology requires an explicit articulation of the *linkage* between individual action and social structures. His formulation of procedures, strategies, and concepts that do so constitutes one of his central strengths. They are the subject of this chapter. The world systems, causal analytic, and interpretive historical approaches all fail to analyze explicitly the manner in which this agency–structure linkage occurs.

Several basic features of Weber's sociology must be examined before this linkage can be comprehended. His "methodological individualism" and concern with the various ways in which action can be oriented by subjective meaning anchors his entire sociology. These familiar aspects, as well as the centrality of "interpretive understanding" (*Verstehen*) throughout Weber's texts, however, do not imply for him a break with structural forces.[3] Rather, as will be discussed in detail, delineated status groups, organizations, and classes crystallize alone from the orientation of action by individuals in *regular and patterned* ways. Furthermore, such action cannot be assumed, as it is by rational choice theorists, to be interest-oriented only, or always to imply an equal motivational intensity. According to Weber, a broad and pluralistic conceptualization of "social action" is necessary.

These foundational components of Weber's sociology – his methodological individualism, "four types of social action," notion of *Verstehen*, and emphasis upon a pluralism of motives – must now be addressed. Having done so, the groundwork will have been laid for an investigation of the three "modes of patterning action" that, for him, tie agency to structure.

The Foundational Components: Methodological Individualism, *Verstehen*, Four Types of Action, and a Pluralism of Motives

Weber's sociology departs from the assumption that persons account for and justify their actions; in doing so, they attach subjective meaning to them. His entire sociology rests fundamentally upon a view of persons as "*cultural* beings endowed with the capacity and will to take a deliberate stand toward the world and to lend it *meaning (Sinn)*" ("Obj," p. 81/180; transl. alt.; emph. orig.). Even in those cases when action appears to be carried out in a seemingly unreflective manner in conformity with established custom, this fact does not itself signify blind acquiescence. Rather, it may imply a conscious acceptance of the custom, and the reasons for doing so may vary. Moreover, the taken-for-granted very often involves values

---

3 On this point, which is debated hotly in the secondary literature on Weber, see pp. 30–2 and note 22 below, and notes 19 and 20 in chapter 3.

and assumptions about which individuals can be made aware.[4] Indeed, in the long run, customs, conventions, values, laws, and even forms of legitimate rulership and entire belief systems will vanish unless persons orient their action to them and endow them with meaning. To ignore the mechanisms by which persons interpret, make sense of, and influence organizations, classes, and status groups, as do the proponents of the world systems, interpretive historical, and causal analytic schools, is to paint a drastically incomplete and "over-socialized" picture. In Weber's sociology, individuals are genuine actors capable of interpreting their social realities and of initiating creative action.

His methodological individualism places the intentions of actors, their potential to influence their social surroundings, and their modes of making sense out of their realities (*subjektiver Handlungssinn*) at the forefront. Individuals act, for Weber, not social organisms or collectivities. Nor can social reality be adequately explained if persons are viewed as merely responding to scientific laws, the "social facts" of Durkheim, evolutionary forces, or the putative necessity for societies to fulfill certain "functions." No "objective meaning" exists in history, neither Hegel's "spirit" nor Marx's dialectical logic of historical change. Meaning is found only in the consciousness of human beings, and "action in the sense of a subjectively understandable orientation of behavior exists only as the behavior of one or more *individual* human beings" (*E&S*, p. 13/6; emph. orig.). The subjective motives of individuals as they constitute a "meaning-complex" is Weber's concern (*E&S*, pp. 8–18/3–9). Fearing greatly the definition of individuals as simply the "products" of societal forces, Weber defines sociology in terms of *Verstehen*, or the interpretive understanding of social action. The "social action" of individuals, which includes *both* a "social" and a "subjective" meaning, comprises its fundamental unit of analysis.

> Sociology . . . is a science concerning itself with the interpretive understanding of social action and thereby with a causal explanation of its course and consequences. We shall speak of "action" insofar as the acting individual attaches a subjective *meaning* to his behavior [*Verhalten*] – be it overt or covert, omission or acquiescence. Action is "social" insofar as its subjective meaning takes account of the behavior *of others* and is thereby oriented in its course. (*E&S*, pp. 4/1; emph. orig.)[5]

4   This remains the case even though "In the great majority of cases *actual* action goes on in a state of inarticulate half-consciousness or unconsciousness of its 'subjective meaning'" (*E&S*, pp. 21–2/11; transl. alt.; emph. orig.).
5   See also pp. 18/9, 1377–8/454–5; "EK," pp. 429, 439–40; *R&K*, pp. 185–6/126. See further e.g. Henrich, 1952; Girndt, 1967; Truzzi, 1974; Albrow, 1990, pp. 199–226. As Bendix points out, in Weber's scheme even action that evidences high conformity to social expectations retains an individual component and, conversely, action motivated mainly by individuals will contain a social element (1962, p. 475; 1984, pp. 40–2; see *E&S*, pp. 22–3/11, 1375–6/441). Weber's term *Handeln* will be uniformly translated here as "action." Parsons's frequent rendering as "behavior" or "conduct" appears to me unfortunate (see Weber, 1947, p. 89n.) in that these terms, especially with the popularization of Behaviorism in the United States, more and more connote simply externally conditioned action. Since this type of action is, for Weber,

For Weber, social action can be best conceptualized as involving one of four types of meaningful action: means–end rational, value-rational, affectual, or traditional action.[6] Each type refers to ideal-typical motivational orientations of actors. He defines action as means–end rational (*zweckrational*) "when the end, the means, and the secondary results are all rationally taken into account and weighed. This involves rational consideration of alternative means to the end, of the relations of the end to the secondary consequences, and finally of the relative importance of different possible ends" (*E&S*, p. 26/13).[7] Similarly, persons possess the capacity to act value-rationally (*wertrational*), even though this type of action has appeared empirically in its pure form only rarely. It exists when social action is "determined by a conscious belief in the value for its own sake of some ethical, aesthetic, religious, or other form of behavior, independently of its prospects of success . . . Value-rational action always involves 'commands' or 'demands' which, in the actor's opinion, are binding [*verbindlich*] on him" (*E&S*, pp. 24–5/12). Affectual action, on the other hand, is "determined by the actor's specific affects and feeling states," and is distinguished clearly from value-rational action as a result of the "consistently planned orientation" of the latter action to values (*E&S*, p. 25/12). Traditional action, "determined by ingrained habituation" and often merely a routine reaction to common stimuli, also lacks a highly self-conscious aspect" (*E&S*, p. 25/12).[8]

Each type of action can be found in all epochs and all civilizations. The meaningful action of even "primitive" peoples may be means–end rational (see, for example, *E&S*, pp. 400/245, 422–4/258–9; "EK," pp. 472–4) and value-rational (see, for example, *E&S*, p. 426/260), and modern man is not endowed with a greater capacity for either type of action than his ancestors.[9] Some epochs, of course, as a result of sociological constellations, may

only one component of *Handeln* (Weber employs, for this component, the term *Verhalten*), Parsons's translation constricts this multi-layered term. In their implied emphasis upon the individual's fragmented responses to miscellaneous environmental stimuli, the terms "behavior" and "conduct" also neglect a potential implied by *Handeln*, namely that action *may* emanate from an inner unity or, in Weber's terms, a "personality" (on this concept see e.g. *R&K*, p. 192/132).

6 As is Weber's sociology as a whole, this study is explicitly concerned with *social* action. Frequently, simply for reasons of style, "social" will be dropped. The terms "social action," "action," and "action-orientation" will be used synonymously throughout.

7 *Zweckrational* appears in the translations also as "instrumental" and "purposive" action. Only "means–end rational" will be employed here.

8 For this reason both traditional and affectual action are viewed by Weber as resting on the borderline of "meaningfully" oriented action and merely "reactive" behavior. He points out that his classification does not seek to exhaust all possibilities, "but only to formulate in conceptually pure form certain sociologically important types to which actual action is more or less closely approximated" (*E&S*, p. 26/13). Weber does not expect to discover empirical cases in which social action is oriented *only* to one of these types of action. On these types of social action, see further *E&S*, pp. 24–6/12–13.

9 Thus, Weber rejects the Enlightenment belief that Reason and Rationality appeared on the stage of human history only with the dawning of the modern epoch.

tend to call forth a particular type of action more than others (see Kalberg 1980, pp. 1169–76; forthcoming c).

This foundational emphasis in Weber's sociology upon a pluralism of motives for action implies a firm rejection of the attention by all organicist and functionalist schools to general societal norms and social structures.[10] Organic theories, according to Weber, are helpful and indeed indispensable, yet, if utilized other than as a means of facilitating preliminary conceptualization, a high risk of "reification" arises: "society" and the "organic whole" rather than the individual may become viewed as the single important level of analysis (see *E&S*, pp. 14–18/7–9). Indeed, for him, a principled disjunction always remains between "external forms" and the motivations of individuals. This may occur to such an extent that an entire range of heterogeneous subjective meanings may be found among persons who orient their action to a single group, class, or organization (see *E&S*, pp. 29–38/14–20, 313/182). The world systems, causal analytic, and interpretive historical schools are all unable to acknowledge this possibility. Weber expresses this fundamental tenet of his comparative-historical sociology in a variety of ways.

In every rulership organization, for example, the search for and legitimation of authority can be anchored in affectual motives (an emotional surrender to the ruler), means–end rational calculations (conformity to conventions or obedience to laws), value-rational motives (the belief in loyalty and duty, and in the rulership as just), religious values, or, as is generally the case empirically, a combination of these action-orientations (see *E&S*, p. 31/16).[11] As is obvious if the functioning of structurally identical bureaucracies is compared cross-culturally, not all functionaries are motivated by the constellation of values implied in the classical "bureaucratic ethos."[12] Likewise, a legal order may endure not only as a consequence of the individual's awareness that a staff of people stand ready to punish all violators, but also for reasons of self-interest, sheer habit, or conformity to convention. This legal order may, though must not, also claim ethical status for its laws. It does so, Weber believes, less often than orders supported simply by adherence to convention (*E&S*, p. 314/183, 36/19).[13] Similarly, an "ethical order" may be upheld by secular value-rational action or by religious value-rational action. This same order, however, might be maintained for "external" reasons: legally, and as a consequence of expec-

10   Motives for Weber are causes of action: "A motive is a complex of subjective meaning which seems to the actor himself or to the observer an adequate ground for the conduct in question" (*E&S*, p. 11/5).

11   Weber's conviction that the diverse sources of legitimation constitute the central issue in respect to authority and rulership, rather than the sheer "external form" of a rulership organization, stands at the foundation of his interest in the subject of rulership (see e.g. *E&S*, pp. 952–4/549–50, 1068–9/623–4, 1104–9/650–3).

12   Bendix provides an example (1962, p. 465).

13   Roth notes correctly that the secondary literature has put undue stress upon Weber's attention to force and legitimacy in social action; see 1968, p. xxix).

tations of legal sanctions (means–end rational action),[14] or, even more importantly, conventionally (traditional action) (see *E&S*, p. 36/19). Individuals may join an ascetic Protestant sect not as a result of sincere belief, but exclusively in order to establish the good character and trustworthiness that, given plans to open a business, will prove quite helpful (see "Sects," pp. 304–5/209–11; *E&S*, p. 30/15). Confucian ethics regarding piety to parents and ancestors were for the most part upheld not by value-rational beliefs in their correctness as absolutes, but because they were accepted as conventions (*RofC*, p. 229/515).[15]

These distinctions in terms of subjective meanings that can be grasped through the four types of social action establish the analytical base Weber employs to conceptualize the great pluralism of action-orientations. They indicate the diverse ways in which, for him, action must be conceptualized. However much it may appear to be similar when viewed externally, homogeneity at the level of meaningful social action cannot be assumed, as it is by proponents of the world systems, causal analytic, and interpretive historical approaches. Weber is extremely insistent upon this position. Even the religious sect, despite the extremely coercive nature of its formal structure, fails to call forth homogeneous action-orientatons.[16] Even when seemingly tightly bonded to social structure, social action can result from heterogeneous motives.

This fundamental assumption underlies, for example, Weber's crucial distinction in *PE* between an "economic form" and an "economic ethic" (see pp. 51–67/33–52). He saw diverse possibilities regarding, for example, the economic form of capitalism and the "traditional" and "rational" economic ethics: the traditional ethic might combine with modern capitalism (Italian capitalism before the Reformation) or with irrational capitalism (the medieval textile entrepreneur), and the rational economic ethic might appear in combination with either modern (nineteenth-century laissez-faire and industrial capitalism) or irrational capitalism (Benjamin Franklin's printing company, the Quaker sects in seventeenth-century Pennsylvania) (see *PE*, pp. 65–9/50–3; 74–5/60; *PE II*, pp. 47, 164). Precisely such observations regarding the complex relationship between structure and subjec-

14   In Islamic theocracies, for example, religiously legitimated legal systems are directly strengthened by the state's coercive powers (see *E&S*, p. 756/443).
15   Weber generalizes this statement: "In the past as well as in the present in the reality of daily life, 'moral commandments' are, in contrast to 'legal commands,' from a sociological point of view normally either religiously or conventionally conditioned maxims of conduct" (*E&S*, p. 325/191; transl. alt.).
16   For example: "The stratum typical of [the brotherhoods of the Occidental Middle Ages and of Islam] were identical: petty bourgeois and especially artisans. Yet the spirit of their respective religions were very different. Viewed externally, numerous Hinduist religious communities appear to be 'sects' just as those in the Occident. The sacred value, however, and the manner in which values were mediated pointed in radically different directions" ("I," p. 292/264).

tive meaning are repeatedly manifest in Weber's substantive analyses. They led, for example, to conclusions regarding the origins of modern capitalism: after comparing capitalism in Florence in the fourteenth and fifteenth centuries (where activity directed toward profit for its own sake was viewed as ethically unjustifiable) with the economic backwardness of eighteenth-century Pennsylvania (where a "spirit" of capitalism was "considered the essence of moral conduct, even commanded in the name of duty"), Weber argued that capitalism alone could not have given birth to a "rational" economic ethic (see *PE*, pp. 74–5/60). Economic ethics and economic forms may stand in fully heterogeneous relationships (see also *E&S*, pp. 70/35, 480/292, 630/378; *PE II*, pp. 31, 171).[17]

A sustained attention to the diverse possible subjective meanings for action sets Weber's sociology apart from all orthodox structural approaches, including the world systems, interpretive historical, and causal analytic schools. The *verstehende* sociologist must "understand" the action of persons in groups under investigation in reference to the pluralism of motives expressed by the four types of action. The assessment of subjective meaning is indispensable even in those cases when statistical analysis yields clear results.[18] A great array of motives within a single "external form" is both analytically and empirically possible – *and* sociologically significant.[19] As will be noted repeatedly, this emphasis upon *varying* motives lays a firm foundation for the attentiveness of Weber's comparative-historical sociology to cultural forces.

This brief discussion of a number of foundational components – Weber's methodological individualism, four types of social action, notion of *Verstehen*, and emphasis upon a pluralism of motives – has revealed fundamental differences between his comparative-historical sociology and that of contemporary schools. It has also laid the groundwork for the central task in this chapter: to examine the manner in which Weber links individual action, or agency, and structure. His procedures, strategies, and concepts for doing so can now be addressed. Three "modes of patterning action" explicitly tie, in Weber's substantive texts, individual action to social structures: "orders," "legitimate orders," and "sociological loci."

17   Only on the basis of such a distinction could Weber have written one of his most famous statements: "The Puritan *wanted* to work in a calling; we *must* do so" (*PE*, p. 181/203; transl. alt.; emph. orig.).
18   "If adequacy in respect to meaning is lacking, then no matter how high the degree of uniformity and how precisely its probability can be numerically determined, it is still an incomprehensible statistical probability, whether we deal with overt or subjective processes. . . . Statistical uniformities constitute understandable types of action . . . only when they can be regarded as manifestations of the understandable subjective meaning of a course of social action" (*E&S*, pp. 12/5–6; see also *R&K*, p. 65/14).
19   It is remarkable how seldom this fundamental aspect of Weber's sociology has been acknowledged in the American reception of Weber.

Agency and Structure: the Modes of Patterning Action

In selecting the social action of individuals as its unit of analysis and opposing all organic, functionalist, and orthodox structuralist approaches,
Weber's sociology appears incapable of articulating a structural dimension.
Nonetheless, the procedures and strategies underlying his comparative-
historical texts can never be understood by reference alone to the subjective
meaning of individuals and the four types of social action. In spite of his
methodological individualism and a strong stress throughout his sociology
upon incessant conflict, Weber never viewed social life as an "endless drift"
of solitary action-orientations. The diverse ways in which individuals act *in
concert*, rather than the mind of the single actor or the social action of the
isolated individual, capture his attention. He sees that patterns of action-
orientations and definitions of "meaning" held by individuals in common
surface frequently and regularly in all societies and throughout history.[20]
Indeed, Weber defines the concern of the sociological enterprise in terms of
action by individuals in delimited groups and the identification of *regularities of action*: "There can be observed, within the realm of social action,
actual empirical regularities; that is, courses of action that are repeated by
the actor or (possibly also: simultaneously) occur among numerous actors
because the subjective *meaning* is typically *meant* to be the same. Sociological investigation is concerned with these *typical* modes of action" (*E&S*,
p. 29/14; emph. orig.; transl. alt.; see also pp. 19–21/9–10; 311/181; "Obj.,"
p. 67/165). They are expressed as ideal types.[21]

For Weber, regular action can result not only from values, but also from
affectual, traditional, and even means–end rational action. The manner in
which action is *uprooted* from its natural random flow and transformed into
regularities anchored in these types of social action constitutes one of his
most central and basic themes. Throughout *E&S*, *PE*, and *EEWR* in particular Weber charts such patterns of action. How, from a comparative and
historical sociological perspective, have various empirical uniformities of
action crystallized despite unending conflict and the perpetual tendency of
social action to lapse into a diffuse, amorphous flow? Under what circumstances has regular action oriented to values and traditions "replaced"
regular action oriented to sheer means–end rational calculations? These
questions stand at the very core of his comparative-historical sociology.
Due to his awkward terminology, his concern with the various ways in
which social action may be oriented in concert and in specific "directions"
is not always apparent.

20   The Anglo-American reception of Weber's methodological individualism and notion of
Verstehen has neglected this fundamental tenet (see e.g. Truzzi, 1974).
21   This foundational concept is pivotal in Weber's sociology as a whole. Ideal types are
constructed "utopias" that involve an accentuation of "the essence" of the empirical action-
orientations. Their formation and major features are discussed in chapter 3; their major usages
are examined in chapters 3 and 4.

Indeed, Weber very often appears, in his substantive texts, to be attending to the structural level alone. The basic orientation in his empirical sociology to the manner in which subjective meaning is formed and influences action is frequently concealed in these texts. This occurs to such an extent that the reader frequently fails to see Weber's methodological individualism and attention to the interpretive understanding of action. At times, his ideal types appear static and even reified. However, far from supplanting his methodological individualism and emphasis upon the four types of action, they always chart the *patterned and meaningful action-orientations* of individuals – and nothing more. Rather than indicating statistical regularities, abstract principles, general maxims, or overarching laws of social life, they "document" the orientation – or "direction" – of meaningful social action of individuals. Weber's ideal type, "the Calvinist," identifies simply sets of uniform action-orientations of individuals (for example, an orientation toward methodical work and an ascetic style of life), as does "the civil servant" (an orientation toward reliability, punctuality, and the impersonal performance of tasks) and "the charismatic leader" (heroism and a rejection of everyday routine).[22] Other – that is, non-meaningful – action is excluded by the ideal type.[23]

The charting of meaningful patterned action by ideal types steers Weber's comparative-historical sociology away from isolated action-orientations on the one hand and global themes, such as societal evolution, social differentiation, and the question of social order, on the other. The multifarious sources of empirical uniformities of action and, in addition, the particular content of such regular action – whether predominantly traditional, affectual, value-rational, or means–end rational – capture his attention rather than overriding developments. Action becomes patterned according to three major modes: through the orientations of actors to "orders," "legitimate orders," and "sociological loci".[24] The explicit linkage of agency and structure in his substantive texts occurs through these *modes of pattern-*

---

22   In order to emphasize this point I will repeatedly employ the expression "action-orientations" (despite its stylistic awkwardness) rather than, as occurs in Weber's texts (and particularly in the English translations), "the Calvinist" or "the civil servant." A debate in the secondary literature has revolved around just this point (see e.g. Rex, 1971; Turner, 1981, pp. 9, 352, 354; Scaff, 1989, pp. 34–5, 78, n. 15). A severe disjunction, it is asserted, exists between Weber's methodological writings, which emphasize methodological individualism and the importance of subjective meaning, and his substantive texts. It is argued that these texts are primarily structural and omit just the emphasis upon subjective meaning so prominent in the methodological writings. Weber's carelessness in respect to formulation (combined with a number of poor translations; notably, this position has been taken by English and American commentators only) indeed would seem to lend credence to this position. Nonetheless, this entire chapter can be viewed as an attempt to rebut this "disjuncture thesis." See also chapter 3, note 19.

23   Such as "reactive" behavior, which is without an element of subjective meaning. See *E&S*, pp. 4–9/1–4.

24   Weber never discusses this issue explicitly in these terms. This is my interpretation. The following sections on "orders," "legitimate orders," and "sociological loci" rely largely upon *E&S*.

ing action. Each defines a way in which action is uprooted from its amorphous flow, becomes directed, and acquires a regular and specific content. *Weber's structuralism* refers simply to these three modes of patterning action. These or other explicit procedures or concepts to tie individual action to social structures are not offered by the world systems, causal analytic, or interpretive historical approaches.

Orders and legitimate orders

An order may be established in three ways: through usage (*Brauch*), custom (*Sitte*) or means–end rational, self-interest calculations (*Interessenlage*) (*E&S*, p. 29/15). These action-orientations introduce regularities that stand opposed to and order random action.

Orders upheld by custom and self-interest are of much greater importance for Weber than those upheld by mere usage. Customs order action and create uniformities simply because a failure to orient actions to them causes petty inconveniences and annoyances of varying degrees of intolerability (*E&S*, p. 30/16). Whatever the motivations of persons to conform to a custom – and they do so of their own free will, whether simply without thinking, for reasons of convenience or whatever other reasons – individuals know that, *should* violations of the custom occur, they will not be confronted by consistent external sanctions, whether conventional or legal; conformity is not "demanded" (*E&S*, p. 29/15). Nonetheless, the adherence of individuals to customs may be so strong that directly opposing laws may be powerless to alter them (*E&S*, p. 320/187).[25]

Weber is quite explicit in particular in respect to the manner in which even a means–end rational expression of self-interests may lead to patterned action. On the one hand, the regularities produced by self-interested action may derive from an actor's orientation to the interests of others; by doing so he hopes that antagonism will not be aroused to such an extent that his own interests will be endangered (*E&S*, pp. 30–1/16). On the other hand, similar action may result simply from a common definition of interests by individuals:[26] "The more *strictly* individuals act in a means–end

25 Weber's acknowledgment of the potential strength of customs leads him, for example, to reject "Bakuninism": "The naive idea of Bakuninism of destroying the basis of 'acquired rights' together with 'rulership' by destroying the public documents overlooks that the settled orientation of *persons* for observing the accustomed rules and regulations will survive independently of the documents.... This conditioned orientation [is] bred both in officials and subjects" (*E&S*, p. 988/570; emph. orig.). He particularly notes that custom can be of immense significance for the "level of economic need" and economic activity (see *E&S*, pp. 319–38/187–98).
26 That interests alone (*Interessenlage*) can lead to uniformities and regularities is also clear from *E&S*, pp. 43/23, 191/112–13, 111/60, and 483/294. Because it neglects entirely Weber's emphasis upon the manner in which means–end rational and traditional action can also introduce patterned action, Parsons's assertion that, for Weber, regularities of action result from a "common orientation to norms" (1937, p. 678) severely misconstrues Weber's sociol-

rational fashion, the more will they tend to react similarly to given situations. In this manner, similarities, regularities and continuities of attitudes and action originate" (*E&S*, p. 30/15; transl. alt.; emph. orig.).[27] Once a course of action has been acknowledged as beneficial in the sense that it satisfies the self-interests of all parties involved, a probability exists that actors will avoid risks that may upset such a satisfactory situation. Such uniform action is often found in the economic arena, though it occurs in all other domains of human action as well.

Means—end rational action calls forth continuity and regularities of action in the rulership domain, for example, when officials of the patrimonial ruler and vassals of feudal princes all pursue the stable authority of their rulers in the hope of thereby securing the legitimacy of their own rule. A parallel situation obtains in charismatic rulership: the blood relatives of a ruler may seek to enhance claims to legitimacy by espousing the charismatic character of his leadership and, ultimately, of an entire sib group (*E&S*, pp. 1143/676–7; see chapter 4, pp. 124–7). Similarly, interests often called forth patterned action wherever ruler, staff, and subjects struggled, as they did in all forms of rulership (*E&S*, pp. 257/150, 1027/595). Interests are also visible in the common attempts by patrimonial monarchs to retain their rulership against the striving for status autonomy by the feudal aristocracy and the attempt by the bourgeoisie to establish economic independence (*E&S*, pp. 1101/647, 1107/652). The priesthood and Church hierarchies as well, in order to secure diverse mundane interests, clashed perpetually with all forms of secular rulership.[28] Even within religions, patterned action in diverse groups may be guided by interests: those of priests, laity, prophets, and theologians (see "I," pp. 288–9/260–2; *E&S*, pp. 439–67/268–85). Weber also sees the interests that called forth common action behind "purely religious forces"; the Torah, for example, was mainly "meant to prevent the enslavement of the peasantry by the wealthy families" (*AJ*, p. 240/256); and mystics preferred "as *little* bureaucracy as possible, for their self-perfection could not possibly be promoted by the busy state policy of civilization [*Zivilisationspolitik*]" (*RofC*, p. 184/469; emph. orig.). In sum:

> Many of the highly visible regularities in the course of social action, especially (though not only) economic action, rest . . . simply on the fact that the type of social action of participants on the average best corresponds, in the nature of

---

ogy. In interpreting Weber as equating social action with normative conformity, as the "de-Parsonizing" critics have argued, Parsons has stretched "the terminological domain of 'norm' until it encompasses virtually every sense of 'ruledness,' regardless of the actor's subjective considerations" (Cohen, Hazelrigg, and Pope, 1975, p. 240). See notes 33 and 39 below.

27 This phenomenon is discussed with specific reference to an exchange of goods at *E&S*, pp. 327–8/192. In clear opposition to the Parsonsian reading, Weber here again emphasizes that, when self-interests are clearly delineated, regularities of action need not rest upon a belief in a binding norm or any legitimate order.

28 The "exemplary case" for the rivalry between religious and political interests could be found in the Holy Roman Empire (see *E&S*, pp. 1159/689, 1173–6/699–702).

the case, to their normal, subjectively estimated *interests....* as these are subjectively perceived.... The regularities in prices in the "free" market, for example, are formed in just this manner. (*E&S*, p. 30/15; transl. alt.; emph. orig.)[29]

The adaptation of individuals to changed *external conditions* constitutes a further example of the manner in which action becomes patterned in reference to interests. An acknowledgment that a new situation has arisen eventually leads individuals to conclude that, if their interests are to be protected and promoted in an adequate manner, new action-orientations are required. Individuals "accept or adapt themselves to the external, technical resultants which are of practical significance for their interests" (*E&S*, p. 1117/658). To Weber, such adaptation to courses of action that ensure "success" constitutes a strong inclination, one that may lead even to the compromising, endangering, or even abandonment of ideals ("EN," pp. 23/ 513, 38/529). The capacity to impose a new situation and, thereby, to transform social action as persons adjust accordingly characterizes, for example, bureaucracies: "Bureaucratic rationalization ... revolutionizes with *technical* means, in principle, as does every economic reorganization, 'from without': the situation and societal orders first are altered; then, since a shifting of the conditions of adaptation has occurred and perhaps even an enhancing of the opportunities for adaptation, the people. This occurs simply through a rational determination of means and ends" (*E&S*, p. 1116/657; transl. alt.; emph. orig.; see pp. 1002/578–9). Similarly, altered "situations of

---

29 Weber's comparative-historical writings note with particular frequency historical examples that illustrate the manner in which sheer economic interests call forth uniform action. Even the priesthood may act clearly in behalf of economic concerns, as occurred, for example, when priests in the Middle Ages sought to appropriate monastic prebends and to transform them into hereditary possessions (*E&S*, pp. 1159–63/689–91, 1173–6/699–702). Because Weber views economic interests as ubiquitous and simply "natural," such examples are neither surprising to him nor problematic. For example: "Naturally the capacity to receive pay for ritualistic instruction was monopolized by the Vaidika-Brahmins of full caste rank" (*RofI*, p. 321/353). He notes the economic interests of Byzantine, Chinese, and Catholic monks as well; see *E&S*, p. 586/354; *RofC*, pp. 8/285, 60/347. Lawyers, as well, often acted in terms of economic calculations, as took place when this stratum in England demanded, in order to protect fees, that new judges be appointed exclusively from its own ranks (*E&S*, p. 1029/597). Weber also notes how the "established jurisdictions" of patrimonial officials resulted mainly from their competing economic interests (*E&S*, p. 1029/596). He further emphasizes the centrality of economic interests in the legal realm when he calls attention to the manner in which bourgeois strata acted to prohibit restrictions upon the marketability of land that would lead to the development of seigneurial rights and benefit feudal strata (*E&S*, p. 694/416). Similarly, he stresses the role played by economic interests in his analysis of the expansion of market freedom (see e.g. *E&S*, p. 84/44), the appropriation of means of production from status groups (see e.g. *E&S*, p. 639/384), and the development of a political community (see e.g. *E&S*, p. 908/519). To Weber, even a socialist economy would not deter diverse organizations and status groups from orienting action in behalf of interests (*E&S*, pp. 202–3/119, 919–20/526). Of great fascination to him are those cases when economic interests either oppose values or become directed and *intensified* by values, such as occurred with the Calvinist entrepreneur (see chapter 2, pp. 63–4). Of course, the protection of economic interests may serve as simply a means toward the fulfillment of a further interest, such as the defense of status.

life and hence its problems" related to external definitions of social honor lead to the conclusion that a new course of action more effectively serves status interests (see *E&S*, pp. 39–40/21, 245/142, 755–6/442). New laws as well lead to assessments regarding their capacity to fulfill interests effectively and, possibly, an alteration of action (see *E&S*, pp. 760–1/445–6). For Weber, just the "deliberate adaptation to situations in terms of self-interest" belongs among the most central ways in which action becomes patterned (see *E&S*, p. 30/15). Depictions of interests – and the uniform action they call forth – can be found on nearly every page of Weber's comparative-historical writings.[30]

However, Weber views the patterned action of individuals not simply in terms of a common definition of subjective interests, as would a rational choice theorist. He also sees that regularities of action arise from its orientation to collectivities. Such orientations may "have a powerful, often a decisive causal influence on the course of action of real individuals" (*E&S*, p. 14/7). A certain inner substance, persistence, and permanence characterizes these regularities of action. The patterns formed when action is oriented to organizations, classes, and status groups with clearly articulated boundaries assume particular importance for Weber.[31] Sociologists can assume, for example, that the laws of the modern state influence action regularly wherever persons believe that the state exists and that its laws are valid (*E&S*, p. 14/7). Even economic actors calculating their material interests are not indifferent to guarantees of legal coercion made by the state, if only because this guarantee enhances the security for economic calculations (see *E&S*, pp. 328–33/193–5). Weber's concept of *legitimate order* encompasses such regular action-orientations.

Although orders based upon custom or self-interest vary in terms of their degree of flexibility,[32] neither of these modes of orienting action in a regular fashion, nor action patterned by usage, includes an obligatory (*verbindlich*) or exemplary (*vorbildlich*) element. Orders that do so are "valid" (*geltend*) or "legitimate." For Weber, the chance that an order will be supported by a group of actors is enhanced considerably when, in addition to whatever other reasons may exist for conformity to it, it is also defined as either an ideal or as morally binding. This valid order more effectively orders social

30 For further examples, see e.g. the analyses of the origins of democratic suffrage (*E&S*, pp. 1127–33/666–9), of the office of justice of the peace in England (*E&S*, pp. 1059/616–17), and of the formal rationalization of law (*E&S*, pp. 809–11/468–9).
31 This emphasis upon the action-orientations of individuals to groups stands, for example, at the very center of *PE*: "In order that a way of life and notion of vocation [*Beruf*] so well adapted to the peculiarities of capitalism could be 'selected out' at all – that is, one that could come to be victorious over others – it first had to originate, and not in single and isolated individuals, but as a mode of acting carried by *groups* of people. This origin is what actually needs to be explained" (*PE*, p. 55/37; transl. alt.; emph. orig.).
32 Weber believes that means–end rational, self-interested action is generally more flexible (*E&S*, p. 31/16).

action into regularities (*E&S*, pp. 31/16, 33/17). Weber explicitly notes the centrality of legitimate orders for "the sociological point of view": "The sociological point of view . . . asks what *actually* happens in a group owing to the probability that persons engaged in social action . . . subjectively consider certain orders as valid and practically act according to them; such persons, in other words, orient their action towards these orders" (*E&S*, p. 311/181; transl. alt; emph. orig.; see also "Obj," p. 67/165).[33]

Typically, Weber's concern mainly involves the various *means* by which a valid order is maintained, rather than the legitimate order itself. In a pivotal dichotomization for the organization of *E&S* and *EEWR* in particular, he classifies the motivations of individuals for supporting a legitimate order as either "internal" or "external," and then notes the several possible modes of regular action that fall within each of these categories. The resulting typology, in respect to "internal motivations," takes the following form:

The legitimacy of an order may be guaranteed by purely internal factors [*rein innerlich*]:
(*a*) purely affectually – through emotional surrender [*gefühlsmässige Hingabe*];
(*b*) value-rationally through the belief in the absolute validity of an order as the expression of ultimate binding [*verpflichtender*] values (whether ethical, aesthetic or whatever other values);
(*c*) religious – through the belief that salvation depends upon maintaining the order. (*E&S*, pp. 33–4/17–18)

The appearance of civil servants in their offices every morning punctually at nine, for example, can – though must not – be a manifestation of their belief in a legitimate order as a value: for them, it may be a matter of duty for all civil servants to be punctual. Considering themselves to be responsible civil servants, they attribute validity to this value and internalize it as a personal ethic. It has, thereby, acquired for them an inner sense of obligation (*innere Bindung*) and action is oriented accordingly. Weber considers the general flexibility of these civil servants to be less than that of others who act simply for reasons of custom or sheer self-interest (*E&S*, p. 31/16).[34] His study of Calvinism illustrates the ways in which he investigates

---

33 Unfortunately, the term *Ordnungen* is frequently translated in *E&S* as "norms," especially in the "Basic Sociological Terms" chapter (pp. 3–62). Weber uses the term *Norm* (the term is the same in German) very rarely (see e.g. *E&S*, pp. 30/15, 36/19). Moreover, although he admits freely that his distinction between orders and legitimate orders is, in empirical reality, fully fluid (*E&S*, p. 31/16), he confuses matters considerably by generally referring in *Wirtschaft und Gesellschaft* to legitimate orders as simply orders.

34 Conformity with the prescriptions of a valid order need not be, Weber contends, the only means by which an actor acknowledges its legitimacy. A thief, for example, "orients his action to the validity of the criminal law in that he acts surreptitiously" (*E&S*, p. 32/16; see "EK," p. 443). Moreover, a single individual may orient his action to contradictory legitimate orders, as does, for example, the follower of a code of honor who decides not only that, in a certain situation, a duel is called for, but also respects the law against dueling by afterwards turning himself in to the police (*E&S*, p. 32/17).

the crystallization of patterned action-orientations in reference to religious values.

Weber sought in *PE* to clarify how Calvinists endowed certain action with subjective meaning. From the point of view of a "natural" attitude toward life that simply and without hesitation takes delight in diverse worldly pleasures, the Calvinist's asceticism could only be seen as quite strange.[35] Indeed, if examined from the perspective of a eudaemonistic attitude, the action-orientations of the ascetic must be judged as totally "irrational" (*PE*, pp. 53/36, 70–2/54–5, 78/62, 119/117).[36] Following the tenets of his *verstehende* sociology, Weber assumed that, if a meaning complex could be reconstructed, even the patterned action of this "type of person" (*Menschentyp*) would be disclosed as subjectively rational. He hypothesized that the religious doctrine of these devout practitioners would reveal how actions putatively "irrational" could *subjectively* make sense, and began an investigation of Calvinism's major theological texts. From these texts, he constructed an ideal-typical believer oriented to the predestination doctrine and then deduced the impact of this "religious [legitimate] order" upon the action – especially the economic action – of believers (*PE*, pp. 98–112/87–106).

Weber's *verstehende* investigations in *EEWR* of the origins of the discrete and unique action uniformities typical of the Confucianist, Taoist, Hindu, Buddhist, and Jew utilize parallel procedures.[37] The withdrawal from the world of the Buddhist mystic, for example, can be understood as "meaningful" if placed within the framework of his perception of the transcendental realm (as dominated by an immanent and impersonal Being rather than an anthropomorphic and omnipotent Deity), his definition of the goal of salvation (immersion in the All-One), and his view of the appropriate means toward its attainment (a "silencing of the soul" through contemplation).

Of course, the regular orientation of action to a legitimate order may also occur as a result of "external" motivations: "The legitimacy of an order may be also – or exclusively – guaranteed by the expectation of specific external consequences; that is, by attention to one's self-interests" (*Interessenlage*). These self-interests here, however, unlike those discussed

35 The enjoyment of eating, drinking, and relaxation was denied to this believer. In addition, the single activity to which he could unequivocally devote his energies – regular and systematic labor in a "calling" – connoted to most people sheer drudgery and pain. Since they constituted threats to the relationship of highest importance – to his God – even the cultivation of friendship and the happiness of intimacy were prohibited to the ascetic Protestant. See *PE*, pp. 104–9/94–101.
36 These passages, which indicate Weber's clear ambivalence regarding inner-worldly asceticism (see also e.g. *PE*, pp. 180–2/202–6), are often unclearly rendered by Parsons's translation.
37 Perhaps Weber's magisterial comparison of the meaning complexes of Calvinism and Confucianism constitutes the best illustration of his procedures in this respect. See *RofC*, pp. 226–49/512–36.

above in relationship to orders lacking in validity, refer specifically to expectations of a specific kind: either in regard to (a) conventions or (b) laws.[38]

The sense of obligation that results when a legitimate order is based upon convention or law originates from the awareness of actors that consistent and decidedly unpleasant consequences will follow should they arbitrarily act in defiance of the specified conventions or laws.[39] A convention guarantees a legitimate order simply because "deviation from it within a given social group will result in a relatively general and practically significant reaction of disapproval" (E&S, p. 34/17),[40] while a legitimate order based on laws is maintained when an individual is aware that failure to do so will result in the application of physical or psychological coercion by a staff of people until compliance occurs or the violation of the law is avenged. In this purely empirical definition, laws exist, for Weber, whenever a staff or a coercive apparatus is present. Such enforcing agencies may exist in the clan as well as in the modern state.[41]

Weber stresses that the patterned internal and external action-orientations that uphold a legitimate order must not be confused with the legitimate orders themselves. If so, their "reification" occurs. Nor are legitimate orders, in empirical reality, guaranteed by a pattern of any single internal or external action-orientation. On the contrary, for him it is self-evident, and a postulate of the greatest significance for his comparative-historical sociology, that the validity of an order can be, and often is, maintained by the most diverse motives (see E&S, pp. 313/182, 35/18).

However, Weber's analysis of the manner in which structure – or patterned action – originates is not exhausted by reference to regular action oriented

38   This entire typology is presented at E&S, pp. 33–4/17–18. I have altered the translation somewhat. Most importantly, I prefer to translate *innerlich* und *äusserlich* uniformly as "internal" and "external." "Innerlich" is also translated throughout E&S as "subjective" (e.g. pp. 35/18, 33/17). Weber stresses the centrality of these terms by often underlining them or enclosing them in quotation marks. These modes of emphasis have not found their way regularly into the English translation.
39   Though seldom referred to, norms are, for Weber, always "valid." He refers explicitly to legal norms (*Rechtsnormen*) as obligatory (E&S, pp. 332/195, 313–14/183). The normative and obligatory power of conventions, as opposed to customs, are contrasted at E&S, pp. 326/191–2. He places both conventions and laws at the conceptual level of norms in "Obj" as well (p. 71/170) and contrasts "usage" and "norm" in a passage on the rise of the conception of gods over spirits (E&S, p. 1008/582).
40   Weber illustrates this definition at E&S, p. 34/18; see further E&S, pp. 319/187, 324/190.
41   Further details in regard to these definitions and the problematic behind them cannot be addressed here. On Weber's definition of law, see E&S, pp. 34–5/17–18, 313–15/182–4, 324/190; Rheinstein, 1954, pp. lxiv, lxvii. On the relationship between law and convention, see E&S, pp. 326/191, 320/187. It cannot, of course, be argued that orientations to law are *generally* stronger empirically than orientations to conventions or religious forces. Weber is convinced that the contrary is often the case; see e.g. E&S, pp. 37/18, 316/184. A sociology of conventions that includes an analysis of their potential autonomy vis-à-vis, e.g. laws, status groups, and classes is concealed within EEWR.

to orders and legitimate orders. He takes a large step beyond these modes
of patterning action in various explorations in his substantive texts on the
origins of empirical uniformities of action. If examined closely, these texts
reveal a deeply contextual dimension that unveils further features of
Weber's structuralism. Yet this structuralism, and unlike that of the world
systems, interpretive historical, and causal analytic approaches, once again
fails to abandon agency: acknowledgment of the varying subjective meanings, the particular type of social action, and the differing intensities of
social action remains central. The notion of a "sociological locus" for action, which implies a situating of action contextually, best conveys this
structuralism.[42] All sociological loci articulate contexts that imply both constraints upon and opportunities for action.[43] Attention to such "social conditions of existence" unveils a further mode, in addition to orders and
legitimate orders, in Weber's comparative-historical texts by which action
becomes patterned. Once again, unlike the world systems, interpretive
historical, or causal analytic approaches, he offers explicit procedures, concepts, and strategies that serve to link agency and structure.

The contextual sociology: sociological loci for action

Weber seeks often to define an array of delimited social contexts in reference to which patterns of action will likely crystallize. The ideal types of
E&S frequently chart not only the recurring action-orientations of individuals, but also social contexts that demarcate constraints upon and opportunities for action.[44] By outlining shared life chances, empirical activities,
routine experiences, the social conditions of existence, and the particular
demands and premiums placed upon the social action of individuals in
specific situations, or delineated contexts of meaningful action, these ideal
types – *sociological loci for action* – imply hypotheses regarding patterned

42   The emphasis upon social contexts throughout Weber's comparative-historical sociology
will be most evident in this section and in chapters 4 and 5. In addition to his insistence upon
four types of social action and the varying intensity of action, this emphasis places his sociology
in the strongest contrast to all rational choice theories (see chapter 2, pp. 62–8).
43   The notion of diverse sociological loci for action is obscured by Weber's failure to discuss
it explicitly in the *E&S* "Basic Sociological Terms" chapter (pp. 4–62/1–30) or elsewhere.
Furthermore, as a result of his habit in *E&S* of interweaving a variety of themes, the central
significance of this concept cannot be easily grasped. Although loci are always either orders or
legitimate orders, I have chosen to introduce this additional concept simply because of the
importance in Weber's comparative-historical texts of the ways in which constraints and
opportunities are placed upon action by social contexts. Sociological loci highlight just this
aspect of orders and legitimate orders. Weber uses this term, though only on a few occasions.
I am not aware of a discussion of loci in the secondary literature on Weber.
44   This expression – "constraints upon and opportunities for action" – is used throughout the
remainder of this chapter. It refers to the diverse ways in which a social context influences and
shapes action by placing demands and limitations on the one hand and by offering opportunities and possibilities on the other.

action.[45] Rather than simply evolving and flourishing as a consequence of the rational choices of individuals, action-orientations acquire, Weber argues, an imprint and shape by milieus.

Each locus not only delineates the manner in which action is severed from its amorphous flow and then directed in ways that, despite its pluralistic sources, endow it with coherence and continuity, but also indicates probabilities regarding the content of such patterned action. To Weber, persons similarly situated who are engaged over time in common everyday activities and experiences, and confront empirical constraints and opportunities, may share not only patterns of affectual, traditional, and means–end rational action-orientations, but also, in some cases, orientations to values. Each locus outlines a social context and then a range of *probable* action-orientations substantively different from the range demarcated by any other locus.[46] Thus, each locus implies an *ideal-typical model* that demarcates chances for regular action-orientations to appear and, more importantly, to endure and become sociologically significant; conversely, each delineates as well likelihoods regarding the circumscription and exclusion of other recurring action-orientations. As such, loci also address the question of what patterns of social action *can* arise in a given setting.[47]

In sum, unlike orders and legitimate orders, this third mode of patterning action points to Weber's frequent tendency to see social action as embedded in and shaped by social contexts. In so doing, it as well articulates the structural dimension – the patterning of meaningful action – in Weber's comparative-historical sociology. It does so, however, because sociological loci chart constraints upon and opportunities for action, in a more graphic and contextual fashion than do orders or legitimate orders. Nonetheless, this structuralism, just as the structuralism articulated by orders and legitimate orders, remains anchored in the four types of social action; as such, it as well bridges agency and structure. A comparable concept does not appear in the world systems, interpretive historical, or causal analytic schools, all of which retain an orthodox structuralism.

Weber's notion of a sociological locus for action, which is central to his

45 It must be emphasized that not all ideal types demarcate a social context for action, and thus not all ideal types are sociological loci. Again, the formation and major features of ideal types will be addressed in chapter 3. Sociological loci are ideal-typical *models*, and thus in a certain sense belong in chapter 4. However, because they are a central mode of linking agency and structure, their scrutiny in this chapter is required.

46 Despite this clearly structural mode of analysis, Weber stresses repeatedly that those regular action-orientations, and particularly value-rational action, that congeal from social contexts cannot be conceptualized as a simple "function" or "reflection" of daily experience or as "determined" by typical and routine activities. To him, a "more basic misunderstanding would hardly be possible" ("I," p. 270/240; see e.g. *AJ*, p. 80/89). These terms are simply too strong. Weber utilizes terms such as "chance," "probability," "likelihood," and "elective affinity" throughout his loci *models*. He never ceases to see choice in human action, indeed even in those cases when a locus for action would seem at first glance to tightly circumscribe action-orientations (e.g. the religious sect; see notes 5 and 16 above).

47 This subject is addressed also in chapters 4 and 5.

comparative-historical sociology, can be grasped fully only through several illustrations. Sociological loci models are most clearly constructed in *E&S*. Only two status groups, two universal organizations, and one form of rulership can be noted.

Status groups: warriors and civic strata   Persons who share a style of life, consumption patterns, common conventions, specific notions of honor, and economic and particular status monopolies comprise a status group (*Stand*). Status differences become apparent whenever the two major measures of social action – *commercium* (or social intercourse) and *connubium* – are restricted or lacking. Stratification by status always implies the "monopolization of ideal and material goods or opportunities" as well as social distance and exclusiveness (see *E&S*, pp. 927/531, 935/536; Kalberg, 1985a, pp. 48–52).

Weber's analyses of "status situation" and "status groups" are not designed exclusively to formulate clear concepts, nor do they relate only to the goal of expanding the base for a theory of stratification beyond material interests to include style of life and social honor, as the secondary literature has emphasized. Rather, he also aims to formulate models that articulate the patterned action-orientations originating in the pragmatic, everyday activities inherent to status situations. A discussion of the status ethics of warriors and civic strata must suffice to illustrate how this occurs. In each ideal-typical model, the ways in which regular action, with a certain likelihood, arises from typical social conditions of existence to orient action will be emphasized.

Perhaps the typical action of *warriors* can be most easily understood as standing in a relationship of elective affinity with certain social conditions of existence. These charismatic heroes gather young followers fully dedicated to them and prove their mighty strength in marauding campaigns of plunder for booty and women. Followers emotionally surrender themselves to their permanent warriors' league and legendary leader, and live together in a communistic warrior community. Since the conduct of war is their single vocation and only the cultivation of the military virtues is considered honorable, the values learned among the fraternity of warriors and in battle typically influence their action: loyalty, bravery, and personal honor. The warrior's loyalty to friends, as praised in hymns and sagas, and his cult of personal bonds are esteemed largely as a result of the loyalty and devotion to the leader learned in warfare.

Precisely their pride in the military virtues inclines warriors to orient their actions to worldly matters and to scorn all metaphysical beliefs. This same pursuit of worldly interests disinclines them to ponder life's meaning through cognition alone, while their high evaluation of loyalty, bravery, and personal honor, as well as their proclivity to seek mastery over events and hardship through decisive action, uproot them from the immediacy to organic processes and natural events typical of peasants. Even though this distance from natural forces fails to direct them, as is the case for intellectuals, toward a search for a total understanding of the universe and its events,[48] it nonetheless predisposes warriors to scorn an immersion in emotional needs and experiences as undignified and opposed to their cult of honor.[49]

No cultivation of the military virtues characterized the typical and patterned action-orientations of *civic* (*bürgerliche*) *strata*: skilled craftsmen and artisans, petty-bourgeois traders and merchants. Although the regular action of these strata remains as this-worldly as that of warriors, it varies considerably. In Weber's model, these patterns of action as well stand in a relationship of elective affinity to social conditions of existence.

Uprooted from magic and taboo, detached from the bonds of nature, and generally torn from sib and caste ties, these strata normally find their home in urban environments. Neither the incalculable events of nature nor the inexplicable creation involved in processes of organic reproduction influence the work of civic strata; rather, it is characterized by a severing of the immediate relationship to vital natural forces. Unlike agricultural work, which is seasonal, variable, and depends upon natural forces neither known nor constant, the regular and rationally organized work of the artisan (potter, weaver, turner, and carpenter) generally involves essentially visible and understandable relationships between means and ends as well as success and failure (see "I," p. 284/256; *E&S*, p. 1178/703).

Weber saw one of the most succinct expressions of the typical uniform action of members of this status group in the adage of Paul, a wandering craftsman: "He who does not work shall not eat" (*GEH*, p. 137/128; *E&S*, p. 499/304; "I," p. 279/251). Founded in the hard necessities of workaday life, this sober attitude endows an entire perspective toward economic transactions with an element of calculability far more stringent than that found among peasants, and it offers a positive evaluation of honesty, work, and the performance of obligations.

> When one compares the life of a petty-bourgeois, particularly the urban artisan or the small trader, with the life of the peasant, it is clear that the former has far less connection with nature. . . . At the same time . . . it is clear that the economic foundation of the urban man's life has a far more rational character, viz., calculability and capacity for means–end rational influence. Furthermore, the artisan and, in certain circumstances, even the merchant lead economic existences which influence them to entertain the view that honesty is the best policy, that faithful work and a performance of obligations will find their reward and are "deserving" of their just compensation. (*E&S*, pp. 482–3/294)

48 Weber notes that chivalrous warriors, as is typical of heroism in general, "have lacked . . . the desire as well as the capacity for a rational mastery of reality." This results in part from their acceptance of a notion of fate as more powerful than even heroic action (see "I," p. 283/255).

49 On the above two paragraphs see *E&S*, pp. 905–8/517–18, 1142/676, 1153–4/684–5; *RofI*, pp. 63/64–5; *RofC*, p. 24/302.

This immersion in daily activities inclines civic strata away from a search for a comprehensive meaning of the world's fragmented happenings or a theoretical mastery of reality, away from a cultivation of military virtues, and away from an indulgence in emotional needs and experiences. Instead, a goal-oriented pragmatism rooted in practical life situations prevails ("I," p. 284/256).

Universal organizations: the household and neighborhood   Similar to status groups, "universal organizations" constitute, for Weber, models that capture the uprooting of action from its random course. The household, clan, and neighborhood comprise the major universal organizations (see *E&S*, p. 48/26).[50] As "undifferentiated forms of life," all are unequivocally endowed with an intense person-oriented, or communal, aspect (*E&S*, p. 375/266). Just as the regular action that arises to congeal into status groups, the patterned action typical of universal organizations crystallizes out of the conditions of social existence and everyday experiences.[51]

The most important universal organization in Weber's empirical texts is the *household*. It provides, as the basic unit of economic maintenance and the most widespread economic organization, the locus for "very continuous and intensive social action" (*E&S*, pp. 358–9/214). The intense bond of intimacy and perpetual interaction between father, mother, and children in the household gives rise to distinct values. The sense of loyalty toward the in-group forms the basis for a strong household solidarity in dealing with the outside world and promotes an ethic of brotherhood that prohibits all financial calculation within the family. The "principle of household communism," according to which "each contributes in relation to his capacities and consumes according to his needs," expresses this sense of in-group loyalty and personal obligation. Blood bonds and continuous social action also form the basis for candor, reliability, and authority (*E&S*, pp. 358–60/213–14, 579/350; *GEH*, pp. 46–50/57–60, 116–22/111–16).

The circle of participants in the *neighborhood* universal organization is far more fluctuating than is the case for the household. Since based on the simple fact that people reside in close physical proximity, the social action it calls forth is far less intensive and continuous than that typical in the household. Indeed, neighborhoods very often lose their open character, in which merely intermittent social action prevails, and acquire firm boundaries only when they become either an economic or an economically-regulatory organization. Although they may only seldom call forth social action and vary greatly in form – scattered farms, a city street, an urban slum, a village – and cohesiveness, neighborhoods, even in the modern city, retain

50 The translations of *Verband* (organizations) have been exceedingly diverse, and thus it is not possible to understand the household, clan, and neighborhood as organizations without access to the original German. See chapter 2, note 15.
51 Weber refers to these organizations variously as communal, traditional, primeval (*urwüchsig*), personal, and universal.

the potential to orient action in defined and patterned ways (*E&S*, pp. 361–3/215–18). Weber's locus model, by examining typical constraints and opportunities, charts these action-orientations.

Simply as a result of the dependence of neighbors upon one another in times of distress, the neighborhood comprises the original locus for an ethic of mutual assistance. Indeed, an "unsentimental ethic of brotherhood" may well arise in neighborhoods. This ethic might also strengthen the household's in-group prohibition upon haggling and dickering.

> The neighbor is the typical helper in need, and hence "neighborhood" is the typical carrier of "brotherhood," albeit in a somber and unpathetic, primarily economic sense. If the household is short of means, mutual help may be requested: the loans of implements and goods free of charge, and "free labor for the asking" [*Bittarbeit*] in case of urgent need. This mutual help is guided by the primeval popular ethic which is as unsentimental as it is universal: "Do unto others as you would have them do unto you".... If compensation is provided, it consists in feasting the helpers.... If an exchange takes place, the maxim applies: "brothers do not bargain with one another." This eliminates the rational "market principle" of price determination. (*E&S*, pp. 361–2/216; see also p. 1188/710)

Thus, Weber sees the "essence of neighborly social action" as involving a "sombre economic 'brotherhood' practiced in case of need" (*E&S*, p. 363/218). The idea of reciprocity – "as you do unto me, I shall do unto you" and "your want of today may be mine of tomorrow" – develops from this ethic of mutual assistance and orients action.

Feudal rulership   Rulership organizations also, as status groups and universal organizations, delineate clear loci for regular action-orientations. Again, typical life experiences and pragmatic everyday activities, according to Weber's ideal-typical model, imply probabilities in respect to the crystallization of patterned action. Only the manner in which feudal rulership does so can be noted.

Both the manorial and benefice forms of feudalism imply full appropriation of the means of administration and extreme decentralization. In both cases vassals tend to cultivate an independence from lords, and obedience remains voluntary rather than coerced. This structural context makes for endemic conflict: a situation within which customs might be called into question and both rulers and vassals attend to their self-interests.[52]

Such high decentralization means that, according to Weber, authority depends upon whether vassals remain faithful to the *Treuebeziehung*, the fraternal relationship of allegiance rooted in a host of values (see *E&S*, p. 256/149). This feudal ethos, which arises particularly in manorial feudal-

---

52 On the various ways in which the ruler in manorial feudalism sought to strengthen his position against his vassals, see *E&S*, pp. 258–9/150–1.

ism, regulates and gives legitimacy to the precarious relationship between lords and vassals. It does so mainly through its demanding code of duties and honors, all of which provide "substantial safeguards of the vassal's interests" and stress action-orientations toward notions of allegiance and loyalty. Moreover, vassals legitimate their elevated status solely through an intact relationship with the lord. Consciousness of status, the privileges and duties incumbent upon status, an exalted conception of status honor, and a solidarity that precludes the imposition of arbitrary obligations upon vassals orient, according to this code, regular action. It is binding upon both parties and formulates, in Weber's terms, an "integrating component" (*E&S*, p. 1081/633; see also pp. 1078/630, 1074–5/628, 1104–5/650).

The inculcation of such an ethos based upon status honor and fealty, in this model, is the subject of an elaborate special education. Military education, for example, is oriented to free camaraderie and chivalry: courage, valor, loyalty, friendship, perfection of personal military skills, and individual heroism in battle are decisive rather than discipline, drill, and the adaptation of each individual to an organized operation, as in mass armies. Preparation for the way of life of the knightly stratum also entails, according to Weber, refinement, cultivation, and an orientation toward individual artistic creation.[53] In general, knightly conventions, pride of status and a high sense of aristocratic sentiment predispose the feudal education to emphasize an heroic individualism. This opposes sharply the patrimonial official's notion of honor based upon services and functions (*E&S*, pp. 1105–6/650–1, 1090/639–40, 1108/653).

These few ideal-typical models must suffice to indicate that Weber's comparative-historical sociology outlines a further mode of patterning action beyond orders and legitimate orders: sociological loci. Indeed, his substantive texts delineate a strongly *contextual* sociology that forcefully and vividly argues, at the level of ideal types, for the acknowledgment of a relationship between routine life chances and empirical uniformities of action.[54] Loci identify social conditions of existence that, because they imply

53 This central aspect endows the manorial feudalism model with a "heroic hostility" (*E&S*, p. 1108/653) toward all commercial relationships, the impersonal and formally rational nature of which bestows upon them, from the point of view of the feudal ethos, an undignified and vulgar character. This feudal way of life exhibits a nonchalance in respect to business affairs rather than a rational economic ethos (see *E&S*, pp. 1105–6/650–1).

54 Status groups, universal organizations, and rulership organizations best illustrate Weber's notion of a sociological locus for action. However, the formulation of models in which *patterned action is situated contextually* by reference to social conditions of existence and routine experience occurs also in a more general sense fairly regularly throughout *E&S*. For example, a propensity to develop salvation religions arises whenever ruling strata have suffered a loss of political power. At such times of enforced or voluntary de-politicization of the educated strata, the socially privileged begin to evaluate their "intellectual training in its ultimate intellectual and psychological consequences [as] far more important . . . than their practical participation in the external affairs of the mundane world" (*E&S*, p. 504/306; for examples, see *E&S*, pp. 504–5/306–7, 592/357). Similarly, Weber's sustained attention to social contexts leads him to

constraints and opportunities, call forth patterned action. Probabilities exist that regular action-orientations will appear and, more importantly, endure and become sociologically significant.[55] Although not all ideal types articulate social contexts, those ideal types that do – the sociological loci – are fundamental throughout Weber's comparative-historical sociology.

Sociological loci, along with orders and legitimate orders, comprise Weber's structuralism. These concepts denote *patterned* action and, in doing so, indicate the manner in which repetitiveness and stability crystallize. In other words, for Weber, they articulate explicitly the ways in which agency becomes linked to structure. The uprooting of action from an amorphous flow and its orientation in clear directions – that is, its formation into *regularities* of meaningful action – constitutes one of the most very basic concerns in Weber's empirical writings.

The Agency–Structure Linkage

In conceptualizing empirical uniformities of action as arising, with varying likelihoods, from demarcated social contexts, the notion of a sociological locus for action reveals another manner in which, alongside orders and legitimate orders,[56] Weber links action to structure. Just as orders and

---

conclude as well that certain settings favor the development of certain values and even religious ethics. For example, values of resignation and passivity become increasingly prominent in religious ethics wherever political circumstances of oppression lead to the utilization of priests as agents to domesticate the masses. Eventually, with an anti-political rejection of the world and a total loss of secular concerns among priests and the educated strata, brotherly love and a renunciation of violence may characterize religious ethics. This occurs all the more to the extent that a religion becomes congregational and popularized, to the degree that great world empires cease their struggles and – with the bureaucratization of rulership – universal pacification characterizes the "external situation," and to the extent that class conflicts are eliminated (see *E&S*, pp. 591–3/356–7). Finally, Weber makes this point also in reference to original thinking. He argues that a favorable milieu for the development of religious thought is provided by marginal social status. Pariah intellectuals (e.g. scribes, wandering poets, the self-taught intelligentsia, the Russian quasi-proletarian peasant intellectuals, petty-bourgeois Puritans, and the Jewish laity, all of whom survived under conditions of minimum standards of living and possess "inferior" education) stand either at the lower end of the social hierarchy or outside of it altogether. As a consequence of their freedom from social conventions, they are capable "of an original attitude toward the meaning of the cosmos" (*E&S*, p. 507/308). Even the very intensity of the "ethical and religious emotion" of this group derives from its outsider status and its unwillingness to be influenced by economic considerations (*E&S*, p. 507/308).

55   For further examples, which abound in Weber's texts, see Kalberg, 1985a. Again (see note 46), Weber refers, in these models, to the *analytic* linkage between shared everyday experiences and uniform action by reference to terms such as "likelihood" and "elective affinity." These regular action-orientations, and particularly value-rational action, cannot be conceptualized as a "function" or "reflection" of daily experience or as "determined" by typical and routine activities, as Weber repeatedly stresses (see e.g. "I," pp. 269–70/240, 284/256, and generally pp. 268–92/238–65; *AJ*, p. 80/89).

56   These are the most central modes of patterning action in Weber's substantive texts. However, they are not exhaustive. Other, and less sociological, modes might include e.g.

legitimate orders, sociological loci demonstrate that, for him, the origin and crystallization of regular action-orientations cannot be accounted for simply by reference to instrumental calculations. These three *modes of patterning action* as well place Weber in strict opposition to the view that uniformities of action originate in a putative necessity for societies to "maintain themselves," create social order, or fulfill certain functions. Weber enunciates a level of analysis distinct from an exclusive focus upon solitary and interest-pursuing individuals on the one hand and "society," global generalities, organic "systems," and a simple orientation to norms on the other. In doing so he combines his attention to subjective meaning and individual action with a distinctly social aspect: an orientation of action to collectivities on the one hand and social contexts on the other.

In clearly linking agency and the regular action of individuals, or structure, Weber avoids a prominent weakness of the world systems, causal analytic, and interpretive historical approaches. All fail to offer explicit concepts, procedures, and strategies that do so. Indeed, because agency scarcely appears in these approaches, structural analyses dominate. Moreover, in articulating his modes of patterning action, Weber never substitutes the abstract, general theory of the structural–functional school of political development and modernization for empirical observation. His orders, legitimate orders, and sociological loci preclude a push toward the ahistorical evolutionism and differentiation processes typical of this approach. The emphasis widespread in the secondary literature on Weber upon global notions, such as "universal rationalization," "irresistible bureaucratization," and an "alternation between charisma and tradition," neglects Weber's concern in his substantive texts with the linkage between individual action and social structures.

Weber's notion of *Verstehen*, or interpretive understanding, lays the cornerstone for his agency–structure synthesis. Tendencies among Ameri-

---

Weber's "legitimation–compensation" social psychology. For him, "any advantage of life," including power, manifests "a generally observable need ... to justify itself" (*E&S*, p. 953/549), and "simple observation shows that in every situation he who is more favored feels the never ceasing need to look upon his position as in some way 'legitimate,' upon his advantage as 'deserved,' and the other's disadvantage as being brought about by the latter's 'fault'" (*E&S*, p. 953/549; see also p. 491/299; "I," p. 271/242). This "general need" is especially visible whenever rulership organizations (see *E&S*, p. 213/122; "I," p. 338/551; *RofI*, pp. 16–17/16–17, 131/131; *AJ*, pp. 231/246–7) and status groups (see *E&S*, pp. 490–7/298–303, 934/536, 953/549; "I," pp. 274–7/245–8) seek to justify advantage. On the other hand, an equally universal tendency exists for "the sense of dignity of the negatively privileged strata naturally [to] refer to a future lying beyond the present, whether it is of this life or another" (*E&S*, p. 934/536). In this future, what is lacking in the present will come into being: a special function, historic mission, or vocation will be assigned to members of these strata, thereby fulfilling their "hunger for worthiness" and significance (*E&S*, p. 491/299). Weber sees also a further *psychological* dimension as central in the case of the patterning of action of intellectuals: an "inner need" to undertake a theoretical mastery of reality (see Kalberg, 1980, pp. 1153–4, 1985a, p. 51; 1990).

can commentators to discuss *Verstehen* exclusively in terms of its epistemological status and to interpret Weber's methodological individualism and stress upon subjective meaning as standing in opposition to all structural considerations have been widespread.[57] This constriction of *Verstehen* has led to a neglect of Weber's articulation, through orders, legitimate orders, and sociological loci, of a unity between patterned action-orientations and social structures. This chapter has sought to define the foundational "agency" components of Weber's sociology clearly – his methodological individualism, notion of *Verstehen*, four types of action, and emphasis upon pluralistic motives – and then to discuss them in reference to these modes of patterning action. In the process of doing so a larger purpose behind his comparative-historical sociology has been disclosed: to assist macro-sociologists in quite practical ways to "understand" putatively "irrational" action-orientations and, thereby, to take cognizance of the importance of subjective meaning.

Wherever sociologists are assisted to see how action is oriented to orders and legitimate orders, and embedded in social contexts, they can more easily *understand* its subjective meaningfulness. Moreover, not merely the understanding of the ways in which persons, for example, orient action to a particular religious doctrine, attribute legitimacy to a given form of rulership, or adhere to a specific status ethic is involved here; rather, Weber's modes of patterning action – orders, legitimate orders, and sociological loci – facilitate also the comprehension of social action even in "foreign" and "strange" environments as subjectively meaningful. Researchers can, once they have reconstructed a setting, assess whether actions approximate one of the types of action. To the degree that meaningful action is identified as located within orders and legitimate orders as well as indigenous contexts of constraints and opportunities, and thereby "understood," it becomes "transformed" from "irrational" action into "plausible" and even, in some cases, "altogether logical" action. Within the reconstructed milieu, individuals can be seen to "make sense" of their situations and act accordingly. Through "interpretive understanding" – a "recapturing" of the experiences of others in a milieu – sociologists grasp the ways in which action becomes motivated in patterned ways, indeed even the *varying motives and intensities* of action.[58] They do so either through "rational understanding," which involves an intellectual grasp of the meaning actors attribute to their actions, or through "intuitive" or "empathic understanding," which involves an understanding of "the emotional context in which the action [takes] place" (*E&S*, p. 5/2).[59] In this way, at the most basic level,

---

57 The notion of *Verstehen* has been appropriated in the American discussion only by Symbolic Interactionism.

58 Although less the case in *AG* and *GEH* than in *EEWR* and *E&S*, reconstructions of meaning complexes that constitute causal motivations for action pervade Weber's substantive texts.

59 Most of the secondary literature has addressed Weber's notion of causality exclusively in

Weber's *verstehende* sociology provides *causal* explanations of action.[60] In doing so – by reference to orders, legitimate orders, and sociological loci – agency and structure are linked.

Having scrutinized this linkage by examining the structuralism of Weber's substantive texts (his three major modes of patterning action) and their agency foundation (methodological individualism, the notion of *Verstehen*, the four types of action, and the pluralism of motives), this chapter has laid the groundwork for his causal sociology. One further foundational component of Weber's comparative-historical sociology must be addressed in a systematic fashion before turning to the strategies and procedures of this causal sociology: the multicausality of his substantive texts.

---

such terms. This imbalance will be addressed and, it is hoped, corrected, by reference to Weber's empirical writings, in chapters 2, 3, and 4.

60   Investigators must not, of course, themselves relive the experience in order to understand the manner in which it causes action: "one need not have been Caesar in order to understand Caesar" (*E&S*, p. 5/2). States of emotional experience, in particular, can be seldom relived. In this case understanding occurs if the emotional context within which action takes place is adequately grasped (*E&S*, p. 5/2; "EK," pp. 428–9). The meanings of the persons under investigation may, of course, vary enormously from those accepted by sociologists as "legitimate" or "correct." Extreme cases, such as that of the Buddhist monk and the Calvinist (see *PE*, pp. 70–1/54–5, 110/103; *PE II*, p. 161), render the "objective" understanding of meaning difficult, all the more so if the sociologist is not susceptible to states of great religious emotion or personally scorns pre-scientific modes of knowledge (see the discussion of *Richtigkeitsrationalität* at "EK," pp. 432–6; "EN," pp. 40–3/532–5). These acknowledged difficulties do not in principle (see *E&S*, pp. 5–6/2), however, call the *method* of *Verstehen* into question.

2
Weber's Multicausality

All assertions of a universal and constant relationship between values and material interests remain foreign to Weber, as do all attempts to establish whether rulership, organizational, religious, legal, status, or economic forces can be said to be generally dominant. For example, economic changes cannot be said to lead generally to new legal forms; rather, these forms must already exist in incipient forms: "the rational patterns of legal technique ... must first be 'invented' before they can serve an existing economic interest" (*E&S*, p. 687/412). Arguing in a parallel fashion, Weber abjures the elevation of religious factors above economic factors: "religion nowhere creates certain economic conditions unless there are also present in the existing relationships and constellations of interests certain possibilities of, or even powerful drives toward, such an economic transformation" (*E&S*, p. 577/349; see also, for example, "I," pp. 268–70/238–40, 286–7/ 259). He refuses as well to offer general causal propositions in respect to distinctly delineated developments (see, for example, *E&S*, p. 577/349).[1] In the concrete case, even the "market may be subject to an order (*Ordnung*) autonomously agreed upon by the participants or imposed by any one of a great variety of different groups, especially political or religious organizations" (*E&S*, p. 639/385; transl. alt.). Thus, Weber accords *analytically* equal weight to, in his well-known phrase, an array of both "ideal and material interests." He does so even while acknowledging the possibility, in a *given empirical* case, of the pre-eminence of a single factor.

Weber's comparative-historical texts attend to a full spectrum of causal factors, as does the interpretive historical school. His writings, however, oppose the attempt by adherents of this approach, particularly Charles

---

1 "It is not possible to enunciate any general formula that will summarize the comparative substantive powers of the various factors involved ... or will summarize the manner of their accommodation to one another" (*E&S*, p. 577/349).

Tilly, to establish causality alone from a detailed richness of description. Given his axiom of value-relevance, an understanding of social reality as inexhaustible, and a preference for ideal types, Weber denies in principle the possibility of doing so.[2]

On the other hand, proponents of the world systems school reject broadly multicausal procedures. They attend above all to the influence of the international economy upon domestic political and economic development. The *interests* of economic and political actors in the core constitute their major concern, as well as the power of multinational corporations. The values of status groups, the family, and religions are accordingly downplayed, as are cultural variations in general in the semi-periphery and periphery areas.

The causal analytic school as well focusses upon structural forces, mainly class relations and the state. Adherents of this approach, in investigating alternative hypotheses, invariably fail to uphold a broadly multicausal methodology. Moore emphasizes classes, changes in class structures, and the interests of ruling classes, while Skocpol stresses national politics and the manner in which states act independently. Neither attends to cultural factors on a regular basis. A complex relationship between values, traditions, and interests is seldom acknowledged. Although not constrained by their Millian research design methodology to reject multicausal procedures, practitioners of the causal analytic approach regularly elevate economic and political factors to positions of causal priority.

Weber's causal investigations *retain* a principled commitment to a broadly multicausal methodology. He insists in particular that the investigation of all enduring structures and economic relations include reference to the beliefs and values that legitimate and uphold them. His analyses of the power, for example, of the sib group in China, the caste order in India, and the German Prussian state are characterized by just such an emphasis. His well-known "types of rulership" involve not simply an examination of external structures, but also a focus upon the manner in which rulership comes to be viewed as legitimate.

Weber's radically multicausal analyses diverge significantly from all recent schools of comparative-historical sociology in further ways. First, his empirical texts exhibit a repeated attention to the variable *intensity* of action. Second, Weber stresses, if action is to become sociologically significant, the indispensability of powerful "social carriers." Indeed, carriers themselves may exert an independent causal impact upon regular action-orientations. However, even while attending to a variety of social carriers of patterned action, Weber's multicausal analyses do not downplay the influence of action oriented to historical events, technological innovations, and geographical factors. These action-orientations will be examined in the

---

2   The axiom of value-relevance and Weber's view of social reality is discussed in chapter 3, pp. 84–6. Ideal types are the main subject of chapter 3.

third section of this chapter. As will become apparent in chapters 4 and 5, Weber insists, even more than the interpretive historical school, that these forces must be placed within a sociological *context*. Finally, his comparative-historical sociology links social carriers to the question of power on the one hand and to the capacity of conflict, competition, and the sheer tension between patterned action-orientations to call forth regular action on the other hand.[3] These themes concern us in this chapter.

The Principled Commitment to Multicausality

Weber's historicist stress upon individual constellations and the dynamics of historical contingency, as well as his refusal to view "abstract uniformities," including even ideal types, as other than heuristic concepts, indicates a deep commitment to a broadly multicausal methodology, as does his explicit rejection of all theories that argue in behalf of the empirical validity and necessary unfolding of universal stages and laws (see chapter 3, pp. 81–3). His unwillingness to postulate necessary causal relationships is visible even in his analysis of the juxtaposition of Calvinism and capitalism: rather than to be understood as the product of a logical evolution or inevitable development, this intertwining of a particular "economic ethic" and "economic form" occurred as a result of concrete historical forces.[4] At first glance, Weber's radical multicausality may not be apparent.[5]

Many commentators have viewed *PE* as evidencing a general "idealist bias"; Weber, however, insists upon the limited task of this case study. Rather than being designed to offer a causal explanation for the origins of modern capitalism, *PE* seeks to investigate the *source* of the methodical attitude toward labor – the "spirit" of capitalism – that replaced the "traditional" economic ethic (*PE*, pp. 48–51/31–3, 55/37, 74–8/60–2). Unable to discover the origin of this "rational" economic ethic in material, biological,

3 Although recent commentators recognize Weber's multicausality, I am not aware of a study in the secondary literature that examines this theme explicitly and in the degree of detail set out here.
4 In particular, as a consequence of rulership and political (power) factors (see e.g. *PE*, p. 278, n. 84/192, n. 1; *E&S*, pp. 630/378, 1196–7/716–17; "IR," pp. 336–7/549–50; *RofI*, pp. 337–8/372). Marshall (1980) makes this quite clear, as does Collins (1981) in his reconstruction of Weber's "last theory of capitalism."
5 Many statements to be found throughout Weber's substantive writings drastically oversimplify his own procedures to establish causality and must be viewed as only embryonic conceptualizations. I am thinking of his not infrequent statements which proclaim the primacy of a single societal domain, frequently the political (rulership and power); see e.g. *E&S*, pp. 845/486, 883/505, 977/564. In *EEWR, GEH*, and *AG* in particular Weber too often reduces the true complexity and power of his causal methodology by treating, for example, religious and material factors in isolation rather than providing an analysis of the complicated ways in which they intertwine. (However, I do not share Alexander's contention [1983] that Weber "retreats" from "multidimensionality." His argument rests upon a failure to understand the differing modes of analysis in the political, comparative, and analytic [*E&S*] writings. See below and chapters 4 and 5.) On this issue generally, see chapter 5. The translations constitute another problem. Most have regularly strengthened Weber's verbs, omitted his quotation marks, and failed to translate the emphasis in statements that qualify causal linkages.

or structural factors, he turned to religious texts and found clear evidence in the exhortations and sermons of the Puritan divines, particularly those delivered by Baxter in the seventeenth century (*PE*, pp. 99–106/90–7). Whether this "ethos" was indeed significant in the rise of modern capitalism in the several countries of its birth was, to Weber, an open question to be investigated empirically and in relation to a host of patterned action-orientations toward rulership, the economy, status groups, universal organizations, and laws. Weber himself never intended to offer a multicausal analysis in this "essay in cultural history"; rather, he intentionally emphasized "ideal" configurations in order to argue forcefully for the necessity of their inclusion into all analyses of the rise of modern capitalism (*PE*, p. 183/ 205; see also pp. 277–8, n. 84/192, n. 1; pp. 283–4, n. 118/205, n. 3; *PE II*, p. 182).

Weber considers *both* the influence of religious doctrine and the "materialist" side in *EEWR*. He notes a variety of non-religious obstacles to economic development in China, such as extremely strong sib ties and an absence of "a formally guaranteed law and a rational administration and judiciary" (*RofC*, p. 85/374; see also pp. 91/381, 99–100/389–91), and in India, such as constraints placed upon migration, the recruitment of labor, and credit by the caste system (*RofI*, pp. 111–17/109–16, 52–3/54–6, 102–6/100–4). He discovers as well, however, an entire host of conducive material forces that nonetheless failed to bring about modern bourgeois capitalism, such as, in China, freedom of trade, an increase in precious metals, population growth, occupational mobility, and the presence of a money economy (*RofC*, pp. 243/530, 54–5/340–1, 99–100/390, 243/529–30, 12/289–90). Thus, he states again his refusal to ignore religious values: "The origin of economic rationalism, just as it is dependent upon a rational technology and rational law, is also dependent upon the capacity and disposition of people to engage in a certain kind of practical-rational *way of life*. Wherever this way of life has been obstructed by inhibiting religious forces, then even the development of an *economically* rational way of life confronts severe indigenous resistance" ("AI," pp. 26–7/12; transl. alt.; emph. orig.). Weber describes the *EEWR* studies as not simply investigations into the complex relationships between the spheres of the economy and religion, but more generally as "studies on the *universal* historical interrelationships between religion and society" (*PE*, p. 284, n. 119/206, n. 1; emph. orig.; see also "AI," pp. 27/12–13).

The very organization and disposition of *E&S* also testifies to Weber's commitment to broadly multicausal modes of procedure. Rather than departing from a notion of "society" or taking the issue of how social order arises and is maintained, this analytic treatise remains focussed upon patterned action by persons in diverse status groups, classes, and organizations. These, in turn, are situated within demarcated *societal domains* (*gesellschaftliche Ordnungen*), each of which is defined by an indigenous problem: the status group, universal organization, religion, law, rulership, and economy domains. An array of ideal types is connected analytically to each domain.[6] As argued in chapter 1, each of Weber's ideal types – for example, the family, civil servants, the capitalist economy, the asceticism path of salvation, and bureaucratic authority – implies *regular* action-orientations with a degree of endurance, directedness, and firmness. Each indicates both a continuity of meaningful action and a clear resistance against random action as well as all competing action-orientations. Thus, likelihoods regarding the persistence of certain uniform action and the exclusion of other action are apparent in respect to each ideal type. In this manner, each charts *empirical possibilities*, and, as patterned, the action-orientations demarcated by ideal types are endowed with an indigenous causal thrust and staying power or, in Weber's terms, an *autonomous* (*eigengesetzliche*) aspect.[7] His substantive texts testify that arrays of independent action-orientations are sociologically significant: each is potentially endowed with empirical causal efficacy.[8]

Because Weber views the sources of patterned action as extremely pluralistic, he rejects all theories of cyclical development and the monocausal materialist theories popular in the Marxist thought of his time. He was especially critical, even while acknowledging its fruitful heuristic value, of the elevation of the Marxian substructure/superstructure axiom to the status of a general and scientific law. For example, although he stressed the influence of carrier strata upon the formation and diffusion of religious doctrines, Weber also argued that belief systems could not be viewed as a mere function of stratum-specific interests (see, for example, "I," pp. 269–70/240–1). An economic ethic, likewise, cannot be understood "as a simple 'function' of a form of economic organization" ("I," p. 268/238; see chapter 1, pp. 28–9). By the same token, a class of formally trained jurists, for example, should not be understood as crystallizing simply from capitalistic interests. As Weber asks: "Why did not the capitalistic interests do the same in China or India" ("AI," p. 25/11)?

He is convinced that a far more complex relationship exists, for example, between legal and economic factors than the Marxian substructure/superstructure axiom allows. The absence of economic interests is by no means

6 The character and organization of *E&S* is noted in detail in chapter 3, pp. 87–91; chapter 4, pp. 95–8 and 102–17; see also chapter 5, pp. 149–51.
7 The centrality of "autonomy" has been obscured by its diverse translations. It appears variously as "lawful autonomy," "own rules," "inherent logic," "intrinsic necessities," and "autonomy." See Kalberg, 1979, 1980, 1985a. Salomon first noted the importance of this notion in Weber's works (see 1945, pp. 597–600); see also Gerth (1946, pp. 62–4), Tenbruck (1980).
8 As the "relations of antagonism" models will demonstrate (see chapter 4, pp. 102–17), Weber makes no assumptions regarding a drift toward harmony. To him, whether a *society* succeeds in creating an overarching cultural order, normative integration, and "value-generalization" (see Parsons, 1966, 1971) does not constitute a central theoretical issue for sociology. Rather, this remains a question to be investigated empirically and on a case-by-case basis (see Kalberg, 1987, 1992, 1993a, forthcoming c). Parsons's reading of Weber, which obviously departs from such questions regarding the maintenance of social order, distorts the Weberian corpus.

the single explanation for the failure of a legal institution to develop, and a legal system's specific types of techniques "are of far greater significance for the likelihood that a certain legal institution will be invented in its context than is ordinarily believed" (*E&S*, pp. 687/412; see also pp. 654–5/395; Weber, 1889, pp. 13–14). The "irrational" modes of thought of Germanic law, for example, favored the invention of certain legal techniques (see *E&S*, p. 683/409), and the "backward" legal devices of medieval law, which were decidedly less rationalized in a logical and technical sense than those of Roman law, facilitated the invention of an array of capitalistic legal institutions (see *E&S*, p. 688/412; *GEH*, pp. 340–3/290–3). In general: "Economic situations do not automatically give birth to new legal forms; they merely provide the opportunity for the actual spread of a legal technique if it is invented" (*E&S*, p. 687/412).[9]

Weber sees that vested interests often pushed legal development along an independent developmental path. "Intrajuristic" conditions, such as "the particular features of the individuals who are in a position to influence, by virtue of their profession, the ways in which the law is shaped," and especially the type of legal education, have been especially important (*E&S*, p. 776/456; transl. alt.). Technically trained notaries developed legal techniques along "their own paths" in the seventh century (*E&S*, p. 683/408). Weber viewed also the differences in methods of legal thought between continental and Common Law as closely bound up with the "internal structure and modes of existence of the legal profession" (*E&S*, p. 889/509). "Intrinsic needs of the administration of justice," including the necessity of rationalizing legal procedures, set into motion a powerful thrust that called forth a stratum of trained jurists who could articulate legal issues unambiguously (*E&S*, p. 853/491). These jurists, in turn, very frequently played an autonomous and influential part in the innovation of legal techniques (*E&S*, p. 776/456).

In steadfastly refusing to assign a rank order to patterned action-orientations, as captured by ideal types, in the status groups, universal organizations, rulership, religion, economy, and law societal domains, Weber contends that all combinations are in principle empirically possible. In introducing his chapters on traditional and charismatic rulership in Part II of *E&S*, for example, he summarizes his aims as involving not only an evaluation of the extent to which the "developmental chances" of the major "structural principles" of each rulership type can be said to be subject to "economic, political or any other external determinants," but also an assessment of the degree to which the developmental chances of the types of rulership instead follow "an 'autonomous' logic inherent in their technical structure" (*E&S*, p. 1002/578). This logic must be viewed as *capable* of

9 Weber points out on many occasions that modern capitalism has prospered equally well in countries with considerably varying legal systems, especially with respect to "principles of formal structure" (*E&S*, p. 889/509). His examples usually relate to continental and Common Law (see *E&S*, pp. 788/458, 892/511, 976–7/563–4).

exerting an independent effect even upon patterned action oriented to the economy (*E&S*, pp. 578/349, 1002/578, 654–5/395). Weber discovered many empirical cases when it was exerted (see, for example, *E&S*, pp. 650/392, 1309/780).

He is especially cognizant of the extent to which the attribution of *legitimacy* to rulership sets an independent driving force into motion. The attempt to legitimize rulership, as well as high social standing, serves normally to bolster entrenched powers. For Weber, just this capacity endows the "very general need" to justify advantage with significant implications in respect to patterned action: the strengthening of rulership and positive social honor provided by the belief in legitimacy dampens the thrust of innovative forces. With their power and prestige bolstered by Confucianism, the Chinese literati, for example, could serve as more effective proponents of familial piety, which, particularly in China, stood starkly in opposition to the unfolding of both modern capitalism and a "spirit" of capitalism (*RofC*, pp. 236–7/523). The *power* of the Brahmins in India did not alone insure that the caste system would endure and stand as a central obstacle against the development of a city economy and a "citizenry" in India; rather, the widespread *belief* that the Brahmins justly possessed prestige and authority proved also central (*RofI*, pp. 90–1/89, 113–14/112, 127–9/127–9). This same notion of legitimacy played a major part in stabilizing feudal domination: "All powerful vassals were so strongly tempted to dissolve the feudal bond altogether that the only fact to be explained is why this did not happen more often than it actually occurred. The reason was the guarantee of *legitimacy* . . . which the vassals found in the feudal association with regard to their land and rulership rights" (*E&S*, p. 636/1085; emph. orig.).

Weber calls attention as well to religious doctrines and salvation paths, each of which might highly influence the practical way of life of believers: for example, the Calvinist belief in predestination, the Lutheran justification through faith, the Indian *karma* doctrine, and the Catholic doctrine of sacrament ("I," pp. 286–7/258–9). To him: "every configuration of religious ideas . . . carries its own lawfulness and compelling power purely its own" (*PE*, pp. 277–8, n. 84/192, n. 1; transl. alt.).[10] Moreover:

> The nature of the desired sacred values has been strongly influenced by the nature of the external interest-situation and the corresponding way of life of the ruling strata and thus by the social stratification itself. But the reverse also holds: wherever the whole way of life has been methodically rationalized, its direction has been profoundly determined by the ultimate values toward which this rationalization has been oriented. ("I," pp. 286–7/259; transl. alt.; see also pp. 268–70/238–41, 286/259 and 290/263)[11]

10 This passage exists in essence in the first (1904) version of the *PE*; Weber's 1920 revision simply strengthened it.
11 See the discussion below (chapter 4, pp. 135–40) of theoretical rationalization processes for examples of the manner in which religion *may* assert an independent empirical impact upon action.

In arguing in behalf of such a full spectrum of potentially causal factors – indigenous to the economy, law, rulership, and religion life-spheres as well as to status groups, classes, and universal organizations[12] – Weber aimed in particular to conceptualize economic action within a broadened theoretical framework and to treat "both sides" of the causal nexus.[13] He is concerned to acknowledge the centrality of economic factors, as are the world systems and causal analytic schools, even while emphasizing the necessity for a radically multicausal approach. He states this clearly, as well as his aversion to all epoch-transcending generalizations, in a key passage in *E&S*:

> Groups that are not somehow economically determined are extremely rare. However, the degree of this influence varies widely and, above all, the economic determination of social action is ambiguous – contrary to the assumption of so-called historical materialism.... Even the assertion that social structures and the economy are "functionally" related is a biased view, which cannot be justified as an historical generalization, if an unambiguous interdependence is assumed. For the structural forms [*Strukturformen*] of social action follow "laws of their own," as we shall see time and again, and even apart from this fact, they may in a given case always be co-determined by other than economic cases. However, at some point economic conditions tend to become causally significant, and often decisively important, for the structuring of almost all social groups, at least those which have major "cultural significance"; conversely, the economy is usually also influenced by the autonomous structure [*Struktur*] of social action within which it exists. No significant generalization can be made as to when and how this will occur. (*E&S*, p. 341/200–1; see also p. 935/537)[14]

Weber's emphasis upon multicausality is tied intimately to his notion of social carriers (*Träger*). If patterned action-orientations are to become

12 For examples regarding status groups and the rulership and universal organizations see the section in chapter 1 on sociological loci.
13 Weber's cognizance of causal complexities is revealed in this passage on the origins of economic ethics: "An economic ethic is not a simple 'function' of a form of economic organization; and just as little does the reverse hold, namely, that economic ethics unambiguously stamp the form of the economic organization. No economic ethic has ever been determined solely by religion. In the face of people's attitudes toward the world – as determined by religious or other (in our sense) 'inner' factors – an economic ethic has, of course, a high measure of pure autonomy. Given factors of economic geography and history determine this measure of autonomy in the highest degree. The religious determination of the way of life, however, is also one – note this – only *one*, of the determinants of the economic ethic. Of course, the religiously determined way of life is itself profoundly influenced by economic and political factors operating within given geographical, political, social, and national boundaries" ("I," pp. 268/238–9; transl. alt., emph. orig.; see also pp. 269–70/240, 286–7/259).
14 Weber expressed forcefully his criticism of Marxism at the first conference of the German Sociological Association in 1909: "I would like to protest the statement by one of the speakers that some one factor, be it technology or economy, can be the 'ultimate' or 'true' cause of another. If we look at the causal lines, we see them run, at one time, from technical to economic and political matters, at another from political to religious and economic ones, etc. There is no resting point. In my opinion, the view of historical materialism, frequently espoused, that the economic is in some sense the ultimate point in the chain of causes is completely finished as a scientific proposition" ("Proceedings of the First German Conference on Sociology," p. 101; quoted in Roth, 1968, p. lxiv).

influential and sociologically significant, a cohesive and powerful carrier for them must crystallize. As he notes: "Unless the concept 'autonomy' is to lack all precision, its definition presupposes the existence of a bounded group of persons which, though membership may fluctuate, is determinable" (*E&S*, p. 699/419; transl. alt.). Moreover, carriers, in Weber's substantive texts, may independently call forth regular action. Thus, carriers stand at the very center of his multicausality; he repeatedly calls attention to them. Weber's notion of social carriers is far broader than that offered by the causal analytic or world systems approaches, and the causal role of carriers is far more explicitly emphasized in his comparative-historical writings than is the case in investigations undertaken by adherents of the interpretive historical school.

Social Carriers

Values, ideas, and currents of thought of every imaginable variety have arisen in every epoch and civilization. Nothing, for example, "in the area of thought concerning the 'significance' of the world and life ... remained unknown in one form or another in Asia" (*RofI*, p. 331/365). Yet cohesive bearers of action are always necessary, according to Weber, if ideas and, above all, patterned action-orientations are to become sociologically significant. In every society, only certain traditional, affectual, value-rational, and means–end rational regularities of action acquire cohesive proponents and become prominent in the social fabric. A powerful and self-conscious bourgeoisie, for example, failed to appear in China to promote an ethic of formal equality (*RofC*, pp. 137/426, 142/430–1), nor could, in a pre-Meiji Japan dominated by the samurai, a firmly-bounded stratum crystallize to serve "as a political force and promote a 'civic' development in the Occidental sense" (*RofI*, p. 273/298).

A great continuity of social carriers across epochs has been characteristic in some civilizations. The patrimonial bureaucracy and literati stratum in China, for example, remained the central carriers of Confucianism for more than two thousand years. In India, the Brahmins carried Hinduism for more than a millennium. In Japan, "the greatest weight in social affairs was carried by a stratum of professional warriors. ... Practical life situations were governed by a code of chivalry and education for knighthood" (*RofI*, p. 275/300).

Status groups, classes, and organizations (*Verbände*) serve[15] in Weber's comparative-historical sociology, as the most significant social carriers. This concept plays a crucial role throughout his substantive texts. Carriers fall into two fundamental categories. The first type is constituted by those status

15 Weber's notion of *Verband* (organizations) is a generic one. He speaks not only of universal organizations (family, sib, and neighborhood), but also of rulership, sect, church, and voluntary organizations. The enterprise (*Betrieb*) also constitutes an organization, as does the state.

groups, classes, and organizations familiar already as *sociological loci* for action (see chapter 1, pp. 39–49). Because they define clear constraints upon as well as opportunities for certain action and likelihoods regarding the crystallization of discrete, specifiable, and regular action-orientations, these carriers often themselves introduce an independent driving force, one endowed with the potential to influence causally an historical case or development. A second type of carrier implies merely an "external structure" or "form." Because this structure fails to call forth specifiable and patterned action, a broad diversity of action-orientations may take place within it. For this reason, this bearer of action does not itself serve as a driving force. These carriers are generally voluntary organizations, enterprises (*Betriebe*), states, sects, churches, and political parties, though Weber also refers to the city, the nation, the caste system in India, and ethnic groups as examples of this type of carrier.

Sects, for example, even though their external structure is everywhere similar and equally rigid and although they accept only religiously qualified persons as members, fail to call forth homogeneous and regular action-orientations ("I," pp. 287–92/259–65, esp. p. 292/264; see chapter 1, note 16 above). Weber's comparative-historical sociology demonstrates repeatedly, however, the unequalled capacity of the sect to *carry*, once they have congealed from religious or political doctrines, action-orientations. Although less rigid in structure, churches have also proven extremely powerful carriers of religious ethics. At the other extreme of this spectrum stand independent cities. Despite their highly flexible external "structure," they became carriers of a central force in the medieval West called forth by urban guilds and civic strata: the notion of citizenship (see *GEH*, pp. 315–37/270–89). Weber also speaks of cities as pivotal carriers of early and medieval Christianity (*E&S*, p. 1034/600).

This type of social carrier has been, according to him, of enormous historical significance. Yet this has been also true of the carrier classes, strata and organizations capable of indigenously calling forth action-orientations and serving as driving forces in history: the sociological loci. These carriers contribute strongly to the broad multicausality of Weber's substantive texts. The values and ways of life of powerful strata may highly influence, for example, even the formation of religious ethics (see "I," pp. 268–9/239–40, 279–82/253–4). This remains the case despite Weber's position that every religious ethic "receives its stamp primarily from religious sources and, first of all, from the content of its annunciation and promise" ("I," pp. 269–70/240, 284/256), and his assertion that religious belief systems may influence and alter status ethics ("I," p. 270/241). The characteristic features of every world religion's original carrier stratum penetrated sharply into the formation of its belief systems and teachings. Only a few examples of how this occurred can be noted here.

The influence of an intellectual stratum was particularly strong in the world religions of the East. The status ethic of a cultured stratum of literati assisted significantly in the formation of Confucian teachings in China (see *RofC*, pp. 107–70/395–458; "I," p. 268/239). In India an hereditary caste educated in Vedic ritual, the Brahmins, strongly imprinted the formation of Hindu salvation doctrine, and the influence of contemplative, itinerant, and mendicant monks can be seen vividly in the teachings of early Buddhism (*RofI*, p. 215/232; "I," pp. 268–9/239). To Weber, the religions of China, India, and ancient Greece involved "representations appropriate to any cultivated intellectual strata" (*RofI*, p. 352, n. 5/136, n. 1). This was also the case for ancient Judaism. The transformation and rationalization in ancient Palestine of old oracles and promises and the introduction of the "characteristically different and independent conceptions" that formulated the intellectual traditions of this religion could not have occurred if an "independent cultured stratum" had not crystallized (*AJ*, p. 205/219).

Other strata have also, in a distinctly different manner, highly influenced religious ethics: "The situation in which strata decisive for the development of a religion were practically active in life has been entirely different. Where they were chivalrous warrior heroes, political officials, economically acquisitive classes, or, finally, where an organized hierocracy dominated religion, the results were different than where genteel intellectuals were decisive" ("I," p. 282/254). The doctrine of early Islam was deeply penetrated by the status ethic of its original carrier stratum: a knight order of disciplined crusaders and conquerors. Christianity's belief system was shaped significantly in Antiquity by its original carriers: itinerant artisan journeymen, petty-bourgeois merchants, and, more generally, urban civic strata.[16] In the later Church, the fact that its functionaries held bureaucratic offices itself influenced the character of ecclesiastical lawmaking (*E&S*, p. 828/480). The impact of the typical action-orientations and ways of life of the middle and lower bourgeoisie upon ascetic Protestantism's doctrines is generally clear ("I," pp. 268–9/239–40; *E&S*, pp. 479–80/292–3, 1180/704), although Calvinism "appears to be more closely related to the hard legalism and the active enterprise of bourgeois-capitalistic entrepreneurs" (*PE*, p. 139/146).

The great impact of the carrier stratum's status ethic upon religious ethics is readily visible also whenever a world religion changes its carrier stratum. As Weber notes, "a change in the socially decisive strata has usually been of profound importance" ("I," p. 270/241). Hinduism, for example, carried in its classical period by Brahmins educated in the Vedas, became a sacramental religion of ritual, belief in saviors, magic, and even orgiasticism in the Indian Middle Ages when plebeian mystagogues and the lower strata became its carrier ("I," p. 269/239).[17] Weber succinctly indicates the importance of carriers for religious ways of life in general:

16 Weber finds "civic" strata the most ambiguous in terms of affinities to any particular type of religion. See "I," pp. 283–5/256–7.

17 On an earlier carrier shift in early Hinduism, see *RofI*, p. 176/183. See also chapter 5, pp. 182–4.

The various great ways of leading a rational and methodical life have been characterized by irrational presuppositions, which have been accepted simply as "given" and which have been incorporated into such ways of life. What these presuppositions have been is historically and socially determined, at least to a very large extent, through the peculiarity of those strata that have been the carriers of the ways of life during its formative and decisive period. ("I," p. 281/253; transl. alt.; see further "I," pp. 279–85/251–8)[18]

Thus, carrier strata constitute in their own right causal forces. They are attended to repeatedly throughout Weber's substantive works and contribute strongly to their radical multicausality. These texts draw explicit attention to the causal significance of patterned action-orientations toward numerous carrier strata, organizations, and classes. Only the interpretive historical perspective takes cognizance of such a diverse array of carriers. Proponents of this approach fail, however, to do so in an explicit and systematic fashion that indicates their analytic independence.

Because, as these few examples indicate, carriers of patterned action can, for Weber, become very important causal forces, his empirical writings regularly attend to the question of *which carriers*, in respect to a specific new development, become "economically available." He is especially attentive to the economic availability of classes and status groups. Since each implies an array of distinct action-orientations, the economic "availability" of a specific class or status group is of great sociological consequence: the extent to which the "external situation" allows a particular class or stratum to participate in a new development may well be decisive in respect to the direction followed by this new development. For this reason, a concern to assess just such availability permeates Weber's substantive texts. Only a few examples can be noted.

His investigation of participation in the political arena addresses the question of "economic availability." Political parties, for example, up until the end of the eighteenth century were normally formed by the older upper class, for only aristocrats were available for service (*E&S*, p. 1130/668). Administration by such "notables" is particularly characteristic wherever bureaucratic forms of organization are not present (*E&S*, p. 291/171). As mass parties arose in the latter nineteenth century, certain classes once again were far more available for leadership roles than others. Journalists, for example, and especially propertyless journalists, simply as a consequence of the "tremendously increased intensity and tempo of journalistic operations" ("PV," p. 97/526), were only seldom available as party leaders. The same must be said of urban businessmen who, because of their economic indispensability, were similarly handicapped, at least until their retirement. On the other hand, simply because they were economically independent, the likelihood that wealthy landowners would become "pro-

18   Of course, as just noted, Weber is not here perceiving a rigorous causal relationship. See also e.g. "I," p. 270/240; chapter 4, pp. 108–11.

fessional" politicians proved much greater.[19] This was particularly the case in England where the rural gentry increasingly leased its property, thereby becoming free to serve as justices of the peace (*E&S*, pp. 1060/617–18; "PV," p. 85/514).[20]

Intimately bound up with Weber's overall multicausality – a radical *pluralism* of forces regularly gives rise to patterned action-orientations – is his assertion that action varies in its intensity, or its capacity vis-à-vis other forces to sustain regular action. This central aspect of Weber's substantive texts constitutes a fundamental component of his multicausal comparative-historical sociology. It places him in the strictest opposition in particular to rational choice theory.[21]

The Variable Intensity of Action: the Opposition to Rational Choice Theory

For Weber, as noted in chapter 1, patterned action results not only from values (*E&S*, pp. 30/15, 32/17), but also from affectual and traditional action. Even means–end rational action in behalf of worldly interests calls forth continuity and regularities of action.

His adherence to methodological individualism, focus upon subjective meaning, and rejection of organic, functional, and orthodox structural

19   Attention to the question of the "availability of classes" points to one of the great dangers faced by democracies. This danger – "the probability that administration will fall into the hands of the wealthy" (*E&S*, p. 949/546) – arises not because the well-to-do are more fit to rule; rather, it originates from the fact that the income of many among the wealthy finds its source in intermittent labor at best. For this reason, they are blessed with both a surplus of leisure time and the availability to perform service tasks for little or no remuneration. A sacrifice of time or income is not required of them (*E&S*, pp. 949–50/546–7).

20   Weber argues along the same lines in respect to other carriers as well. A few examples can be noted. The time-consuming training for magical charisma or heroism remained a possibility for young men from diverse strata only to the extent that the economy could run smoothly without them. Because more frequently dispensable, the wealthy often acquired a monopoly on charismatic education (*E&S*, p. 1146/679). Similarly, he sees that only men of means emancipated from intensive work are available for participation in Hinduism's elaborate rituals of devotion and piety (*E&S*, p. 530/322). Moreover, he concludes: "In the midst of ... culture[s] ... rationally organized for a vocational workaday life," the acosmic search for salvation of the mystic can take place only among the "economically carefree strata" ("IR," p. 357/571). Agrarian slaves in Antiquity are also viewed in terms of their availability, in this case in respect to military service: just the necessity for them to sustain themselves as well as a feudal lord rendered this stratum ill-suited to serve as a permanent military force (*E&S*, p. 1015/587). He examines warfare as well in part in reference to the question of the availability of classes and status groups. Unless overwhelmed by ideological passions, the acquisitive and propertied strata in urban areas became less and less available for war wherever the "intensity and strain" of labor increased.

21   A concern to define action is seldom manifest in recent comparative-historical investigations. Mann is an exception. He states his underlying rational choice assumptions clearly (see 1986, pp. 4, 30). Notably absent, as is the case with all proponents of rational choice theory, as well as values, is an analysis of the strength of tradition. See chapter 1, pp. 32–9.

schools, as well as his observation that interests alone may lead to sustained regularities of action, might seem to bring Weber's sociology into a close affinity with rational choice assumptions. Rational choice theorists firmly uphold methodological individualism and explain action by reference to the costs and benefits to individuals of a certain course of action as opposed to those of an alternative course of action (see, for example, Coleman 1990; Hechter, 1987; Friedman and Hechter, 1988, 1990; Cook, 1990; Kiser and Hechter, 1991).

Despite this common front, Weber's sociology diverges in significant respects from rational choice theory.[22] Even in its more broadranging versions (see, for example, Friedman and Hechter 1988; Coleman, 1990), this approach generally emphasizes "purposive" and intentional – or means–end rational – action to such an extent that the motivating capacities of traditional, affectual, and value-rational action are all downplayed or omitted. To Weber, all *four* types of social action stand in principle on an equal plane; all are endowed with an independent power to direct action.[23] Indeed, a central tenet runs throughout his comparative-historical writings: the orientation of action to values and traditions is not easily altered by means–end rational action, and often this action is powerless in the face of value-rational and traditional action.[24]

Weber's attention to the subjective meaning individuals attribute to their actions led him to this conclusion. He wishes to know what meaning – in terms of the four types of social action – is involved for the actor. This issue acquires for him sociological significance not simply because subjective meaning varies, but also because meaningful action diverges in respect to its intensity, a point also neglected by rational choice theorists as well as adherents of the world systems, interpretive historical, and causal analytic schools.

That the adventurer and Calvinist capitalists conform to the price-fixing rules of the market economy, for example, is not, for Weber, a matter of great significance. For an investigation of the *origins* of modern capitalism, however, the fact that these actors supported this economic order as a result of radically different action-orientations is of immense consequence. "The Protestant ethic thesis" does not concern simply the introduction of a new type of means–end rational action with Calvinism, one influenced by religious premiums; rather, decisive was the fact that the Calvinist's orientation to the economic realm was now rooted, due to his search for *signs* of his

22   A further manner in which Weber's substantive texts stand in opposition to rational choice theory will be noted in chapters 4 and 5 in those sections where his emphasis upon social contexts is addressed (see chapter 4, pp. 98–117; chapter 5, pp. 168–77). See also, in this regard, chapter 1, pp. 39–46.
23   It should be mentioned, however, that affectual action is somewhat less prominent in Weber's substantive texts.
24   This major pivot in Weber's comparative-historical sociology will become especially clear in chapter 4.

"election," in value-rational action. Only this type of action could introduce the *methodical rational* way of life (see Kalberg, 1980, pp. 1164–8; 1990). The combination of a designation of the economic realm as the arena for "proof" of the state of grace plus the methodical character of the Calvinist's way of life accounted, in Weber's argument, for this religion's *extreme* orientation to "world mastery." In this case, particular action-orientations – those of the Calvinist – possessed, as a consequence of their greater intensity and thus *singular* capacity to shatter the traditional economic ethic,[25] world-historical implications (see *PE*, pp. 51–2/33–4, 125–6/125, 176–7/ 197–9, 196–7, n. 12/38–40, n. 1; *E&S*, pp. 542/328, 575/348).

Thus, all regular action-orientations do not exhibit, in Weber's comparative-historical sociology, the same intensity or stability.[26] Although he sees action in the marketplace as capable even of calling "forth uniformities and continuities of action . . . often far more stable than . . . action . . . oriented to a system of norms and duties" considered to be binding (*E&S*, p. 30/15), in general action-orientations anchored by values prove more stable than those rooted in means–end rational or traditional action: "An order which is adhered to *only* from means–end rational motives is generally far more unstable than one upheld in the end on the basis of custom, or simply as a consequence of the habitual nature of a certain mode of behavior. Yet the latter is in turn much more unstable than an order which enjoys the prestige of being considered exemplary or obligatory" (*E&S*, p. 31/16; transl. alt.; emph. orig.).[27]

Weber's methodological individualism and his emphasis upon four types of social action also empower his sociology, unlike rational choice theory, to assess the manner in which the *combination* of different action-orientations affects the intensity of action. For him, an orientation to values above and beyond an orientation to material interests tends, as just implied, to enhance the stability of action. This characterizes not only the action of Calvinists; it is also the case, for example, wherever civil servants are punctual not simply as a consequence of a means–end rational calculation (tardiness may lead to dismissal), but also because they *believe* in punctuality as a value (see chapter 1, pp. 35–7). On the other hand, material interests intertwine regularly with and strengthen – or weaken – values (see,

25   In Weber's technical terminology, this greater intensity was rooted in "psychological premiums" placed upon action. These premiums were an *irrational* consequence of the doctrine of predestination (see *PE*, pp. 62/78, 98–104/87–93, 155–77/163–99). Fatalism would have been the rational response. It was Richard Baxter's revisionism that alone allowed believers to escape this fatalism, as well as the extreme anxiety that accompanied uncertainty regarding one's salvation status, and to seek a *sign* – worldly success – of their predestined status.
26   For examples that concern variations in intensity in respect to, for example, the types of rulership, see *E&S*, pp. 1068–9/623–4, 1104–5/650, 1108–9/652–3.
27   For further examples of the manner in which action-orientations vary in intensity see the discussion of "orders" and "legitimate orders" in chapter 1. These concepts are foundational in Weber's sociology in respect to both agency–structure linkages and his multicausality.

for example, *RofI*, pp. 228–9/248–9; *E&S*, p. 30/15). Similarly, the infusion into Confucian teachings by orientations to magic enhanced significantly their capacity to resist change, including even technological innovations.[28] Conventions, no less than laws, may be magically or ritually *stereotyped*, in which case, when broken, the social and legal sanctions incurred are all the more strictly and severely applied (see *E&S*, pp. 405–6/249, 577/348–9, 815/471–2).[29] Weber's substantive texts abound with such examples.[30]

His notion of "ethical rationality" illustrates especially well the attention of his empirical writings to different intensities of action. He defines an "ethical" standard as "a specific type of value-rational *belief* among individuals which, as a consequence of this belief, imposes a norm upon human action that claims the quality of the 'morally good' in the same way that action which claims the status of the 'beautiful' is measured against aesthetic standards" (*E&S*, p. 36/19; transl. alt.; emph. orig.). When believed in value rationally, the ethics of solely this-worldly and secular value postulates, such as communism, are designated by Weber as ethically rational, no less than the ethics of all but the most "primitive" religions, regardless of whether a monotheistic God or pantheistic gods held sway (see *E&S*, pp. 429/262, 518/314, 325/191).

Ethical rationality does not involve simply a cognitive element, such as comes into play when rules are memorized for proper conduct. Instead, ethical action is far stronger and implies, first, an imperative for conformity to a moral good that is felt to be internally binding or obligatory and, second, a disjunction between a normatively valid canon that claims ethical status and the empirical flow of fragmented realities. According to Weber, daily action can be decidedly influenced by ethical rationalities even if "external" guarantees for them are lacking and even, at times, in spite of strong opposing traditions and interests (*E&S*, pp. 36/19, 528/321; "I," pp. 286/258–9, 293–4/266, 280/252; "IR," p. 324/537–8).

Because ethical action implies always an internally binding expectation, it opposes all traditional, affectual, and means–end rational action. If an entire configuration of ethical values arises and if these are systematized into an internally consistent unity, action may be comprehensively influenced by these values. The "meaningful total relationship of the pattern of life" (*E&S*, p. 578/349) that results is itself endowed with a strong capacity to guide action. In Weber's terminology, an "ethic of conviction" (*Gesinnungsethik*) appears. In this case, not "stereotyped individual norms"

---

28 Weber argues, for example, that "the dominance of magic . . . is one of the most serious obstructions to the rationalization of economic life" (*GEH*, p. 361/308). He particularly emphasizes its role in obstructing the development of a rational economy and modern science in China (*RofC*, pp. 227–9/513–15, 235/521, 196–8/481–3; *GEH*, p. 361/308). See also "AI," pp. 26–7/12.

29 According to Weber, conventions acquired, with greater likelihood, a ritual character in civilizations thoroughly stratified by status, such as many Asian civilizations (see e.g. "I," p. 301/275).

30 For further examples, see chapter 5, pp. 168–78.

but ultimate values and an "inner state" give rise to regular action-orienta-tions. Empowered not only to sanction different patterns of action in differ-ent situations, this state may, depending upon the particular way of life called forth by the ethical values, strongly oppose interests and even tradi-tions. Ethical values grounded in a religion may influence action in this way, though also other ethical values may do so, such as those typical of feudal-ism (see *E&S*, pp. 1068/623) or Marxism (*E&S*, pp. 486/296, 515–16/313–14, 873–4/501).[31]

Thus, ethical rationalities in the secular arena also vary in value content, degree of comprehensiveness, and internal unity. Persons, for example, may elevate an ideal of friendship to the level of an ethical standard and consider themselves internally bound to uphold all the standards of broth-erhood, despite the practical difficulties of doing so. When "value-rational-ized," secular ethical rationalities may exhibit a more general applicability that influences social action more comprehensively. The Renaissance rejec-tion of traditional bonds and its faith in the power of the *naturalis ratio* ("I," p. 293/266) permeated diverse social domains, as did the Enlightenment's faith in Reason and classical liberalism's credo of the Rights of Man and freedom of conscience (*E&S*, pp. 1209/725–6). Similarly, the upholding of egalitarianism as a value may affect not only its adherents' purely political and legal activities, but also their social and even economic endeavors.

Whenever further rationalized, such ethical rationalities become compo-nents within more comprehensive and internally unified ethical rationali-ties. This occurs if, for example, the orientation of action toward social justice as an ethical ideal is value-rationalized to such an extent that a closed world view implying an explanation of all past, present, and future human misery arises. Secular political, social, and philosophical movements of this total degree of comprehensiveness and inner consistency blossomed in nineteenth-century Europe. In Marxian socialism, for example, the ideals of brotherhood, egalitarianism, and social justice no longer remain isolated ethical principles or vague hopes, but fused into a systematically unified world view that explains past and present suffering. It also promises, if the tenets laid down are correctly implemented, the future abolition of all earthly hardship. As a unified belief system that claims absolute truth, Marxism, when believed in value-rationally, ethically orders all regular action "from within." For Weber, the power of such a secular ethic of conviction to order all action in behalf of its values is far more effective than means–end rational, traditional, or cognitive orientations and no less strong than that of a religious ethic of conviction. Of critical importance in each case is an acceptance of the ethic on faith and a belief in it as an absolute beyond all compromise.

---

31 On those empirical occasions when ethical values call forth a methodical rational way of life and these values place a premium upon worldly activity in a comprehensive sense, they undertake to mold and master social reality (see *E&S*, p. 578/349).

Only ethical rationalities are capable of permanently suppressing "practical–rational" regularities of action[32] or, just as important, intensifying them by transforming them into "practical–ethical" action.[33] In addition, only ethical rationalities set value-rationalization processes into motion that lead to the formulation of comprehensive, internally unified value configurations. Ethical substantive rationalities alone are capable of calling forth *methodical rational* ways of life (see Kalberg, 1980, 1990). For Weber, action may be – with unmistakable sociological consequences – "routinized" from ethical to traditional or utilitarian/means–end rational action, and then "rationalized" back to ethical rationalities and even back to the methodical rational way of life.[34]

Just such distinctions in respect to *intensities of action* are crucial for an understanding of the multicausality throughout Weber's comparative-historical sociology. The worldly wisdom and utilitarian common sense of an Alberti could not have given birth to a "spirit" of capitalism, nor can the initial impulse for social, philosophical, or religious movements that profess to alter given realities crystallize from practical rationality alone (see *PE*, pp. 76–8/61–2; 194, n. 12/38, n. 1; 262, n. 16/168, n. 3). Such regularities of action rooted in means–end rational orientations are also never alone capable, Weber asserts, of giving birth to ethical rationalities, value-rationalization processes, or a unified way of life. Ethical action governed by an internalized standard, regardless of whether it involves a circumscribed ethical rationality such as friendship or an ethic of conviction, never results solely from means–end rational action.

Moreover, neither the means–end rational action that provided the foundation for practical and formal rationality,[35] nor value postulates devoid of an ethical aspect, can rupture traditional ways of life and attitudes and then transcend and order daily routine to a degree sufficient to set a comprehensive and continuous rationalization of action into motion. Such a development can emerge only after value-rationalization processes

---

32   Or regularities of action rooted in means–end rational action that are directed "toward the world." See Kalberg, 1980, pp. 1151–2.

33   In the societal domain of religion, practical–rational action patterns were consistently, and for all believers, awarded psychological premiums only by the ascetic Protestant churches and sects and Catholicism's virtuoso dogma for monks. In placing enormous premiums on disciplined work and methodical ways of life, these doctrines comprehensively sublimated practical–rational action, whether in the monastery or "in the world," into practical–ethical action (see *E&S*, p. 551/334; *RofC*, pp. 247/553–4; *PE*, pp. 197, n. 12/38–40, n. 1).

34   Weber occasionally substitutes the term "sublimated" (especially in "IR"; see e.g. p. 328/541).

35   I have noted (1980, p. 1158) that practical rationality always indicates a diffuse tendency to calculate and to solve routine problems by means–end rational patterns of action in reference to pragmatic self-interests. Formal rationality, on the other hand, ultimately legitimates a similar means–end rational calculation by reference back to universally applied rules, law, or regulations, such as those in bureaucracies.

rooted in an ethical rationality have led to the formation of at least an incipient value standard. In reference to this standard, and irrespective of its particular content, everyday routines can be qualitatively assessed, found wanting, and rejected ("I," pp. 293–4/266). Weber's concept of ethical rationality, and his emphasis upon the divergent directions followed by rationalization processes rooted in values, accounts for his opposition to all explanations of "Western rationalism" as a manifestation of either adaptation to given realities or the conflict of sheer interests.[36]

Numerous other examples could be cited. The rational choice, world system, interpretive historical, and causal analytic schools all neglect such considerations pivotal throughout Weber's comparative-historical sociology. Their neglect of agency–structure linkages precludes the formulation of a set of concepts for doing so. However, Weber's principled commitment to multicausality is not exhausted by recognition of the variable intensity of action, its pluralistic bases, and the central significance of sociological carriers.

Historical Events, Technology, and Geography

Weber's empirical texts endow well-known forces – historical events, technology, and geography – as well with the capacity to serve as significant causal factors. Indeed, for him, in a given empirical situation, each contains the potential to become decisive. His comparative-historical sociology, in this respect, moves closer to the interpretive historical school and away from the structuralism and general focus upon a limited number of causal forces, normally the state or the economy, of the world systems and causal analytic approaches.

In light of Weber's view of social reality as pervaded by unceasing conflict and constituted from patterned action-orientations indigenous to universal organizations, a multiplicity of status groups, and the religion, economy, rulership, and law spheres of life, it is not surprising that he avoided broad lawful generalizations and took great cognizance of historical events and even historical "accident." Weber's appreciation of the unpredictability of history convinces him that the imponderable and the unexpected appear on a regular basis and are endowed with sociological significance.

Thus, he attended closely to the causal significance of delimited historical events. The defeat of the Persians by the Greeks at the Battle of Marathon proved pivotal for the development of Hellenic culture and thus for the entire course of Western history ("Logic," pp. 171–4/273–7, 184–5/286–7). The eucharist at Antioch was as well of "tremendous importance." Because

36 This entire discussion of ethical rationality is indebted to my article (1980), which examines these themes in more detail.

the commensalism of the Lord's Supper cut across all ritual barriers of exclusion, this historical event demonstrated the universalism of the Pauline mission. In doing so, it provided the "hour of conception" for the Occidental notion of citizenship (*RofI*, pp. 37–8/39–40; Kalberg, 1993a). This mission also brought about the adoption of the Old Testament by Christianity. Had this not occurred, no Christian Church or ethic could have been formulated and the Christian congregation would have remained simply one among many Jewish pariah sects (*AJ*, pp. 4–5/6–8).

Weber acknowledged the importance of historical events in Asia as well. The conversion in India of King Ashoka in the third century AD to Buddhism, for example, led to a pacifistic welfare state and proved the first impetus toward the development of Buddhism as a world religion (see *RofI*, pp. 238–42/256–62), and the Dai-Bing rebellion (1850–64), had it been successful, might well have set the history of East Asia onto an entirely different track (see *RofC*, pp. 294–5, n. 52/505, n. 3).[37]

The importance Weber attributes to technology and geography is most clearly visible in *AG*, *GEH*, and *RofC*.[38] *AG* discusses frequently the great influence of technological change upon military organization. In Antiquity, for example, the introduction of the horse was instrumental in creating the Near Eastern conquest state and the knightly society of the Mediterranean, and this same innovation in China proved pivotal in introducing an "Homeric" age of heroic combat. The utilization of iron in weapons in Antiquity played a crucial role in calling forth mass armies as well as, ultimately, in the creation of the ancient "citizen polis" (*AG*, pp. 352–3/ 266–7; *RofC*, p. 24/302).[39] Technological innovation in agriculture – better tools for threshing, ploughing, and harvesting – was particularly significant in the ancient Near East for increasing the production of labor (*AG*, pp. 354/268–9). Many further examples could be noted. Weber states his general position in respect to the role of technology succinctly: "Everywhere . . . the influence of technical rationalization processes on displacements of the entire external and internal conditions of life must be taken into consideration" ("EN," p. 38/530; transl. alt.).

Weber viewed *geography* as not only capable of setting distinct para-

37 Weber sees an epileptic seizure at the "militarily decisive moment" as having prevented the defeat of a beaten Peking government (see *RofC*, p. 219/505).

38 Weber dealt with the causal impact of technology and geography relatively seldom in *E&S*. This fact, however, by no means signifies a denigration of their importance. Rather, his downplaying of these factors results largely from the delimited purposes of this treatise. Planned as a single volume within the multi-volume *Outline of Social Economics* series, *E&S* aimed to "consider actual human activities as they are conditioned by the necessity to take into account the facts of economic life" (*E&S*, pp. 311–12/181). This goal distinguished *E&S* clearly from the other two sections in the *Outline* table of contents: "economy and nature" and "economy and technology." See Schluchter, 1989, pp. 433–63.

39 Weber sees that natural resources themselves can as well, in certain circumstances, play a causal role. In the context of the natural economy, for example, even the possession of only a modest supply of precious metals could have "extraordinary significance for the rise and power position of a state" (*E&S*, p. 1093/642).

meters to social action – ones that, moreover, could remain effective over long periods of time – but also as itself constituting a causal force. He pointed out, for example, that the shift of capitalism from the Mediterranean area in Antiquity to the inland economy of middle and northern Europe in the Middle Ages involved a distinct and significant difference in respect to consumption: the more severe climate of Europe kept people indoors and altered the "minimum physiological necessities" (*AG*, pp. 356–7/270–1). Nor does Weber underestimate the importance of geographical factors when he turns to the pivotal question of why "economic rationalism" did not develop in Asia: "The lack of economic rationalism in Asia is predominantly conditioned by the *continental* character of the social order as it was called forth by the geographical structure" (*RofI*, p. 340/375; emph. orig.; transl. alt.). Indeed, in respect to the "external conditions" relevant for the development of capitalism, geographical factors must be allocated a central place. The high cost of transportation associated with all inland trade inhibited severely the possibility for profits in India and China, whereas an inland sea – the Mediterranean – and a network of interconnecting rivers favored (*begünstigte*) international commerce in Antiquity (*GEH*, pp. 354/301–2).

Weber also directly acknowledges the very crucial role played by geographical forces in respect to the transformation of rulerships. This is apparent, for example, in his analysis of the alteration in classical China away from a situation of decentralized rulers and "political feudalism": the compelling necessities to regulate enormous rivers and to expand the area of cultivation required a centralization of labor and a general rationalization of the irrigation economy, factors that "worked in favor of semi-bureaucratic political patrimonialism" (*E&S*, p. 1091/640; see also *RofC*, pp. 33–47/314–30). The need to administer any large inland empire may itself lead to the spread of patrimonial bureaucracies, as occurred in Russia and ancient Rome as well as in China. The different geographical setting in northern Europe – one that required the clearing of forests if new land was to be acquired – "favored the manorial system and therefore feudalism" (*E&S*, p. 1091/640). That Weber perceived geographical forces as important causal factors is evidenced as well in his sociology of religion. He notes, for example, that innovative religious beliefs and practices crystallize frequently not in cosmopolitan centers, as one would expect, but in urban areas adjacent to great world empires. An advantage, Weber surmises, as a consequence of distance from the great centers of thought, is bestowed upon residents outside these centers: namely, the possibility to disentangle themselves from accepted dogma, to be awakened to religious questions, and to speculate (*AJ*, pp. 206–7/220–1).

These forces – historical events, technological innovations, and geographical factors – further contribute to Weber's broad multicausality. They endow it with an expansive causal breadth and testify to his unwillingness to elevate particular factors to positions of general causal priority. While regularly acknowledging the causal significance of historical events, technological innovations, and geographical factors, the world systems and causal analytic approaches consistently favor a limited number of forces, particularly the economy and the state. Several further fundamental aspects of Weber's substantive texts must be examined briefly: the central positions of power, conflict, and competition testify as well to his broad multicausality.

Power, Conflict, and Competition

Although all social carriers may be capable of independently calling forth regular action, Weber never sees a determinant relationship between them and empirical historical change. Rather, as will be discussed in chapter 5, entire configurations of patterned action-orientations must crystallize. However, one force in particular is tied closely to social carriers and to the emphasis upon a radical multicausality throughout Weber's comparative-historical sociology: power, or the capacity to carry out one's will. In his classical formulation, Weber defines power thusly: "Within a social relationship, power means any chance (no matter whereon this chance is based) to carry through one's (individual *or* collective) own will (*even* against resistance)" (*E&S*, p. 53/28).[40] A certain minimum of power always exists as a prerequisite for success against opposing carriers of regular action. Weber sees power as ubiquitous in social life.

Officials in patrimonial and bureaucratic forms of rulership, for example, particularly as a result of their struggles against rulers, often develop their own vested interests and domains of power. They seek to monopolize the prerogatives of their positions and to appropriate privileges and power, indeed to such an extent that a regular obstruction of the ruler's wishes may take place. Whether rulers succeed in resisting this tendency depends largely upon power,[41] and especially military power (*E&S*, pp. 232–5/134–6, 1040/604, 1042/605, 1028/596). Even priests seek to secure power when they, for example, adjust religious doctrines to the emotional needs of the laity (*E&S*, p. 457/279), strongly support a traditional economic ethic and patriarchal authority against all forces that seek to rationalize the economy (*E&S*, pp. 584–5/353), and coalesce with the petty-bourgeoisie in order either to confront great capitalist families, as occurred in Antiquity and the Middle Ages (*E&S*, pp. 1180–1/704), or to pacify the masses (*E&S*, pp. 1161–2/690–1; *RofI*, p. 236/254). Priests also seek to organize the social

40   This is the translation by Walliman *et al.* (1980) in their excellent discussion of the proper rendering of *Macht*. For Weber's earlier formulation, see *E&S*, p. 926/531.
41   Just this theme is central in Weber's discussion of patrimonial rulership in Egypt, China, England, Russia, and other areas, though he also examines a variety of other forces (e.g. the role of the army and the size of the country); see *E&S*, pp. 1044–69/607–24; "I," pp. 298/271–2.

order in behalf of their own power interests.[42] Members of the aristocracy might also act in reference to power interests, as took place when they supported established religions because they offered an instrument to control the masses, or when local notables in France opposed the rise of disciplined and organized political parties that would encompass the entire country and threaten their influence (*E&S*, pp. 516/314, 984/568).

Power is central as well in respect to the question of whether the compromises carried out between political and hierocratic organizations result in caesaropapist or hierocratic forms of rulership, whether feudal princes are successful in limiting or forbidding subinfeudation, and whether the routinization and transformation of charismatic education results in the formation of an ecclesiastic institution. Similarly, the development of law from "primitive" to patrimonial law very often depends upon the relative power of rulers against other social carriers: sib organizations, status groups, and the Church hierocracy.[43]

On the other hand, new action-orientations frequently fade or become the victims of suppression by opposing coalitions if power is lacking and alliances fail to take place. Buddhism in India comes to mind, as does the suppression of the Old Confederacy's patriarchalism by Solomon's patrimonial monarchy in ancient Israel. Rulers are particularly adept, according to Weber, at forming alliances with the sole purpose of maintaining and aggrandizing power. As a matter of course, they seek to balance classes, status groups, and organizations off against one another. Priests and religious intellectuals were frequently sought out by kings and princes, if only because these classes, if controlled, were capable of leveling and pacifying the masses.[44] The dominance of priests at the beginning of Persian rule, for example, "was connected with a quite consistently pursued policy of the Persian kings always to place the priesthood in the saddle as a useful tool for taming the dependent peoples" (*AJ*, pp. 348–9/364). Hinduism, in particular, in providing a religious justification for a caste system that effectively opposed fraternization and the ascendance of guilds, both of which could mend the cleavages of Indian society and pose clear threats to rulers, was exploited for reasons of sheer power by princes throughout India.[45] Similarly, the interests of rulers in the "domestication" of the masses played a significant causal role in the spread of Buddhism throughout large areas of

42   "The priesthood, when it had the power, as was the case in India, organized the social order to correspond to its indigenous dynamic features; i.e., *ritually*. After the downfall of the Shogun in Japan the priesthood was no longer powerful enough to regulate the way of life of the knighthood more than in a purely external sense" (*RofI*, pp. 333–4/368; transl. alt.; see also pp. 128–9/128–9).

43   On these examples, see *E&S*, pp. 1015/586, 1021–2/591, 1027–8/595–6, 1174/700, 1144/677, 258/150, 883/505; "I," p. 298/271.

44   On the manner in which caesaropapist rulers – i.e. rulers who possess supreme authority in ecclesiastic matters – utilized monasticism to domesticate subjects, see *E&S*, pp. 1170–1/697–8.

45   As Weber notes: "It is not difficult even at this point to guess the political interests which had a hand in the game during the transformation to monopoly rule of the caste system" (*RofI*, p. 39/41). See also chapter 5, pp. 177–92.

Asia (*RofI*, pp. 257–9/280–2, 271/296). Foreign conquerors especially sought to acquire the support of the priesthood in order to diminish attacks against them as oppressors without legitimacy, undermine the leading strata of the conquered, and domesticate their new subjects (see *AJ*, p. 130/140; *E&S*, pp. 1160/689–90, 1176/701). Nobles and the lower classes, depending upon circumstances, were also exploited for power purposes: whenever a tendency toward feudalization became clear, kings frequently attempted to co-opt the secular or priestly nobles. On the other hand, when patrimonial tendencies became ascendant, positions of political power were filled by lower-class upstarts (*RofI*, pp. 72/73, 74/75; *E&S*, pp. 1070–81/625–34, 1107/652).

Both the world systems and causal analytic schools also emphasize the central significance of power. The interpretive historical approach offers a more contextual mode of analysis and endows power with a less pivotal role. Unlike Weber, all contemporary schools omit a systematic treatment of power (see *E&S*, pp. 53–4/28–9, 926–48/531–45).

Weber examines, in his analytic treatise *E&S*, two major bases for actors to realize their own wills despite resistance: power arises from the possession of goods or marketable skills, and from the "power to command and duty to obey" (*E&S*, p. 943/542).[46] While not limited to it, interest compromises in the marketplace and the formation of economic interests into constellations of such interests and property typify the former source of power. The purest exercise of power takes place in this case as a result of monopoly positions. This basis of power is illustrated by the capacity of a large central bank to define terms of credit. Even though subject to monopoly conditions, those persons dominated are not subject to an authority in the strict sense of "submission"; rather, formally free persons, as a result of their need for credit, submit to given terms and, in so doing, "rationally pursue their own interests as they are forced upon them by objective circumstances" (*E&S*, p. 943/543). This type of power is also exemplified by the imposition by entrepreneurs, despite competition, of prices upon exchange partners, by the dependence of craftsmen upon knowledgeable exporters, and by the "voluntary" acceptance by office-workers of contracts drawn up by their employers (*E&S*, p. 945/543).[47] To Weber: "It is the most elemental economic fact that the way in which the disposition over material

46 Instances of a general exercise of power – such as those exercised in charitable relationships, on the lecture platform, or in scientific discussions – are ubiquitous, according to Weber (*E&S*, pp. 53/28–9, 943/542). He views this concept, when employed in such a general sense, as possessing little scientific utility. Weber does not claim here that the two definitions of power above offer an exhaustive inventory of the bases for power (see *E&S*, pp. 943/542, 945/544).

47 Weber places "voluntary" in quotation marks in order to indicate his awareness of the way in which the mode of distribution favors owners and leaves the propertyless, who can subsist only by bargaining their labor, to accept terms offered by employees. "Property" and "lack of property," Weber states, "are . . . the basic categories of all class situations" (*E&S*, pp. 927/531–2). He also notes that such contracts are signed by parties that are only formally equal (*E&S*, p. 945/543).

property is distributed among a plurality of people, meeting competitively in the market for the purpose of exchange, in itself creates specific life chances" (*E&S*, p. 927/521).

Interest constellations and possessions may also, of course, take forms unrelated to property or the market's exchange relationships and still serve as the root of power, as occurs, for example, when wealth is combined with a style of life to create prestige and the resulting social honor enables the exercise of power. This power may then be utilized in behalf of the creation of wealth and economic power, though it may also be used in order further to enhance social honor. To Weber, "man does not strive for power only in order to enrich himself economically," and the power of money alone is generally not acknowledged as an adequate basis for social honor. For this reason, he argues, in opposition to Marx, that status groups as well as classes must be recognized as carriers of power (*E&S*, p. 926/531).

Whereas this first type of power is based upon possession and usually upon the formally free interaction of persons with market interests, the second type of power originates from the "authoritarian power of command" (*autoritäre Befehlsgewalt*). Power in this case concerns rulership (*E&S*, p. 946/544). Exemplified by the patriarch, patrimonial monarch, village chief, and judge, rulership takes place by virtue of authority and obedience. Dominant actors claim submission on the basis of authoritarian power and without respect to the interests of the dominated.[48]

In either form, power plays a central role in Weber's multicausal analyses of how new patterns of action arise, spread, and set historical developments into motion, as well as in his investigations of how action-orientations become circumscribed and rendered less influential. Even though no reliable generalizations can be formulated and "fateful events play a tremendous role" (*E&S*, p. 1176/702), power remains crucial for Weber. As an all-pervading force in all social groupings, power weaves throughout his comparative-historical sociology as a pivotal causal force.

48 Power relationships based upon constellations of interests may be transformed into ones involving rulership, particularly if rulership was based originally upon a monopoly. This takes place, for example, when "A bank . . . in order to control more effectively a debtor corporation . . . demand[s] as a condition for credit that some member of its board be made a member of the board of the debtor corporation. That board, in turn, can give decisive orders to the management by virtue of the latter's obligation to obey" (*E&S*, p. 944/543). Similarly, if a bank, on the basis of its monopoly over credit institutions, succeeds in establishing regulations and special agencies and thereby acquires control of the business cycle, its formal rulership approximates that of a government. Rulership on the basis of authority and obedience also occurs if publishers form a cartel with the power to dispense and withdraw the retail licenses of book dealers, or if coal and oil producers acquire the same degree of power over coal and oil dealers. Likewise, this type of rulership arises if the craftsman becomes subject to the authoritarian regulation of his labor in a sweatshop and if the ancient debtor's dependency on his creditor develops into formal servitude (see *E&S*, p. 944/543). The transitions, according to Weber, from power based upon interests to power as a result of authority and obedience are often very gradual.

Conflict and competition

As is the case for adherents of the world systems and causal analytic schools, conflict and competition are viewed in Weber's substantive texts as intrinsic features of social existence and independent causal forces. Action-orientations toward classes, status groups, and organizations compete against one another unceasingly throughout his empirical writings.[49] Indeed, struggles among competing social carriers, for example, may themselves in a variety of ways call forth new patterned action-orientations. This occurred, for example, when competition among the feudal warring states in pre-classical China led to administrative rationalization (*RofC*, pp. 37/318–19). Similarly, the competition for markets in China compelled the rationalization of private enterprise, and struggles for political power set a rationalization of the economy and economic policy into motion both in the Occident and in pre-classical China (*RofC*, pp. 61–2/348–9). Competition as well gave rise to regular action when struggles between priests, prophets, and laity led to the creation and refinement of religious doctrines (see "I," pp. 288/260–1; *AJ*, pp. 216/231, 235–49/251–65).[50] In many cases, competition among religious groups for economic resources proved instrumental in the shaping of religious teachings (see, for example, *RofC*, p. 112/401). Weber sees the struggle of Confucians and Taoists for offices as a good example (see *RofC*, pp. 193–4/477–9). He is particularly lucid in noting the manner in which competition for power tended, once the process of capital formation had been set into motion, to facilitate the development of capitalism (see *E&S*, p. 1103/649).

Such examples can be found with great regularity throughout Weber's substantive texts. He emphasizes in particular the capacity of the sheer tension between competing societal domains – for example, religion, the economy, and rulership – to serve as a causal force capable of calling forth new action-orientations. This competition *itself*, as a consequence alone of the tension that characterizes the perpetual interaction and jousting between bounded realms with indigenous problematics, calls forth pat-

49 Conflict permeates Weber's works. For him: "Conflict pervades . . . potentially all types of social action with no exception" ("EK," p. 463). On Weber's belief in the ubiquity of conflict generally, see "SV," p. 152/609; Honigsheim, 1968, pp. 128–32. For an analytic discussion of the ubiquity of conflict in his comparative-historical sociology, see the section in chapter 4 on "relations of antagonism" (pp. 102–17). Weber defined conflict in *E&S* thusly: "A social relationship will be referred to as 'conflict' insofar as action is oriented intentionally to carrying out the actor's own will against the resistance of the other party or parties" (*E&S*, p. 38/20). Peaceful conflict constitutes competition, or a "formally peaceful attempt to attain control over opportunities and advantages which are also desired by others" (*E&S*, p. 38/20; see generally, pp. 38–40/20–1).
50 Examples of this mode of competition recur repeatedly throughout *EEWR*, though also in the "sociology of religion" chapter of *E&S*. Even monastic communities developed in part as a consequence of competition among opposing religious groups (see e.g. *RofI*, pp. 229/249, 303/333).

terned action. Just how this can occur may be illustrated by a scrutiny of the tension between, in Weber's terms, "world" and "religion."

Salvation religions of brotherliness have always clashed with mundane values. This clash with "the world" has been more sharp to the extent that the demands of these religions have been consistently carried through: "The tension has . . . been the greater the more rational in principle the [religious] ethic has been and the more it has been oriented to *inward* sacred values as means of salvation. In other words, the tension has been greater the more religion has been sublimated from ritualism and toward an 'ethic of conviction' [*Gesinnungsreligiosität*]" ("IR," p. 328/541; trans. alt.).[51] Nonetheless, the conflict between "world" and "religion" has been less acute as long as the worldly domains – the universal organizations, status groups, and the spheres of rulership, the economy and law – remained less rationalized, that is, more rooted in sheer means–end rational, traditional and affectual action and more engulfed in magic (*RofC*, p. 226/512), as in China and India for example. A split between "religion" and "world" became more apparent to the degree that the worldly domains acquired an independence from the religious realm – that is, to the extent that patterned action-orientations "in the world" broke from, above all, traditional action-orientations (primarily conventions and customs) anchored in magic and ritual and became rationalized and sublimated. Autonomous worldly paths of development in the economy, rulership, and law domains could then crystallize ("IR," pp. 328/541, 330/544). "The world," at this point, became a very distinct "problem" for religion: "With the increasing systematization and rationalization of social relationships and their substantive contents, the external teachings of compensation provided by the notion of theodicy are replaced by the conflicts involving the autonomy of the particular worldly domains against the religious teachings. The more intense the religious need is, the more these teachings present the world as a problem" (*E&S*, p. 578/349; trans. alt.).[52]

As the worldly domains moved more and more toward modern capitalism, logical formal law, bureaucratic form of rulership, and modern states, a conflict between their typical impersonal, formal rationality and the emphasis of religious ethics upon person-oriented values and a substantive rationality became overt and intense (*E&S*, pp. 578–9/349–50; see "IR," p. 339/552). To Weber, precisely the tension introduced into "worldly conditions" by religious ethics of brotherliness *itself* constitutes a "strongly dynamic developmental aspect" (*dynamisches Entwicklungsmoment*) (*E&S*, p. 579/350) empowered to call forth new regularities of action.[53]

51   Weber describes this sublimation in more detail at "IR," pp. 330/543–4. See also Kalberg, 1990, pp. 75–80.
52   Only inner-worldly asceticism and mysticism succeeded in offering consistent solutions to this conflict (see "IR," pp. 332–3/545–6, 340/553–4; *E&S*, pp. 587–9/354–5, 593–7/357–9; Kalberg, 1990).
53   The translation in *E&S*, "social evolution," is incorrect and misleading. Weber also makes this point at "IR," p. 328/541.

In sum, unlike the world systems and causal analytic schools, Weber's substantive texts discuss and utilize a full spectrum of independent causal action-orientations. The ideal types formulated in *E&S* in the religion, rulership, economy, law, status groups, and universal organizations societal domains; the social carriers (classes, status groups, and organizations); customs, conventions, interests, and values; historical events, technological innovations, and geographical forces; and, finally, power, conflict, and competition – all constitute potentially independent sources for patterned action-orientations and thus all are sociologically significant causal forces. All must be included in the comparative-historical enterprise and no statement can be made regarding a general causal priority of a particular factor. Orientations, for example, of action to the values of the sib group, one of the most prominent universal organizations, are not "automatically" weakened over time and displaced by orientations to laws, the economy, or a status group, as the case of China in particular illustrates for Weber. Nonetheless, and despite this principled commitment to a broad multicausality, Weber insists that one or another factor *may*, in a given *empirical* situation, possess a greater causal weight (see chapter 5).

His unwillingness to elevate single factors, or even a demarcated cluster of single factors, to causal priority status does not convince Weber that causal explanations of particular cases and developments cannot be attained. This remains the case despite his conviction that conflict, unforeseen consequences, and historical accident may upset tendencies that look firm to the sociologist. In this respect he strongly agrees with advocates of the interpretive historical approach. Yet Weber emphatically rejects the mode of establishing causality advocated by Charles Tilly: attention to a detailed richness of description. While cognizant of empirical reality's vast complexity, Weber steadfastly traces the intertwining of events and unexpected occurrences with patterned social action, as documented by ideal types. This focus leads him to an array of causal procedures and strategies to establish causality (see chapter 5). On the other hand, Weber forgoes all attempts to formulate a general theory. Again, to him, "fateful events play a tremendous role."

To provide causal analyses of cases and developments constitutes the overall purpose of his sociology. Having examined foundational and general features of Weber's empirical writings, the groundwork has been laid for an investigation of the ways in which his substantive works offer complex procedures and strategies, as well as a theoretical framework, to assess causality. Part II of this study turns to this subject.

Weber's "causal sociology" can best be understood if divided into three separate discussions. Chapter 3 examines his predominant level of analysis: the ideal type. Its formation, major features, and capacity to define empirical cases are addressed. Weber asserts repeatedly that, without clear definitions, all causal explanation remains impossible. Chapter 4 addresses a further capacity of ideal types, one seldom noted: their power to construct hypothesis-forming models that facilitate conceptualization of the case or development under investigation. A vast array of such models are formulated in *E&S*; each is designed to assist comparative-historical research. Chapter 5 reconstructs the mode of causal analysis actually practiced in Weber's empirical texts. It offers as well a detailed illustrative case: the rise to dominance of the caste order in India. All of Weber's causal strategies and procedures testify to the universal range of his sociology. Their contribution to comparative-historical sociology today will be highlighted by repeated comparisons to the world systems, interpretive historical, and causal analytic schools.

PART II

The Causal Sociology: Strategies and Procedures

3

The Level of Analysis: the Ideal Type

Ideal types distinguish Weber's level of analysis and separate his empirical writings clearly from the world systems, causal analytic, and interpretive historical schools. This chapter aims to demonstrate that his entire causal sociology takes place at the level of ideal types.

In his substantive texts, causal explanations are not provided alone by the central notion of *Verstehen*. The exploration of subjective meaning must be supplemented by causal procedures and strategies that capture empirically observed factors. In this regard, the ideal type plays a crucial part: "Even the most perfect adequacy on the level of meaning has causal significance from a sociological point of view only insofar as there is some kind of proof for the existence of a probability that action in fact normally takes the course which has been held to be meaningful. For this there must be some degree of determinable frequency of approximation to ... a pure type" (*E&S*, pp. 12/5–6).

Before turning to a discussion of the formation, major features, and capacity of ideal types to define empirical cases, a brief examination of the overall goal of Weber's sociology is in order: to offer causal analyses of cases and developments. As will become apparent, this goal accounts for the central status of ideal types in his substantive texts. This heuristic tool assists the isolation and precise definition of the causal origins of cases and developments.

The Aim of Causal Analysis

Weber shares with the interpretive historical and causal analytic schools a clear emphasis upon discrete problems and the causal analysis of specific cases and developments or, in his terms, the "historical individual." The proposal that the causal explanation of the unique case and development should serve as sociology's primary aim is stated just as unequivocally in Weber's methodological as in his substantive writings.

> The type of social science ... *we* wish to put forth is an *empirical science* of concrete *reality* [*Wirklichkeitswissenschaft*]. We wish to understand the reality that surrounds our lives, in which we are placed, *in its characteristic uniqueness*. We wish to understand on the one hand its context [*Zusammenhang*] and the cultural *significance* of its particular manifestations in their contemporary form, and on the other the causes of it becoming historically so and not otherwise. ("Obj," p. 72/170; transl. alt.)[1]

> The aim should ... be ... to identify and define the *individuality* of each development, the characteristics which made the one conclude in a manner so different from that of the other. This done, one can then determine the causes which led to these differences. (*AG*, p. 385/288; emph. orig.; see *E&S*, p. 10/5)[2]

Throughout his substantive writings, Weber inquires repeatedly into the *uniqueness* of a case or development and seeks to identify the determinants of this uniqueness.

As the interpretive historical approach, Weber opposed strongly the numerous positivist schools of thought in his day that sought to define general laws of history and social change and then to explain all specific developments by deduction. He rejected forcefully the position that sociology should aim "to construct a closed system of concepts which can encompass and classify reality in some definitive manner and from which it can be deduced again" ("Obj," p. 84/184; see also pp. 56–7/153–4, 72–5/171–4, 80–1/179–81; *E&S*, pp. 263–4/154). His opposition to the view that laws themselves comprise causal explanations was as well adamant. Because concrete realities and individual cases cannot be deduced from them, laws are incapable of providing the knowledge of reality that would offer causal explanations. Due to their abstract and general character, laws possess no explanatory value even if a "closed" and "complete" system of laws – a theoretical possibility that Weber denies – could be formulated.[3] Only a lexicon would result from such a system. Indeed, the more abstract and general the laws, the less are they capable of providing explanations of individual cases. These can be explained causally, in Weber's sociology, only by "other equally individual configurations" ("Obj," pp. 75–6/174–5; see also pp. 79–80/178–80; *R&K*, pp. 63–6/12–15; "Logic").

> The question of causality is not a question of laws but of concrete causal *relationships*: it is not a question of the subsumption of the event under some general rubric as a representative case but of its imputation as a consequence

---

1   I have retained Weber's emphasis and dropped the emphasis that appears in the English translation.

2   Weber here demonstrates his deep indebtedness to the German historicist tradition, particularly Dilthey (see Tenbruck, 1959).

3   Weber denies this possibility due to the "value-relevance" in terms of which all reality is necessarily observed (see note 9 below).

of some constellation. Wherever the causal explanation of a "cultural phenomenon" – an "historical individual" – is under consideration, the knowledge of causal *laws* is not the *end* of the investigation but only a *means*. . . . In the cultural sciences, the knowledge of the universal or general is never valuable in itself. ("Obj," pp. 78–80/178–80; emph. orig.)[4]

Similarly, Weber's focus upon the individual nature of social phenomena led him to oppose, with particular vehemence, the use of analogies. Thus, he criticized sharply analogies between ancient, medieval, and modern institutions (e.g. capitalism, slavery) simply because they neglected the distinctive context within which each existed. He avoided as well analogies between the biological and social levels entirely.[5] Parallels, historical constants, universal stages of development, as well as analogies and laws, fail to offer explanations of distinctiveness.[6] These "abstract uniformities" fulfill an instrumental purpose on the route toward the goal of establishing causal relationships: they can serve alone as *means* to elucidate and facilitate comparisons that aim to identify where similarities between two social phenomena end and differences begin (see "Logic," p. 135/237; *GAzSW*, pp. 517, 524).[7] To Weber, abstract concepts can be utilized as heuristic instruments only if anchored closely to history: "The existence of a connection between two historical occurrences cannot be captured abstractly, but only by presenting an internally consistent view of the way in which it was concretely formed" (Weber, 1891, p. 2; see also "Logic," p. 135/237). This level of concrete causality pervades Weber's historically-saturated causal sociology.

Nonetheless, Weber retains a level of analysis that separates his empirical writings clearly from the contemporary approaches most intent upon "giving history its due": the causal analytic and interpretive historical schools. It is distinguished at the outset by its reliance upon ideal types. For

4 It should not be concluded, from this goal, that Weber's sociology is overly modest compared to approaches that aim to construct laws of social behavior. On the contrary, for him, "unique cases and developments" refer to research projects that would today, in an age of severe specialization, be considered overly ambitious. His own works explore, for example, the causal origins of the caste order in India (see below), Confucianism and patrimonialism in China, formal rational law and the bureaucratic form of organization in the West, as well as the rise of modern capitalism and Western rationalism.
5 On Weber's use of analogy, see *AG*, pp. 39/4 (Weber's term *Analogien* is translated here as "comparisons"), 341/257, 385/288 (translated also at Roth, 1968, p. xxxi); Roth, 1971a, pp. 256–7.
6 In respect to parallels, for example, he succinctly articulates their preliminary purpose in his critique of Roscher, as well as in his adherence to the historicist focus upon the "historical individual": "If we strive for intellectual understanding of the reality about us, of the way in which it was by needs individually determined in a necessarily individual context, then the analyses of those *parallels* must be undertaken solely from the viewpoint of elucidating the specific meaning of concrete culture elements with regard to concrete, intelligible causes and consequences. In this case, the parallels would merely be a means of comparing several historical phenomena in their full individuality for the sake of identifying their specific character" (*R&K*, pp. 64–5/14; this is the translation by Roth, 1971a, p. 254).
7 Roth has translated the latter passages; see 1968, p. xxxviii.

him, ideal types explicitly serve the purpose of defining "individual concrete patterns" and uniqueness: "We have . . . purposely considered the ideal type essentially, if not exclusively, as a mental construct for the measurement and systematic characterization of *individual* – that is, significant in their uniqueness – contexts [*Zusammenhängen*], such as Christianity, capitalism, etc." ("Obj," pp. 99–100/201; see also pp. 72/170–1). The formation, major features, and most fundamental usage of ideal types – to define empirical cases – now captures our attention.

The Level of Analysis: the Ideal Type

Ideal types anchor Weber's sociology in empirical reality rather than a theoretical scheme. They do not seek to capture overarching differentiation, universalization, or grand-scale evolutionary processes, nor do they aim to document a global shift from "traditional" to "modern" societies or from the *Gemeinschaft* to the *Gesellschaft*. By conceptualizing *patterned* orientations of meaningful action, ideal types aim neither to provide an exhaustive description of empirical reality nor to introduce general laws or theories. They distinguish Weber's level of analysis from the problem focus of the interpretive historical and causal analytic approaches on the one hand and the pre-formulated theory of the world system school on the other.

How are ideal types, his major heuristic tool throughout his substantive texts, formed? What are their major features?

Ideal types: their formation and major features

The ideal type can best be discussed by first turning briefly to Weber's view of social reality.

The impression of excessive fragmentation often fostered by the focus of Weber's sociology upon a distinct pluralism of action and vast diversity of themes appears confirmed by his fundamental view of reality. Rather than "whole" or "organic" or a finite system of delineated, pre-existing structures or laws that the individual adapts to and is socialized into, Weber perceives basic social reality as an unending flow of concrete occurrences, unconnected events, and punctuated happenings. Amidst this maze, persons are confronted by a chaos of inexhaustible realities that overwhelm them in an endless stream of both fragmented and interwoven appearances. Looked at closely and particularly if causal questions are asked, all social phenomena flow together. Because no scientific investigation can ever fully capture the empirical world's concrete individuality, no exhaustive depiction of reality "as it actually exists" or "as it actually occurred" is possible. Consequently, any possibility of discovering unambiguous and "natural" points of division inherent to this reality itself is precluded. Any "laws" are of necessity incomplete reductions. The complexity, infinity, and intertwined character of empirical events effectively prevent even the most painstaking efforts of social scientists to ever "know," in its full complexity, even a selected slice of this forever changing reality.[8]

Given this view of reality, concepts for Weber serve to assist research rather than to capture reality accurately. Selection and arrangement occur inevitably. Rather than being endowed with the capability to "replicate" the external world or define any particular phenomenon, ideal types are constructed "utopias" that alone aim to facilitate empirical inquiry. Thus, Weber's conceptualization, for example, of "the civil servant" or "the Calvinist" portrays accurately the action-orientations of neither a particular Calvinist or civil servant nor all civil servants or Calvinists (*E&S*, pp. 19–22/ 9–11). How are ideal types formed?

As means toward the "end of understanding phenomena which are significant from concrete individual viewpoints" ("Obj," p. 105/207; see p. 90/190), ideal types accentuate those aspects of the empirical case of particular interest to the researcher. In this manner, investigators acquire a "purchase" upon empirical reality by means of its "simplification." Indeed, an ideal type of the patterned action oriented to a specific social or cultural phenomenon may assume various forms simply as a consequence of the fact that the "points of view" according to which the phenomenon becomes of interest to social scientists vary across a broad spectrum (see "Obj," pp. 90– 1/190–2, 101/202; *PE II*, p. 304). In fact, diverging viewpoints demand different ideal types. This fundamental Weberian tenet of "value-relevance,"[9] as well as Weber's conviction that every epoch examines history from the vantage point of particular values and new points of view emerge continuously, precludes the formulation of an exhaustive system of ideal types that captures reality in a conceptual scheme ("Obj," pp. 83–5/183–5, 105–7/207–9; *E&S*, p. 263/154). It also precludes the construction of universal uniformities as well as all general theorizing in the mode of Marx, Parsons, or the world systems theorists (see Salomon, 1935b, p. 68; Zaret, 1980; Mommsen, 1974b, pp. 224–7).

In examining the world religions, for example, Weber notes that his presentation of religious ethics remains "unhistorical" in the sense that it

8 "Now, as soon as we attempt to reflect about the way in which life confronts us in immediate concrete situations, it presents an infinite multiplicity of successively and coexistently emerging and disappearing events, both 'within' and 'outside' ourselves. The absolute infinitude of this multiplicity is seen to remain undiminished even when our attention is focused on a single 'object,' for instance, a concrete act of exchange, as soon as we seriously attempt an *exhaustive* description of *all* the individual components of this 'individual object,' to say nothing of explaining it causally" ("Obj," p. 72/171; transl. alt.; emph. orig.; see also pp. 78/177, 84/184–5, 111/213–14; *E&S*, p. 945/544; Oakes, 1977, p. 12).

9 Literally, that the values of the researcher determine what social issues or problems become *of interest* to the researcher. See "Obj," pp. 67–85/165–85, 104–5/206–7; "Logic," pp. 152–6/254–9; Burger, 1976, pp. 78–82.

follows more systematic and internally consistent lines than ever occurred in the course of their actual unfolding. Nonetheless, because not carried out in an arbitrary fashion, this "simplification" cannot be judged either "purely subjective" or an historical "falsification." Rather, as Weber states explicitly, his interest in a specific question – the manner in which religion influenced the *practical* way of life of believers – expressly guides his research and provides the criterion of selection for the formulation of ideal types. His entire discussion retains this focus (see "I," pp. 292/265, 294/267) and thus his underlying assumptions are clear. Other researchers with a similar interest would replicate Weber's ideal types. For each world religion he examined an array of sources specifically from this limited perspective and integrated his findings into internally consistent and acknowledged "typological simplifications" (see, for example, "RR," pp. 323–4/536–7).

However, by no means should the ideal type be understood as an "average type." Not simply a summarization of elements common to empirical phenomena is involved, nor merely a classification of events. Rather, and although its construction is rooted thoroughly in empirical reality, it is formulated on the one hand through a conscious exaggeration of *essential* features of the significant action-orientations for the research task at hand,[10] and on the other hand through a synthesis of these diffuse characteristic action-orientations into an internally unified and logically rigorous concept. After having examined a number of historical cases, the sociologist formulates ideal types from "historical judgments" based upon "rules of experience." While inductive procedures from empirical observations are followed in the formation of the ideal type, deductive procedures guide the logical ordering of the essential patterns of action into a unified and precise construct. Nonetheless, the anchoring of ideal types empirically, as well as their historically relative nature and their capacity to be reformulated and improved upon in respect to empirical reality, precludes their understanding as "abstract" or "reified" concepts ("Obj," pp. 92–107/193–209).[11] As Weber notes: "Concepts are primarily analytical instruments for the intellectual mastery of empirical data and can be only that" ("Obj," p. 106/208). This is the level of analysis that prevails throughout his comparative-historical texts.

The formulation of such "clear concepts" stands at the foundation of his

10   "The goal of ideal-typical concept-construction is always to make clearly explicit not the class or average character but rather the unique individual character of a cultural phenomenon" ("Obj," p. 101/202).

11   As well as the labelling of Weber as a nominalist. See Warner, 1973, pp. 50–1; Burger, 1976, pp. 176–9; Zaret, 1980, p. 1188. Parsons fails to acknowledge ideal types as empirically-informed and thus views them as "atomized" (1963, pp. lxiii–lxvii). For commentary upon and criticism of ideal types see Schelting, 1922, 1934, pp. 329–33, 353–61; Watkins, 1953; Janoska-Bendl, 1965; Roth, 1971a, 1971b; Bruun, 1972; Burger, 1976, pp. 115–80; and Smelser, 1976, pp. 54–7, 116–21. The ideal type will remain a focal concept throughout this study. Criticisms have focussed upon Weber's failure to offer adequate objective controls for the formation of ideal types.

causal sociology: "Causal explanation requires as an indispensable preparation the isolation (that means, abstraction) of the individual components of the course of events, and for *each* component the orientation toward *rules* of experience and the formulation of *clear concepts*, without which any degree of certainty of causal attribution is *nowhere* possible" (*AG*, p. 385/288; emph. orig.). The central question of why the unique empirical case occurred "historically so and not otherwise" can be ultimately answered only if clear definitions are formed at the outset. What is the most fundamental usage of ideal types in Weber's substantive texts?

The yardstick usage of ideal types: the definition of empirical cases

Once formed as clear concepts that capture regular action-orientations, ideal types anchor Weber's entire causal sociology in a fundamental fashion: they enable the precise definition of empirical cases. Special attention to systematic procedures for the definition of empirical cases is scarcely to be found in the world systems, interpretive historical, or causal analytic approaches.

Utilized as "yardsticks," ideal types serve to define discrete empirical cases. Each can be employed as an orientational instrument that provides a clear "standard" against which given patterns of action can be "measured." Through an assessment of their deviation, these cases can be defined clearly:

> The constructed scheme . . . serves the purpose of offering an ideal-typical means of orientation. . . . Such constructions . . . enable us to see if, in particular traits or in their total character, the [historical] phenomena approximate one of our constructions: [we] determine the degree of approximation of the . . . phenomenon to the theoretically constructed type. To this extent, the construction is merely a technical aid which facilitates a more lucid arrangement and terminology. ("IR," pp. 323–4/537)

Instead of "capturing reality," the ideal type, as a logical construct that documents patterned action, establishes clear points of reference and orientational guidelines against which a given slice of reality can be compared and measured. An examination of the ways in which the regular action-orientations under investigation approximate or diverge from those "documented" by the concept discloses the characteristic features of the empirical case and defines it clearly: "[The ideal type] has the significance of a purely ideal *limiting* concept with which a real situation of action is *compared* and surveyed" ("Obj," p. 93/194; emph. orig.; see also "EN," p. 43/535). And:

> All expositions, for example, of the "essence" of Christianity are ideal types enjoying only a necessarily very relative and problematic validity when they are intended . . . as the historical portrayal of facts. On the other hand, such

presentations are of great value for research and of high systematic value for expository purposes when they are used as conceptual instruments for *comparison* and the *measurement* of reality. They are indispensable for this purpose. ("Obj," pp. 97/198–9; emph. orig.)[12]

Through the use of the heuristic tool, discrepancies from a researcher's conceptualization of economic action under capitalism as purely means–end rational, for example, are, in effect, "thrown into relief" and can be seen to be rooted in "errors": in the sheer strength of traditions, values, or emotions and "misinformation, strategical errors, logical fallacies [and] personal temperament" (*E&S*, p. 21/100).[13] Similarly, the distinctive attributes of patrimonialism in China, Japan, India, the Near East, ancient Egypt, and the West can be isolated and defined clearly through comparison to the ideal type of patrimonialism. Weber states this general mode of procedure explicitly: "[We] . . . proceed from the most rational forms reality *can* assume; [we] attempt to find out how far certain rational conclusions, which can be established theoretically, have been drawn in reality" ("IR," pp. 324/537–8; emph. orig.).

In all such cases, this *yardstick utilization* of ideal types involves a comparison of observed action with ideal-typical depictions of patterned action formulated on the basis of specific premises ("I," p. 294/267). A construct indispensable for a grasp upon "infinite and multifarious historical life" is provided ("I," p. 300/273).[14] Moreover, without these heuristic instruments to serve as standards, it is not possible to conduct comparative "mental experiments" that seek to isolate, on a rigorous basis, significant causal patterns of action. Thus, although ideal types exist in Weber's comparative-historical sociology exclusively as heuristic means rather than ends, without them all causal attribution remains impossible ("Obj," pp. 101–2/202–4). The world systems, causal analytic, and interpretive historical schools all fail to offer such "organizing mechanisms" designed to enable a purchase upon diffuse realities and to provide systematic procedures for defining empirical action-orientations.

At times, single ideal types standing alone may not adequately serve as standards; the divergence between the real world and the logically consistent ideal type may be so large that recurring meaningful action can be accurately described only by combining two pure types into a sub-type (see, for example, *E&S*, pp. 954/550, 1070/625). In these cases, Weber forms "mixed," or compound, ideal types. Because, for example, office-holding in

12 See also *R&K*, p. 189/130. Weber makes this general point further in the chapter on rulership in Part I of *E&S*: "Hence, the kind of terminology and classification set forth above has in *no sense* the aim – indeed, it could not have it – to be exhaustive or to confine the whole of historical reality in a rigid scheme. Its usefulness is derived from the fact that in a given case it is possible to distinguish what aspects of a given organized group can legitimately be identified as falling under or approximating one or another of these categories" (*E&S*, pp. 263–4/154; emph. orig.).
13 See also *E&S*, pp. 6–7/2–3; "EN," pp. 43–4/536–7; Bruun, 1972, p. 223. Weber sees action as following the "laws" of "pure economic theory" only in unusual cases (*E&S*, p. 9/5).
14 Roth has called this the "blueprint" usage (1971b, p. 126). See also Albrow, 1990, p. 157.

Chinese patrimonialism involved qualifying examinations and official certificates of conduct, Weber calls this mixture of bureaucracy and
patrimonialism "patrimonial bureaucracy."[15] The formulation of mixed
types must be carried out simply because action-orientations very frequently belong in part to one ideal type and in part to another ("I," pp. 299–
300/273; *AG*, pp. 78/43–4; *E&S*, pp. 20/10, 954/550). Weber constructed
such types throughout his comparative-historical sociology.[16] Once formed,
they as well serve the fundamental purpose of facilitating the precise definition of empirical action-orientations (*E&S*, p. 1070/625).[17]

The yardstick usage characterizes all ideal types in Weber's sociology,
even though they vary broadly in scope, or "degree of specificity." Some
aim to grasp the uniqueness of regular action connected to a specific social
reality, such as the ideal types of the Chinese literati, the Brahmin intellectuals, the "spirit" of capitalism, the medieval city, the caste system, ancient
capitalism, the Calvinist sect, and the ancient polis ("historical type"),[18]
while others are more abstract, "universalized," and general in range:
priests, bureaucratic and feudal rulership, the neighborhood, the oikos, and
the family. Although also grounded in empirical reality, these ideal types
are bound neither to a specific social context nor era. Formulated as trans-
epochal and transcultural concepts ("pure types"), they serve as analytic
instruments that enable much broader comparisons.[19]

15 "We shall be compelled again and again to form expressions like 'patrimonial bureaucracy' in order to make the point that the characteristic traits of the respective phenomenon
belong in part to the rational form of rulership, whereas other traits belong to a traditionalist
form of rulership" ("I," p. 300/273). Other mixed types include "hierocratic" rule (salvation
religion, routinized charisma, and bureaucratic rulership; see *E&S*, pp. 54–6/29–30, 1158–93/
688–714; "I," pp. 294–5/267–8) and the converse historical case: "caesaropapism" (see *E&S*,
pp. 1159–63/689–92).
16 His penchant for doing so, it must be stressed again, never implied an attempt on his part
to capture historical reality completely and to force the infinity of social life into a schematic
net ("I," p. 300/273). Such an aim stood "as far as possible" from his own (*E&S*, p. 216/124).
Nor did he wish to create a situation in which either the "pure" type or the mixed type could
be confused with empirical reality. On the contrary, he emphasized that the level of analysis
implied by ideal types – they are *analytic constructs* – should be always kept in mind and that
such a confusion would strike a fatal blow to their correct utilization ("EN," pp. 44/536–7;
"Obj," pp. 106–7/208–9).
17 Roth refers to this usage as the "battery approach" (1971b, p. 127; 1971c, pp. 92–3).
18 These ideal types are more common to, though not limited to, *AG*, *EEWR*, and *GEH*.
Mommsen (1974b, pp. 182–232) calls these "individual" ideal types; see also 1989, pp. 124–36.
19 These latter ideal types are more common in *E&S*, especially Part I. Although they
include less illustrative historical evidence than those formulated in Part II and although the
expressions "pure type" and "universal type" are found more frequently in Part I, which was
written later, I disagree with Rex (1971), Turner (1981), and others who have argued that such
alterations indicate a break with Weber's earlier methodological and substantive writings,
indeed even an abandonment of methodological individualism as well as the axiom of value-
relevance and a reformulation of sociology's aim as involving pure systematization.
Mommsen's circumspect response (1974a, pp. xiii–xiv, 10–11, 18–21; 1974b, pp. 229–31; 1989,
pp. 127–32), while charting the development of the ideal type toward a more "formalized
shape," emphasizes the continuity between Weber's earlier and later writings (see also Zaret,
1980, p. 1187; Bruun, 1972, p. 227; Fulbrook, 1978; Scaff, 1989, pp. 34–5). This debate cannot
be addressed here.

The yardstick usage of ideal types anchors Weber's entire causal sociology. All (*a*) facilitate a purchase upon diffuse empirical reality, (*b*) assist the ordering and clear conceptualization of the particular empirical problem under investigation, and (*c*) enable the identification of significant causal action-orientations. A formulation of rigorous procedures that fulfill these foundational tasks is not to be found in the world systems, interpretative historical, and causal analytic schools. Nor do they offer an analytic treatise, such as *E&S*, which formulates broad arrays of ideal types.

This three-volume, 1500-page treatise must be viewed as Weber's attempt to systematize the knowledge acquired from his case studies into ideal types. All are designed to aid sociologists engaged in comparative-historical work. However, owing to the poor organization and unfinished character of *E&S*, this aim is not always apparent (see Tenbruck, 1975, 1977; Roth, 1979; Schluchter, 1989, pp. 433–63). Weber never informs the reader of his goals and this opus is organized along thematic and procedural lines only marginally. Although *E&S* offers an analytic framework for comparative-historical research that moves far beyond "modernization processes" or the relationship of the state to the economy, and provides the researcher with an array of ideal types of such abundance as to encompass nearly the entire range of significant macrosociological action, their actual usefulness for contemporary empirical research is frequently not apparent. Weber very often, in formulating his concepts, confuses matters as a result of the extremely detailed character of his historical knowledge, his perfectionist impulses, and his compulsive thoroughness. In order to convince the reader that he has indeed discovered the *essence* of regular action-orientations, he frequently, in the process of weighing a whole series of historical cases, becomes immersed in historical and illustrative details. This is especially the case in Part II. Indeed, Weber's perpetual concern to offer empirical illustrations at times leaves the impression that history constitutes his real interest in *E&S* rather than the formation of ideal types. It also hinders the reader's attempt to discover where historical discussions end and the formulation of ideal types begins.[20] For these reasons many ideal types need to be "extracted" from *E&S* and reconstructed in clear form.[21]

20 Two further reasons account for the lack of clarity of many ideal types. First, amidst the historical detail, Weber too often, and especially in Part II, turns to particular debates, definitional questions, and technical issues in the secondary literature and polemicizes on behalf of a certain position. Even though these repeated diversions shed light upon the more technical issues involved, all tend to disrupt the thematic and conceptual flow in *E&S*. Second, the impression of procedural disorganization in respect to the formation of comparative concepts is reinforced by the division of *E&S* into two parts and the differing emphases in each part. Part I's (1918–19) ideal types are more abstract and universal, whereas the individual ideal types that predominate in Part II (1911–13) are constructed in a less formal manner and more in relation to specific historical epochs and civilizations (see Mommsen, 1974a, pp. 182–232). See the above note. All of these problems account for the extreme difficulty of *E&S*.
21 To do so would constitute a genuine service to comparative-historical sociology.

Only the most fundamental usage of ideal types has been noted in this chapter's investigation of Weber's level of analysis. As constructs, all overcome the historical narrative of the interpretive historical school. However, they establish the analytic power of his comparative-historical sociology in a further, more important manner: as delimited *models* that articulate empirically-testable hypotheses regarding patterned social action.

Although anchored securely in empirical reality, such models of regular social action endow Weber's causal sociology with a broad-ranging *theoretical* capacity fully lacking in the interpretive historical and causal analytic schools, though one quite distinct from that offered by the world systems approach. Unfortunately, the secondary literature has often discussed ideal types in terms of their yardstick usage alone.

4

Ideal Types as Hypothesis-Forming Models: Weber's *Economy and Society*

Hypothesis-forming models of patterned action-orientations postulate delineated, empirically-testable causal relationships. In doing so, according to Weber, they render a central contribution to comparative-historical sociology. They are explicitly formulated throughout *E&S* and directly serve the overall purpose of Weber's substantive sociology: to offer causal explanations of unique cases and developments. Delimited hypotheses, together with clear definitions, constitute indispensable means for the isolation of significant causal regularities of action.

An emphasis upon a broad variety of limited analytic generalizations distinguishes Weber from the interpretive historical and causal analytic schools,[1] both of which retain a focus upon discrete problems. While ideal types are anchored in empirical reality, they also, as hypothesis-forming models, insert a *consistently theoretical dimension* into the very core of Weber's comparative-historical sociology. A dynamic of hypothesized relationships inheres in each model. For him, the sociological enterprise emphatically involves the theoretical framing of problems. On the other hand, unlike the theoretical model of the world systems approach as well as the overarching and evolutionary models of the earlier structural–functional school of political development and modernization, Weber's models of regular action serve heuristic purposes only: they do not claim to capture empirical developments. Rather, they are *useful* to comparative-historical sociologists as analytic constructs that assist the precise theoretical framing, in behalf of causal analysis, of cases and developments. Indeed, the model building capacity of ideal types enables Weber to resolve a conundrum confronted by the causal analytic approach: by proposing a rigorous research design methodology, this school hopes to construct explanatory

---

1 I will be using the terms "model," "construct," and "limited analytic generalization" synonymously.

theories or generalizations that move beyond the cases investigated; its problem focus, however, hinders its capacity to do so.[2]

The distinct character of *E&S* must again be emphasized. This "grandiose work of empirical sociology" (Salomon, 1935b, p. 67) must be seen as the "theoretical yield" of Weber's vast cross-civilizational and cross-epochal empirical studies. It constitutes an explicit attempt to draw, from these investigations, analytic generalizations. This defining feature is more clear in Part I, which Weber wrote later and in response to the suggestion by friends to render this theoretical yield quite explicit. Part II, although also focussed upon the construction of models, includes many more diversions, mainly ones in which Weber (*a*) refers to a vast array of historical cases before formulating his model, (*b*) addresses historical cases that qualify the model, and (*c*) conducts, through comparative analysis, brief (and normally incomplete, by his own standards; see chapter 5) causal analyses. In fact, a great deal of "history" is included in Part II, indeed to such an extent that Weber's model building aim is not always apparent (see chapter 3, pp. 89–90).

"Dynamic," "contextual," "affinity," "antagonism," and "developmental" models, all of which are formulated in the *E&S* analytic treatise, stand at the very center of Weber's comparative-historical sociology and render a pivotal contribution to its rigor, analytic power, and uniqueness. They are systematized and, in the case of several developmental models, reconstructed in this chapter. The world systems, interpretive historical, and causal analytic approaches all fail to offer demarcated orientational models, let alone a treatise such as *E&S* that constructs a broad array of models capable of orienting multiple and diverse research agendas. As heuristic aids, these models of recurring action-orientations, as ideal types generally, facilitate the researcher's grasp upon and comprehension of an amorphous and ceaselessly flowing reality and assist the clear conceptualization of the particular case or development under investigation. In addition, however, they offer delimited hypotheses that can be tested against specific empirical cases and developments, thereby isolating discrete and significant causal regularities of action. To Weber, sociologists otherwise immersed deeply in empirical realities *require* such constructs. By constructing arrays of models – primarily in *E&S* – that theoretically frame patterned action-orientations, he aims to draw the comparative-historical endeavor decidedly *away* from an exclusive focus upon problems and a heavy reliance upon historical narrative and rich description. However, his models must not be equated with those formulated by the world systems approach. They differ owing to (*a*) their origins in empirical reality rather than a theoretical scheme, (*b*) their purely heuristic purposes, and (*c*) the

2   Of course, from the point of view of causal analytic practitioners, Weber's "solution" to this conundrum – hypothesis-forming models – is not satisfactory, for the generalizations they seek are *empirical*. Weber's basic view of reality and anti-positivist methodological presuppositions prevents the formulation of such generalizations. See chapter 3, pp. 84–7.

delimited character of their generalizations. All axiomatic statements on the nature of social change are scorned. What are the major *types* of models formulated in *E&S*?[3] Ideal types are employed as models in four major ways.

Their *dynamic* character is the focus of Weber's first type of model. Rather than being static, each ideal type is constituted from an array of regular action-orientations. Relationships – delimited, empirically-testable hypotheses – among these action-orientations are implied.

Second, Weber constructs *contextual* models in *E&S*. These models articulate hypotheses regarding the impact of specific social contexts upon patterned action.

Third, when examined in reference to one another, ideal types may articulate *logical interactions* of patterned action. Models of "elective affinity" (*Wahlverwandschaften*) and "antagonism" across ideal types abound in *E&S*. In all cases, demarcated hypotheses are formulated.

Fourth, Weber utilizes ideal types to chart analytic *developments*, even ones driven by indigenous action-orientations. Models anchored in and thrust forth by interests (the closure of social relationships and the routinization of charisma) and formal (the development of the market and the state) and theoretical (the development of religion) rationalization processes are prominent in his empirical writings. Each model hypothesizes a *course* of regular action, or a "developmental path."[4]

These models distinguish Weber decisively from the world systems, causal analytic, and interpretive historical schools. By erecting a delineated theoretical framework,[5] every model facilitates a conceptual grasp upon otherwise diffuse realities and formulates causal hypotheses regarding pat-

---

3   His analytic, model building essays in *EEWR*, "I," and "IR," supplement, in this regard, *E&S*. This chapter can in part be read as a critique of the traditional view that *E&S* can be understood simply as an elaborate "taxonomy" that fulfills the single preparatory task of formulating clear concepts.

4   With the exception of the sociological loci models (see chapter 1, pp. 39–46), this chapter attempts, in terms of *types* of models, to be comprehensive. Of course, all *examples* for each type cannot be noted. *E&S* must be viewed as a resource to be referred to by comparative-historical sociologists. Nonetheless, the following sections (especially those on the affinity, antagonism, and developmental models) go into a fair amount of detail. I am doing so at this point not only because the fundamental importance of models in Weber's comparative-historical sociology requires such a discussion, but also because the character of *E&S* should be conveyed. Such a systematic examination of these models is not to be found in the entire commentary upon Weber.

5   All of Weber's models are ultimately formulated in reference to a research agenda that centered on his value-based, fundamental interest to explain the origins and development of Western rationalism. His model building stands consistent with the "value-relevance" postulate (see chapter 3, pp. 84–5). This fundamental fact, however, does not preclude the utility of these models (e.g. feudalism, the bureaucracy, charisma and its routinization, the elective affinity between civil servants and an anti-religious posture, the relationship of antagonism between charismatic rulership and the rational economy) for the investigation of a wide range of themes and problems. An assessment of appropriateness (that is, the extent to which the model can serve an orienting purpose and even theoretically frame diverse empirical realities) must be made in respect to each model and each research task.

terned action-orientations in respect to empirical cases, relationships, or developments.[6] These limited generalizations also affirm the universal range of Weber's comparative-historical sociology. It extends far beyond the focus of contemporary schools upon the transformations over the last few centuries to capitalism, democracy, and the nation-state. His empirical studies encompass the ancient civilizations of the Occident as well as the present and the East as well as the West. They do so, however, without postulating a sociology either of universal laws or of evolutionary stages.

Ideal Types as Dynamic Models

Constellations of meaningful action-orientations comprise each ideal type. Far from unilinear, each constitutes an assemblage of patterned actions that dynamically interact one with another. This dynamic aspect is incorporated into each ideal type. Hypotheses are formulated regarding causal relationships. Propositions about regular action in empirical reality, in other words, are contained within the ideal type. Only two illustrations from the dozens offered in *E&S* can be noted.[7]

Bureaucracy

Far from static, as the secondary literature often assumes, Weber's model of the bureaucracy implies the interaction of a variety of regular action-orientations, and postulates diverse relationships. A number of hypotheses are articulated. Those regarding the relationship of this form of rulership to democracy are among the most central.

Basic features of bureaucracies call forth a "leveling" of social and economic differences and "passive democratization." The exercise of authority in bureaucracies takes place in accord with abstract rules and regulations that apply universally. An "'equality before the law' in the personal and functional sense [and] hence [a] horror of 'privilege'" reigns (*E&S*, p. 983/567; see also pp. 225/129–30). Action oriented toward an impersonal administration of tasks and a demand for equal treatment vis-à-vis a bureaucratic regulation or law prevails in respect to decision-making rather than, as in feudal rulership, arbitrariness and personal relationships. None-

6   As a consequence of the manner in which the ideal type is formed (empirical induction on the one hand and synthetic systematization on the other hand), as well as its purely heuristic character, a particular empirical disconfirmation of an hypothesis formed by a model does not necessarily imply a refutation of the model's usefulness.

7   Of course, the dynamic character of ideal types varies a great deal. Some include far less internal tension between their patterns of action-orientations and thus fewer hypotheses can be constructed regarding possible relationships. These illustrations are among the most dynamic.

theless, and even while postulating such passive democratization, Weber's model as well hypothesizes the likelihood of a high concentration of power in the hands of the bureaucracy's functionaries. As this stratum becomes cohesive, a group closure process is set into motion (see below, pp. 120–7) and patterned action oriented toward a strong defense of status and "rights" appears that opposes democratization. A dynamic tension – one indigenous to this ideal type – exists between the bureaucracy's "principle of equality" and the assertion of special rights by its carrier stratum.

Yet Weber's model includes as well a third component, namely the societal-wide call, in the face of the concentration of power in the hands of functionaries, toward substantive justice. Just this appeal injects a further tension: between functionaries now oriented toward a defense of vested interests and the bureaucracy's clientele. As Weber stresses on a number of occasions and despite its unintended promotion of bureaucratization (see *E&S*, pp. 983–91/567–72), democracy's relationship to the "rule" of bureaucracy is characterized by ambivalence: democracy favors a reliance upon substantive expertise as evaluated through examinations and certificates, yet fears the tendency of the bureaucracy to create a privileged "caste." Its opposition may become manifest in the formation of obstacles to bureaucratic organization (see, for example, *E&S*, pp. 985/568, 991/572, 999/576, 1081/633). On the other hand, as noted, the growth of bureaucracies calls forth passive democratization: "a *leveling of the governed* in the face of the governing and bureaucratically articulated group" (*E&S*, p. 985/568; emph. orig.). Indeed, Weber's model hypothesizes that, as bureaucratization proceeds, local and intermediary powers are either eliminated or transformed into functionaries responsible to a central authority (see *E&S*, pp. 985–6/568–9; "I," p. 288/260). To Weber: "everywhere bureaucratization foreshadows mass [passive] democracy" (*E&S*, p. 226/130).

In charting these tensions, Weber's dynamic model formulates causal hypotheses regarding an entire spectrum of recurring action within the bureaucracy. It provides one illustration of the manner in which a theoretical framework allows the clear conceptualization of a diffuse and ceaselessly flowing reality. In this case, hypotheses are constructed regarding, on the one hand, the typical empirical tensions within bureaucracies and, on the other hand, between bureaucracies and clients.

Patrimonialism

Weber's ideal type of patrimonial, or monarchical, rulership as well must be understood as a dynamic model that implies a set of hypotheses. Pivotal are postulates in respect to the centralization and decentralization of power and the extent to which power and offices are appropriated by the monarch's administrative officials.

The boundaries of the patrimonial office remain invariably unclear. The offices held by officials and the powers they exercise, which under patrimonialism are understood as *personal* rights and privileges, emanate from a relationship to the ruler rather than from impersonal interests and an orientation to objectively defined and functional tasks, as in bureaucracies (*E&S*, pp. 1040–2/604–5, 1082/633–4). To eradicate the resulting unclarity, each member of the administrative corps, Weber's model hypothesizes, seeks to establish an uncontested jurisdiction for his office. This can be accomplished, however, insofar as the prescriptions of sacred traditions do not apply, only through competition with other officeholders (*E&S*, pp. 1026–31/594–8).

His model also postulates, on the other hand, that officials, if they slowly acquire power, will set aside their internal bickering and develop into a closed status group. This group will then take action to suppress feudal landlords, as well as any other groups that aspire to a particularistic sense of honor independent of patrimonial rulership. In addition, it may stand united in opposition to the patrimonial ruler himself. The staff might obtain the power to determine appointments to new offices, establish fixed rules to circumscribe the monarch's rulership, and define services and fees to its advantage. Although they may continue to accept the "patrimonial norm" in principle – "an official must not contradict his ruler" – rulers, of course, see the integrity of their rulership threatened by their staff's tendency to appropriate offices. If not curtailed, this process leads to a disintegration of their powers into a bundle of powers, and these as well may be appropriated. Officeholders may eventually succeed in becoming an independent status group of dignitaries and notables (see *E&S*, p. 1027/595).

In these ways Weber's model of patrimonial rule acknowledges a continuous tension between rulers and officials; it views the distribution of power as always an unstable one and postulates various outcomes. Indeed, unavoidable struggles are built right into the ideal type (*E&S*, pp. 1107/652, 1044/606–7).

Yet Weber's ideal type is dynamic in a further fashion as well. His model also formulates hypotheses in respect to the relationship of the patrimonial ruler to his subjects. Custom dictates that the social action of subjects be oriented toward support of the ruler, even to an economically and personally unlimited extent if necessary, and that he in turn provide "services" and humane treatment. However, the normal obligations of subjects – compulsory labor, military services, and the paying of taxes – all harbor a significant potential for open struggles in which subjects oppose the ruler's desire to maximize power and maintain their dependent status (*E&S*, pp. 1010–11/ 583, 1020–1/590–1). Given these tensions typical of patrimonial rulership's very principle of organization, a ruler's success in maintaining centralized rulership depends, in Weber's construct, largely upon his personal ability and military strength. These factors, in turn, are also weighed against the relative social prestige and independent power of local officials as well as notables and landlords within their own districts, groups also in perpetual conflict with the ruler (*E&S*, pp. 1039–40/604, 1042/605).

Far from being static, Weber's dynamic model of patrimonialism considers all these forces. A theoretical framework is constructed, one that, as in the case of his model of the bureaucracy, enables a clear conceptualization of amorphous empirical action-orientations and formulates an abundance of hypotheses. Causal analysis in respect to specific cases is thereby facilitated.

These two examples must suffice to indicate the dynamic, model building capacity of Weber's ideal types.[8] By charting arrays of patterned action-orientations that interact with one another, they formulate delimited hypotheses. As theoretical frameworks that facilitate the clear conceptualization of empirical cases, relationships, and developments, and the formation of delimited hypotheses regarding causal relationships, they separate Weber's comparative-historical sociology from the pre-formulated theory of the world systems school and the problem focus of the interpretive historical and causal analytic approaches. Weber's sociology emphasizes the central importance of framing empirical problems theoretically. Having done so, the researcher can then embark upon an in-depth causal investigation in order to test hypotheses.

Hypothesis-forming contextual models are also prominent in *E&S*.

Ideal-typical Contextual Models

All of Weber's substantive texts testify that contexts of regular action are endowed with the capacity to allow, utilize, and even cultivate new patterns of action or, on the other hand, to circumscribe and hinder them. In some contexts, certain regularities of social action may be critical in respect to a certain outcome; in others they may be insignificant. Never important as such, patterned action becomes causally significant only within a specific context of regular action. Depending upon this context, action-orientations may disappear, merge, or become transformed – only to reappear in their original form. Should a cluster of action-orientations undergo just a slight shift as a result, for example, of historical events, an accumulation of power, or charismatic personalities, regularities of action presumed to have disappeared entirely "may come to light in an entirely new context" (*AG*, p. 366/ 278).[9] Quite different results obtain given a change in the social milieu within which regular action exists.

Weber's concern to identify the social contexts of patterned action constitutes a central focus, on behalf of his aim of constructing causal analyses

8   *E&S* constitutes a reservoir of such models designed to orient macrosociological research. This section remains short simply because this feature of ideal types is no longer neglected in the secondary literature. See e.g. Roth (e.g. 1971b, pp. 121ff.; 1971c, pp. 86ff.), Smelser (1976, pp. 121, 125, 129,133, 135), and Warner (1972, 1973).
9   The point of reference for this quotation is the Mediterranean–European civilization of Antiquity, yet it expresses Weber's more general position.

of cases and developments, throughout his comparative-historical texts. This concern is apparent as well in his model building in *E&S*. Weber formulates an array of contextual models in this analytic treatise. As theoretical frameworks that articulate delimited hypotheses regarding specific social contexts and regular action, all serve to assist conceptualization and the isolation of significant causal action-orientations. Only a few examples must suffice.

Weber's model regarding the *impact of law* implies a number of hypotheses. The embeddedness of patterned action-orientations and the varying influence of contexts of uniform action upon new action regularities (see generally, *E&S*, pp. 316/184, 322–3/189) is emphasized. An assessment whether, for example, the extension of the legal concept of freedom of contract – "the possibility of entering with others into contractual relations the content of which is entirely determined by individual agreement" – signifies "a decrease of constraint and an increase of . . . the individual's freedom to shape the conditions of his own life" (*E&S*, p. 729/439), as is usually thought to be the case, requires not only the study of formal legal institutions, but also an evaluation of whether a constellation of action-orientations is present. If the development of this legal concept is to imply more than simply formal possibilities, a context must be present within which freedom of contract regarding the exchange of goods as well as work and services becomes a viable possibility available to all. Wherever great differences regarding the distribution of property exist, a formal right of workers to enter into contracts fails in practice to enhance their freedom to determine the conditions of their work; rather, employers remain empowered to offer jobs on a "take it or leave it" basis (*E&S*, pp. 729–31/439–40).

Weber's model of the transformation of the social *prestige of age* also illustrates the importance of the social context. If a high orientation of social action to convention, customary or sacred law, and traditions exists in communities, then the household, clan, or neighborhood elders, simply as a consequence of their broad life-experience and knowledge of traditions, will possess high prestige. This prestige remains uncontested, Weber's model postulates, as long as rough economic parity among the community's members prevails. The resolution of disputes depends, above all, on the voices of the elderly. However, if food is scarce, warfare chronic, or political revolution appears, the elderly become a burden and a gradual "democratization" in favor of younger and more active males may develop. This development takes place all the more wherever religion is too weak to provide sustenance to sacred traditions and wherever economic and status differentiation has advanced to the extent that new *honoratiores* crystallize as cohesive groups (see *E&S*, pp. 950–1/547). The prestige of age, it is hypothesized, will decline.

The *E&S* model of the *relative prestige of civil servants* as well formulates a number of hypotheses, all of which attend to the contextual dependence of action-orientations. The social and economic context within which bureaucracies are placed is central. Prestige, it is hypothesized, tends to be high wherever a need exists for specialized administration, officials are recruited from privileged strata, and qualification for office is based upon educational certificates. This is all the more the case in old civilizations characterized by stable social differentiation and strong status conventions as opposed to newly settled areas where weaker status group conventions allow greater social mobility, such as the United States. Moreover, where opportunities abound for the accumulation of wealth and power, the social esteem of officials suffers, if only because their interest in economic security stigmatizes them as cautious, passive, and even cowardly (see *E&S*, pp. 959–60/553; see also p. 962/555).

Such delimited models that formulate hypotheses regarding the ways in which social contexts influence patterned action-orientations abound throughout *E&S*.[10] They reveal that, for Weber, social settings alter and shape patterns of social action. This must be acknowledged, he asserts, in all attempts to provide causal explanations. Model building that assists the identification of the context of patterned action-orientations is evident as well in *E&S* when Weber turns to major macrosociological themes: stratification, bureaucratization, and capitalism.

A model that postulates a close relationship between types of stratification, or "stratification principles," and social context is especially prominent in *E&S*: stratification by status is favored whenever relationships of production and distribution are stable, and naked class situation becomes prominent in epochs of great technological and economic change. Moreover, when the tempo of such transformations recedes, a reinvigoration of status structures occurs as well as an enhancement of the salience of social honor (*E&S*, p. 938/539). Communities highly "segregated in terms of honor," it is further hypothesized, tend to evidence a great indifference to pecuniary

10 Just this feature of Weber's comparative-historical sociology leads him also to reject all assessments of "indispensability" as adequate to explain unique cases and developments. Common among proponents of structural-functionalism, such assessments for him constitute only preliminary and heuristic steps. The modern bureaucracy, for example, as he notes repeatedly, is indispensable in the industrial society characterized by the necessity for large organizations (see e.g. *E&S*, p. 988/570), yet this very fact does not tell us a great deal. In respect to the crucial sociological issue – the *power* of the officialdom in those societies where developed bureaucracies exist – a contextual analysis is necessary. A number of questions must be asked in each particular case. Is democracy in the form of representative bodies successful in creating "palpable breaks in the bureaucratic pattern and impediments to bureaucratic organization" (*E&S*, p. 991/572)? Are lay representatives and a variety of non-official experts consulted regularly? Does only a poorly informed parliament stand opposite the expert knowledge of officials (*E&S*, p. 993/573)? Similarly, cognizance of the indispensability of a working class under capitalism fails to inform us regarding the "social and political power position of [this] class" (*E&S*, p. 991/572; see the quotation excerpted from Weber's letter to Robert Michels at *E&S*, p. 1003, n. 8), as little as does the acknowledgment that, in a slave economy, slaves are indispensable. Only a consideration of the *setting* within which the slave or working class is located allows an evaluation of the power – that is, causal significance – of these classes. Because incapable of demarcating a social context clearly, the notion of "indispensability" remains only a preliminary tool.

income as well as to entrepreneurial activity generally (see *E&S*, pp. 306–7/180, 935–7/537–9).

Nor can the influence of bureaucratic rulership upon capitalism – a theme central in Weber's comparative-historical works – be said to be a simple or linear one, according to another contextual model in *E&S*. Rather, whether this relationship is one of alliance or antagonism depends upon a host of contextual action-orientations. For example:

> In political and especially in state formations, too, bureaucratization and social levelling . . . have in modern times frequently benefitted the interests of capitalism. . . . In general, a legal levelling and destruction of firmly established local structures ruled by notables has usually benefitted the scope of capitalist activity. But, on the other hand, there is also an effect of bureaucratization that meets the petty-bourgeois interest in a safe traditional "living," or even a state-socialist effect that strangulates opportunities for private profit. This has undoubtedly been active . . . particularly during Antiquity. (*E&S*, pp. 989–90/571; see also *AG*, pp. 363–5/275–8)

Whether economic monopolies stimulate or impede the formation of private capital also depends upon contextual factors. The former took place, Weber's model postulates, when trade and colonial monopolies, owing to their unique capacity to guarantee sufficient profits for the success of capitalist enterprises, facilitated the spread of capitalism during the Middle Ages and in early modern times. Monopolies often, however, create obstacles to capitalist interests. This occurred when Ancient and Eastern civilizations resorted to status-liturgies, when guilds became strong in the late Middle Ages, and, in particular, wherever states, especially highly bureaucratized states, protected monopolies through subsidies (*E&S*, p. 351/209).

These few illustrations indicate Weber's attention in *E&S* to contextual models, each of which charts the importance of contexts of action-orientations.[11] The causal significance and very substance of patterned social action, according to these models, varies depending upon the social milieu. Weber notes, having studied a variety of similar cases, the contextual dependency of patterned action-orientations and then formulates this dependency as a delimited model – or theoretical framework – that implies causal hypotheses. These hypotheses can then serve as heuristic guidelines for the empirical investigation of the fate of such regular action in a given case.[12]

11   See chapter 5, pp. 168–77 for a discussion of the important role attributed to social context in Weber's mode of causal analysis. The *sociological loci* examined in chapter 1 (pp. 39–46) also constitute contextual models (albeit ones with a different emphasis). They belong as well in this chapter. However, their central role in respect to Weber's linkage of agency and structure required their discussion in chapter 1.

12   The above examples indicate a *style* of contextual analysis endowed with great complexity. Of course, more familiar examples from *E&S* all testify to the important part played by contextual models in this treatise: for example, the linkage between marginal social status and the development of religious thought (see *E&S*, p. 507/308), the loss of political power by

"Affinity" and "antagonism" models constitute Weber's third type of hypothesis-forming model. These models are organized specifically in reference to "intra-domain" and "inter-domain" logical interactions. Because less familiar, they must be illustrated in more detail.

Analytic Relationships: Affinity and Antagonism Models

Once formed as clear concepts, ideal types can be compared to one another. This occurs in Weber's writings, for example, when the Confucian literati are compared to the Brahmins, the medieval city to the polis, Catholicism to Lutheranism, and the "traditional" work ethic to the "rational" work ethic. Such comparisons, which can be found on nearly every page of Weber's substantive texts, isolate the distinctiveness of patterns of action.[13] As Weber notes: "One can only define the specific characteristics of, for example, the medieval city . . . after one has established which of these characteristics were lacking in other cities (classical Chinese, Islamic). That is a general rule" (Weber, 1914, pp. xxxiv).

After the distinctiveness of a particular empirical case has been defined through assessments of similarities and differences across a series of cases, the task of causal explanation of this uniqueness can begin. Thus, comparative investigations precede and make possible causal analysis. To Weber: "A genuinely critical *comparison* . . . should be concerned with the *distinctiveness* of each of . . . two developments that [are] finally so different, and the purpose of the comparison must be the causal *explanation* of the difference" (*AG*, p. 385/288; emph. orig.).

This experimental comparison of ideal types constitutes their most familiar usage as fundamental comparative tools for causal analysis. A less well-known application is treated in this section. Ideal types often chart, when examined in reference to one another, *analytic* relationships. These "logical interactions" of patterned action constitute, for Weber, hypothesis-forming models. As such, they formulate further theoretical frameworks that assist conceptualization of amorphous realities and empirical action-orientations. Weber describes these analytic relationships[14] as ones of "elective affinity" or "antagonism." They, as well, are constructed in his analytic treatise, *E&S*.

---

ruling strata and the development of salvation religions (see *E&S*, pp. 504–5/306–7, 592/357), and the domestication of the "masses" by priests during periods of political oppression and the subsequent development of values of resignation and passivity, as well as even religious ethics of brotherly love and a renunciation of violence (see *E&S*, pp. 591–3/356–7). Such examples, however, border on an orthodox structuralism and fail to convey the multidimensionality of Weber's contextual models.

13   For a vivid example, see *RofC*, pp. 248–9/535–6.

14   In this section I will be using the terms "logical interactions," "interaction analytic," and "analytic relationships" synonymously with "models."

A compatible intermingling of two or more ideal types indicates the existence of an *elective affinity* model. A non-deterministic though typical and reciprocal interaction of regular action is hypothesized. Inner relationships of "adequacy" are implied. A mutual favoring, attraction, and even strengthening is involved whenever ideal types coalesce in a relationship of elective affinity, and this attraction does not result from a common opposition to externally constraining forces. Each such interaction model involves an *inner* affinity between two or more separate ideal types.[15] Antagonistic relationships, on the other hand, indicate hypotheses of "inadequacy" and a clash, a hindering, and even an excluding of the patterned action-orientations implied by each ideal type.[16] As a result of such irrevocable antinomies, Weber's model building forecloses a dissolution of fundamental antagonisms in an ideal, or higher, synthesis, as occurs in Parsonsian functionalism.[17]

Analytic relationships of affinity and antagonism do not occur in *E&S* in a random manner. Rather, they take place in reference to the *societal domains* (*gesellschaftliche Ordnungen*) around which this analytic treatise is organized: the major universal organizations, classes, and status groups on the one hand and the religion, law, economy, and rulership life-spheres on the other hand.[18] According to Weber's massive empirical investigations, patterned social action has occurred, in a *sociologically*-significant manner, in these analytically independent realms, or, more accurately, in reference to the arrays of ideal types Weber sees as analytically located within each of

15 Empirical coalitions, such as occurred, for example, between the priesthood and urban petty-bourgeoisie in Antiquity and the Middle Ages, or between invading conquerors and domestic priests, are obviously not the concern here. Such historical alliances may result, Weber makes clear, as a consequence of a vast multiplicity of action-orientations (see e.g. *E&S*, pp. 1160/689, 1180/704).

16 Weber employs a wide array of terms as synonyms for "relations of antagonism" (*antagonistische Beziehungen*), including "in opposition to" (*im Gegensatz zu, entgegengesetzt, steht innerlich gegenüber*), "hostile to" (*feindlich zu*), "rejects" (*ablehnt*), "stands in a relationship of inner tension" (*innere Spannung*) or "inner contradiction" (*innerer Gegensatz*), "foreign to" (*fremd*), "suspicion of" (*misstrauen*), "antagonism of inner meanings" (*innerliche Sinnfeindschaft*), "estrangement" (*Entfremdung*), and "less accessible" (*weniger zugänglich*). Attention to relations of antagonism is very prominent also in the "IR" essay.

17 Precisely in this regard Parsons viewed his own work as "completing" Weber's "work, [which] was left unfinished . . . not a rounded system [and] logically perfected" (1937, p. 502). See Buxton, 1985.

18 *E&S* is explicitly organized around such domains. Weber refers to them variously as *Lebensordnungen* and *Lebensmächte*. *Lebenssphären* (life-spheres), which is also used throughout *E&S* though also broadly in his other substantive texts (as is *Wertsphären*), refers more specifically to the economy, law, religion, and rulership domains. The original title of *E&S* (and now the title of its major section, Part II) indicates Weber's focus upon domains: "Die Wirtschaft und die gesellschaftlichen Ordnungen und Mächte" (The Economy and the Societal Orders and Powers). (I prefer "societal domains" over "societal orders" to avoid confusion with the "orders" and "legitimate orders" examined in chapter 1.) This feature of *E&S* – its focus upon and organization around a set of central societal domains – has been acknowledged in the secondary literature, though not widely. See e.g. Salomon, 1945, pp. 597–600; 1935b, pp. 68–9, 72; Eisenstadt, 1968a, pp. xxxvi–xxxvii, xlii; Roth, 1979; Schluchter, 1989; see also Kalberg, 1980, 1989.

these domains: the paths to salvation in the sphere of religion (through a savior, an institution, ritual, good works, mysticism, and asceticism) (see Kalberg, 1990), the types of law ("primitive," traditional, natural, and logical formal), the stages of development in the economy (the agricultural and industrial organization of work; the natural, money, planned, market and capitalist types of economies) (see Kalberg, 1983), the types of rulership (charismatic, patriarchal, feudal, patrimonial, and bureaucratic), the types of universal organizations (the family, clan, and neighborhood), and major classes and status groups (such as intellectuals, civil servants, and feudal nobles).[19]

From the vantage point of sweeping comparisons across the empirical histories of social groupings ranging from Antiquity to the present and from East to West, Weber concluded that patterned, or causally significant, social action very often occurs in reference to these domains and their respective ideal types. No ontological assumptions played a part. As a sociologist, he attends to causal forces that have been *repeatedly* significant empirically. Moreover, he does not seek to capture all causal forces. In light of the "meaningless infinity of the world process," to attempt to do so would only lead, he is convinced, to an infinite regress (see "Obj," pp. 72–3/170–2, 81/180–1; chapter 3, pp. 84–5).[20]

Of course, a particular society or epoch may be characterized by the prominence of a societal domain or ideal type not included among those Weber assesses in his analytic treatise as sociologically most significant.

19 This, of course, is again Weber's short-hand terminology. Each ideal type documents simply the patterned action-orientations of delimited groups of people.
20 Thus, his criteria for their selection, as well as for the various ideal types within them, did not begin with a pondering of the necessary functions every society must fulfill if social order is to be maintained. Rather, a universal *empirical* assessment – one guided necessarily by his overriding interest in the development of Western rationalism (on the postulate of value-relevance, see chapter 3, pp. 84–5) – governed his selection procedures. The political sphere is omitted simply owing to Weber's long-range historical emphasis: as a distinct and autonomous sphere of life, this domain split off from the rulership domain only relatively recently, namely with the rise of the modern state in the last two centuries (see *GEH*, pp. 338–43/289–93). Before this period, this domain (the realm of the monopolization of force) remained subordinated to the family, the clan, and, in some cases, the neighborhood and even religious groups, to warrior and feudal status groups, and to charismatic, patriarchal, feudal, and patrimonial forms of rulership (see e.g. *E&S*, pp. 901–10/514–20; and below, pp. 131–5). Science is omitted for similar reasons: it attained a degree of autonomy as a distinct domain only in the West, and here only within the last century. Although empirically-based knowledge, strict observation, and contemplation of the world has occurred in a variety of civilizations and epochs, a "rational" science endowed with a potentially autonomous influence arose only in the modern West (see e.g. "AI," p. 13/1; *GEH*, p. 313/270). Similarly, the differentiated organizations, such as the enterprise (*Betrieb*) and voluntary organization (*Verein*), are omitted because they appear primarily in the modern West and not universally. The city, to which Weber devotes a large chapter (see *E&S*, pp. 1212–1372/727–814), constitutes analytically a marginal case in respect to the central issue here: whether the ideal types of cities (e.g. the Occidental, patrician, and plebeian) imply patterned social action. Some cities appear to do so (Weber ties the notion of citizenship closely to the medieval city, yet even more so to its economy and Christianity), while the action-orientations associated with other types appear analytically indigenous to status groups and sib, rulership, and religious organizations.

E&S does not aim to be exhaustive, "complete," or "eternally valid";[21] rather, the inventory of major societal domains and domain-specific ideal types it offers is designed to be helpful to comparative-historical sociologists. This delimited theoretical framework, in addition to the theoretical frameworks offered by the types of models,[22] serves as a guide that assists hypothesis formation and the acquisition of a purchase upon and clear conceptualization of the empirical patterns of action under investigation. In this manner it facilitates the establishment of their *analytic location*. The identification of probable causal action-orientations can then proceed (see chapter 5).

Affinity and antagonism models appear in *E&S* in reference to the societal domains and domain-specific ideal types. Logical interactions are postulated, for example, between types of rulership and types of economies, salvation paths and types of economies, types of law and types of economies, types of rulership and types of law, universal organizations and salvation paths, universal organizations and types of economies, and specific status groups and types of economies. Even though proponents of the interpretive historical and causal analytic schools remain highly cognizant of the *empirical* interactions of patterned action-orientations, neither approach offers such a *theoretical framework* capable of facilitating their clear conceptualization and analytic location. Thus, neither school uproots comparative-historical sociologists in principle from the empirical reality at hand and engages them in a continuous back and forth movement between an historical situation and an analytic framework. In doing so, Weber's comparative-historical sociology stands squarely in opposition to the focus upon problems of these approaches. On the other hand, the centrality of ideal types in this theoretical framework prevents Weber's sociology from moving toward the pre-formulated theory of the world systems school.

A full inventory of *E&S*'s affinity and antagonism models cannot be undertaken here; once again a few illustrations must alone suffice. These models do not take Western modernization processes or the development of the state as their point of reference. Instead, a universal range, from the classical civilizations of Antiquity to the present and from East to West, constitutes the landscape from which they have been formulated. In all cases, and even though these models remain strictly separate from empirical reality

21 Weber's principle of value-relevance prohibits such an attempt.
22 Again, dynamic, contextual (including sociological loci), elective affinity, antagonism, and developmental models have been isolated. Thus, two separate and distinct theoretical frameworks are apparent in *E&S*: those provided by models and those provided by domains and domain-specific ideal types (see chapter 5, note 13). Weber's repeated warnings in respect to the ideal type hold just as emphatically for these theoretical frameworks: it *must* not be confused with actual empirical reality (see e.g. "Obj," p. 94/195). The domain-based theoretical framework is discussed in more detail in chapter 5 in reference to Weber's mode of causal analysis.

where all logical relationships perpetually intersect, the hypotheses of antagonism and affinity they formulate assist the identification of empirical relationships of regular action and their analytic location. Causal analysis is thereby facilitated. Each hypothesized interaction can be tested through an in-depth investigation. Unlike models of elective affinity, antagonistic relations exist both *within* and *across* each separate societal domain.

Intra-domain models of antagonistic relationships

Each ideal type in *E&S* stands in an analytic relationship of antagonism to all other ideal types within the same societal domain, and each of Weber's intra-domain antagonistic models formulates delineated causal hypotheses regarding patterned action that can be empirically investigated. Only a few can be scrutinized here. Selected antagonistic relationships within the domain of rulership will be turned to first.

The bureaucratic ethos – duty, discipline, reliability, punctuality, etc. – and the formally rational procedures of bureaucratic authority strictly oppose the patriarchal, feudal, and patrimonial forms of rulership, all of which imply action-orientations to person-based and particularistic values, such as loyalty and respect. Because patrimonial rulers and officials, for example, hand down decisions in reference to sacred tradition and persons, this form of rulership remains, from the point of view of the impersonal rules typical of bureaucratic rulership, "irrational" ("I," pp. 296/269–70; *E&S*, pp. 1041/604, 958/552, 1007/580–1).

A clear analytic antagonism exists as well even among the various forms of traditional rulership, and in spite of the fact that the personal values cultivated by each may overlap. Weber's models hypothesize that patriarchal, feudal, and patrimonial types of rulership remain in relationships of strict opposition to one another, if only because each implies unique patterns of orientations. Wherever patrimonialism reigns, for example, officials subjugate the charismatically-qualified noble families and their vassals. The status consciousness in feudalism and its perpetuation through an autonomous system of education and code of honor is viewed by patrimonial rulers and officials as suspect and in opposition to their authority, their function-based honor, and their expectation of devotion to "the father of the people" (*E&S*, pp. 1106/651, 1074/628).[23]

A further model examines charismatic rulership, whether in the form of prophecy, a great warrior, or a political leader. This type of rulership is vehemently hostile to all forms of traditional as well as bureaucratic rulership, whether sacred or secular (*E&S*, pp. 1115/657). In part this is due to the unique and anti-status quo character of the value constellation it articulates, and in part to the sheer intensity of the affectual action it

23 Weber notes the opposition of feudalism and patrimonialism, as well as feudalism and bureaucratic rulership, in a succinct passage. See *E&S*, p. 1081/633.

inspires. Civil servants, for example, because entrenched within the modern state and accustomed to the formal rationality of their bureaucracies, stand firmly against the rise of charismatic figures, whether more religious (see "I," p. 283/255) or more political (see *E&S*, pp. 1130–3/668–9).

Analytic antinomies within the legal sphere parallel those found in the realm of rulership: the formal rationality of logical formal law, *E&S* postulates, stands in a relationship of clear hostility to the personal and particularistic values of "primitive," traditional, and natural law. Moreover, the constellations of values indigenous to each of these types of law stand in relationships of mutual antagonism. Similarly, with capitalism, the economy sphere called forth the purest formal rationality, one that, because characterized by a predominance of means–end rational action, strictly opposed the orientations of action to persons in both the natural and planned economies.

The major antinomies Weber's models hypothesize within the religion domain, the universal organizations, and among status groups are rooted largely in the confrontation of discrete value configurations, nearly all of which are characterized by particularistic and person-oriented values. The paths of salvation, which generally refer to constellations of values implicitly or explicitly articulated by doctrines, place premiums upon certain action in such a manner that not only the mystic and ascetic choose courses of action radically different; in addition, action in reference to the other salvation paths – salvation through a savior, an institution, ritual good works, and faith – is mutually exclusive (see *E&S*, pp. 529–34/321–4, 557–72/337–46). Even the values of intimacy originating in the universal organization ideal types – the family, sib group, and neighborhood – stand in a relationship of inner tension, as becomes visible, for example, whenever the kin group serves as a protective organization against an authoritarian household (see *E&S*, pp. 365–9/219–22). Finally, by definition, each status group in *E&S* implies a distinct style of life rooted in a clearly delimited configuration of values, and these styles of life, viewed analytically, clash (see *E&S*, pp. 305–7/179–80; 932–9/534–40).

These same ideal types point to models of antagonism as well within the single societal domains in respect to delimited *themes*. For example, the values indigenous to feudal and bureaucratic forms of rulership imply quite different hypotheses in regard to *military skills*: the feudal warrior's perfection of individualized military skills and his spontaneous heroism in battle contrasts to the discipline, drill, and adaptation of each individual to the organized operations found in bureaucratized armies (see *E&S*, p. 1105/651). Similarly, Weber's models of feudalism and patrimonialism hypothesize opposing views of *upward mobility*. Whereas feudalism's strong stress upon status conventions and honor places this type of rulership in an analytic relationship of strict antagonism to all upward mobility, "typical of patrimonialism is the determined rise from rags, from slavery and lowly service for the ruler, to the precarious all-powerful position of the favorite" (*E&S*, p. 1107/652). Weber also postulates quite different *views of the supernatural* according to the typical action-orientations indigenous to the types of authority. For example, the heroic gods regularly called forth by feudalism stand in relationships of clear antagonism to the immanent view of the supernatural typical of patrimonialism (see e.g. *E&S*, p. 431/263; "I," p. 283/255).

These few examples must suffice to convey the tenor of Weber's *E&S* intra-domain antagonistic models. As logical interaction constructs, each assists the clear identification of empirical relationships of regular action and formulates delimited, testable hypotheses. In their latter capacity in particular, and given their rootedness in a limited array of pivotal societal domains and domain-specific ideal types, they permit the theoretical framing of a relationship, theme, or problem. The *inter*-domain models serve comparative-historical sociology in the same manner. Moreover, by also offering demarcated theoretical frameworks, these models as well further distinguish Weber from the world systems, interpretive historical, and causal analytic schools.

Inter-domain models of affinities and antagonism

Weber's inter-domain models are characterized by both affinity and antagonism. Although no attempt can be made here to discuss these interactions as presented in *E&S* in an exhaustive fashion, several illustrative analytic relationships can be examined in succinct form. Selected inter-domain affinity and antagonism models between (*a*) religion and status groups, (*b*) charismatic rulership and the rational economy, and (*c*) the universal organizations, the economy,[24] and religion capture our attention. Again, theoretical frameworks for empirical investigation are articulated. As Weber notes, for example, in respect to antagonisms across societal domains: "The constructed scheme . . . only serves the purpose of offering an ideal-typical means of *orientation*. . . . The theoretically constructed types of conflicting 'life orders' are merely intended to show that at certain points such and such internal conflicts are *possible* and 'adequate'" ("IR," pp. 323/536–7).

24 A great many of the *E&S* logical interactions play critical parts in the reconstruction of the analytic course of the rationalization of action in the West undertaken in Kalberg (forthcoming c). Antagonistic relationships are noted in respect to several salvation paths and the rational capitalist economy, the status ethics of several status groups and the rational capitalist economy, and feudalism and patrimonialism and the rational capitalist economy. An elective affinity relationship between the rational capitalist economy, logical formal law, and bureaucratic rulership is systematized. These will not be repeated here.

Religion and status groups   Weber's religion/status groups models postulate affinity tendencies between certain salvation paths and intellectuals as well as peasants, yet an analytic antagonism between the life-sphere of religion and other strata: civil servants, feudal nobles, and large-scale traders and financiers.

Despite wide diversity, Weber hypothesized in *E&S* a series of elective affinities between the status ethic of intellectuals and certain salvation paths. Owing to the typical tendency of members of this stratum to ponder the world passively, to search for a comprehensive meaning to life, and to deplore the meaninglessness of empirical reality (see "I," p. 281/253; *RofI*, p. 352 n. 5/136 n. 1; *E&S*, pp. 500–17/304–13), rather than to undertake "tasks" and act regularly *in* the world as "doers," their "specifically intellectualist quest" generally implies a predisposition to formulate notions of salvation "more remote from life, more theoretical and more systematic than salvation from external need, the quest for which is characteristic of non-privileged strata" (*E&S*, p. 506/307; transl. alt.). This predisposition to search cognitively and passively for salvation, Weber's model postulates, contains a dual aspect: the attempt to conceive the world as a meaningful universe and to explain suffering follows the imperative of rational consistency on the one hand and pure contemplation and mysticism on the other.[25]

The status ethic of peasants as it relates to religion can be viewed analytically, in many respects, as the polar opposite of that of intellectuals. Ac-

---

25   In the former case, Weber hypothesizes, the typical striving of intellectuals for a unified answer to the problem of meaning and unjust suffering inclines them toward the formulation of a salvation doctrine and a continuous rationalization of its various components, including salvation paths, in behalf of internal consistency. Paths for salvation from an unjust and "senseless" reality in all religions highly influenced by intellectuals had to be in harmony with the higher order purposes of the universe, for only then could members of this stratum acquire a meaningful relationship with the cosmos and the transcendent realm. Thus, men of knowledge, whether theologians, priests, or monks, frequently sublimated and theoretically rationalized methods for redemption from suffering, as well as relations to the supernatural realm in general. (These endeavors set this stratum in unequivocal analytic antagonism to all "irrational" religions: due to their fragmented, disjointed character to magic and ritual and, due to their emotional character, to orgiasticism and ecstasy [for examples, see e.g. *RofI*, pp. 149–50/ 150, 185–6/195, 192/202, 236–7/255, 334–5/369].) Nonetheless, the hypothesized proclivity of intellectuals to ponder the world at a distance might as well lead away from a cognitive confrontation with terrestrial "senselessness" and toward, as characteristic of mysticism, the inward surrender to and possession of an impersonal divine power. Indeed, Weber stresses that "every pure intellectualism bears within itself the possibility of . . . a mystical development" (*E&S*, p. 593/357; see further, p. 505/306; "I," p. 285/257; *RofI*, p. 177/185). Whether the contemplative proclivity of intellectuals became expressed empirically through the salvation path of mysticism or through the rationalization of salvation doctrines remains a subject for empirical investigation. (The affinity of intellectuals toward the salvation path of mysticism has become manifest empirically in Pythagorean esoterics and Orphism in Hellas, for example, as well as in Taoism in China. It was intensified wherever an impersonal and immanent conception of the divine prevailed, as in Indian religions [see *RofI*, pp. 162/167, 166/171–2, 185/193]. Weber notes a concomitant intense antagonism to the natural, the physical, and the sensual, all of which constitute, to mystics, temptations that threaten distraction from salvation pursuits [*E&S*, p. 505/307; "RR," *passim.*].)

cording to Weber's *E&S* model, peasants are less able to distantiate themselves from a cycle of organic processes and thus seldom offer a unified explanation of suffering or a comprehensive understanding of the universe as a totality. Instead, his model postulates an elective affinity between their status ethic and religions rooted in magic (see *E&S*, pp. 482–3/294; "I," p. 283/285).

Peasants exhibit another tendency in direct contrast to the status ethics of intellectuals: a predisposition to understand given events through emotional experience and emotional needs rather than through cognitive and abstract processes. According to Weber's model, this proclivity creates an affinity, especially in periods of great crises, toward idolatry, ecstasy, and orgiasticism. "States of possession" produced by drugs, alcohol, or dances characterize the massive popular orgiasticism of peasants. Once attained, they enable a magical manipulation of supernatural spirits, demons, and gods, and even self-deification ("I," p. 283/255).

This orientation among peasants to orgiasticism and magic in Weber's model creates a direct antagonism toward ethical salvation religions as well as ethical rationalization processes. Accordingly, their religion typically manifests an affinity to this-worldly orientations and remains strongly penetrated by a *do et des* ritualism. Nor can a distinct notion of sin or salvation be found generally among agricultural strata, and the gods of peasants are typically not ethical but, like man, amoral. Very often, Weber's *E&S* model postulates, a living savior and the veneration of saints are far more important in worship than absolutely transcendent gods or other beings (*E&S*, pp. 469–70/286, 1178–9/703, 488/297; "I," pp. 277/248–9, 283/255; see *RofI*, pp. 326/360, 320/352, 335/370).

These elective affinity relationships must be viewed as models that articulate hypotheses regarding the religious orientations of specific strata.[26] In providing to the investigator a purchase upon ceaselessly flowing realities, each hypothesis offers a theoretical framework that facilitates clear conceptualization and provides an analytic location for the particular relationship of regular action under investigation. This procedure formulates hypotheses that can be investigated empirically through an in-depth historical exploration; in doing so it assists the identification of significant causal action-orientations. Weber's *antagonism* interaction models in *E&S* postulate different relationships between patterned action-orientations to reli-

26   It may appear to the reader of *E&S*, pp. 468–517/285–314 that Weber is here merely formulating, on the basis of his immense comparative and historical erudition, empirical generalizations (see Fulbrook, 1978, p. 77) rather than hypothesis-producing models. This impression arises as a result of his concern in this treatise to justify in every case the typical relationships postulated between status ethics and religious tendencies by providing an array of illustrative historical examples. Indeed, at times in *E&S* it appears that the empirical level constitutes his main concern. Yet this is far from the case, and to view these sections in *E&S* in this way denies the analytic purpose of this treatise.

gion and patterned action-orientations to a social stratum, yet serve parallel purposes: to provide theoretical frameworks that aid clear conceptualization and causal analysis. Only the analytic opposition between religion and civil servants, feudal nobles, and traders and financiers can be noted here.

Weber hypothesizes that civil servants are bearers of a basically non-religious and even anti-religious posture. A particular animosity toward orgiastic ecstasy and a scorn for magical manipulations is typical in this model. Just the "sober rationalism" and pragmatic nature of action within bureaucracies implies, if this stratum becomes the carrier of a religion, a predominance of ritualism: "For all civil servants, religious duties have ultimately been simply official or social duties of the citizenry and of status groups: ritual has corresponded to rules and regulations, and, therefore, wherever a bureaucracy has determined its nature, religion has assumed a ritualist character" ("I," p. 283/255, transl. alt.; see also *E&S*, pp. 1162–3/691). Similarly, feudal nobles become the carriers of ethical religions only seldom. The notions of sin, salvation, and religious humility oppose their sense of status honor, as do all demonstrations of deference to prophets and priests. According to Weber's model, the aristocratic nobility is uprooted from its religious apathy only during periods of intense religious fervor.[27]

Finally, Weber postulates a typical relationship of antagonism between the status ethic of large-scale traders and financiers and religion (see *E&S*, pp. 477–9/291–2). Rather than carriers of ethical rational, congregational, or salvation religions, these capitalists are typically indifferent and sceptical toward religion. Indeed, the more privileged their position, the less the "commercial class . . . evince[s] an inclination to develop an other-worldly religion" (*E&S*, p. 478/291). Instead, a *Realpolitik* opposed to all ethical rigor in the economic sphere typifies this stratum, as can be seen particularly in the mockery of the papist prohibition upon usury by medieval merchants and the trade practices of the Dutch "lords of trade." Not surprisingly, given this antagonism to religion, this stratum showed either no respect for gods, as was the case for the maritime nobility of ancient Greece, or paid allegiance to gods of a purely magical character, such as the god of wealth in Taoism.

These elective affinity and antagonism models of *E&S* illustrate typical logical interactions that exist between regular action-orientations specific to the domains of religion and social strata. An array of delimited hypotheses has been formulated. Each can be employed as an organizing guidepost by researchers seeking to conceptualize and analytically locate historical interactions of action. Moreover, each can be empirically investigated. Only two further illustrations of Weber's logical interaction models can be noted

---

27   As a rule: "A knighthood practically always had a thoroughly negative attitude toward salvation and congregational religion" (*E&S*, p. 475/289; see also pp. 472–3/288).

here: the model of antagonism between charismatic rulership and the rational economy, and the affinity and antagonism models that chart the interactions of universal organizations with ideal types in the economy and religion societal domains.

The antagonism of charismatic rulership and the rational economy
Although "indeterminant consequences" characterize the analytic relationship between the bureaucracy and rational capitalism (see *E&S*, pp. 989–90/571; see above p. 101), *E&S* charts clear elective affinities and antinomies between the other forms of rulership and the economy. Only the logical antagonism of charisma to all economic action can be examined.

Pure charisma stands in a relationship of antagonism to regular economic activity. By its very nature, it is "basically an extraordinary and hence necessarily non-economic power" and "specifically foreign to economic considerations" (*E&S*, pp. 1120/660, 244/142). Wherever economic interests and a concern with regular sources of income become predominant, the vitality of the charismatic movement is imminently threatened. Not salaries, benefices, or orderly compensation of any other kind typifies the economic action of the possessor of charisma and his followers; rather, donations, contributions, endowments, and booty enable their survival, and these are distributed in a communal fashion: "From the point of view of rational economic activity, charismatic want satisfaction is a typical anti-economic force. It repudiates any sort of involvement in the everyday routine world. It can only tolerate, with an attitude of complete emotional indifference, irregular, unsystematic acquisitive acts" (*E&S*, p. 245/142).

Of all the types of economies Weber analyses, only the "booty capitalism" of colonial exploitation, slave trading, risky financial transactions, piracy, and adventurism bears any degree of affinity with charisma. Because they require a certain steadiness and constancy, all others, as well as the typical means of organizing agricultural and industrial work (see *E&S*, pp. 122–37/67–77; Kalberg, 1983, pp. 259–66), stand in strict opposition to charismatic rulership. In particular, all methodical economic activity is viewed as undignified. For this reason, Weber describes pure charisma as "*the* strongest anti-economic force" (*E&S*, p. 1113/656). The formal rationality of the market and capitalism, this model hypothesizes, is rejected unequivocally by this form of rulership with its typical action-orientations rooted in sentiment, deep emotion, and inspiration.

The universal organizations: relations to the economy and religion The capacity of universal organizations – the household, kin group, and neighborhood – to call forth a coherent fraternal ethic shapes their analytic interaction with the economic sphere. Because compatible with this ethic, the planned and natural economies stand in a relationship of elective affinity with these organizations, while the formal rationality of the market and capitalist economies makes for a severe tension. Only this model of antagonism can be illustrated.

The person-oriented, communal relationships and value constellations dominant in the household, kin group, and neighborhood stand in the strictest logical opposition to the formal rationality of the market and capitalism. In prohibiting exchanges based upon the sheer calculation of gain, the ethics of brotherhood indigenous to these "primeval groups" construct barriers against the typical economic action dominant in the market and under capitalism. Rather than oriented to the impersonal associations of the marketplace, action in these groups remains predominantly traditional, affectual, or value-rational, and therefore "economically irrational" (*E&S*, p. 636/383). The pure economic exchange characterized by dickering, as well as marauding raids, is permitted only with outsiders to whom the ethic of brotherhood does not apply: "non-kinsmen, non-'brothers'; in short, non-comrades" (*E&S*, p. 673/402; see also *E&S*, p. 107/58 and Nelson, 1949).[28] The "absolute objectification" of human relationships in this exchange, its exploitation of interest constellations and monopoly positions, and its unrestricted haggling constitutes an abomination to every fraternal ethic.[29] What hypotheses characterize the *E&S* model of the relationship of the universal organizations to the domain of religion?

In a certain sense, logical interactions of elective affinity typify all relations between the universal organizations and both magical and salvation religions. Magical religions simply appropriated the general virtues practiced in the family, kin group, and neighborhood, such as fraternity, truthfulness, loyalty to the sibling, respect for older generations, and reciprocal assistance. Salvation religions typically bestowed distinctly positive premiums upon the brotherhood ethic. In all cases, personal relations and person-oriented values predominated.

Despite this inner compatibility, an analytic tension between the universal organizations and salvation religions also appears. The "greatest achievement" of these religions, according to Weber, was to "shatter the fetters of the sib." In demanding the total loyalty of believers, they espoused the superiority of the community of faith over that of the sibling and other close personal relations, thus requiring the faithful to stand closer to religious leaders and brothers in the faith than even to blood relatives (see *E&S*, p. 580/350; "IR," pp. 329–30/542–4).[30] The general solidarity of the

28   "Where the market is allowed to follow its own autonomous tendencies, its participants do not look toward each person but only toward the commodity; there are no obligations of brotherliness or reverence, and none of those primary human relationships as carried by the universal organizations. They all would just inhibit the free development of the bare market relationship. . . . The rational, means–end pursuit of interests influences market proceedings to an especially high degree" (*E&S*, p. 636/383; transl. alt.; see also *E&S*, pp. 361–2/216, 365–6/219–20; "RR," pp. 331–3/544–6).

29   More specifically on this antagonism between the rational economy and the household, see *E&S*, pp. 359/214, 377/277–8, 1118/659; between the rational economy and the kin group, see *E&S*, pp. 365–6/219–20, 361–2/216; and between the rational economy and the neighborhood, see *E&S*, pp. 362/216, 1188–9/710.

30   For example: "I came not to send peace, but the sword." And: "Whoever does not leave his own father and mother cannot become a follower of Jesus." Both were said in this context (see *E&S*, p. 580/350; "IR," p. 329/542).

religious community and the injunction of brotherly love rested upon this demand as well as the suffering common to all believers.[31] Moreover, in articulating notions of *universal* brotherhood, the fraternal ethic practiced in many ethical salvation religions clashed with the strict insider – outsider division typical of the brotherhood ethic in the universal organizations.

In these ways, Weber's *E&S* elective affinity and antagonism models postulate typical logical relationships between the universal organizations and the economy and religion. Each model enunciates demarcated hypotheses that can be empirically investigated. Each limited generalization as well, in offering a theoretical framework, assists the clear conceptualization of interacting patterns of action-orientations. In this manner, and in light of their rootedness in a spectrum of central societal domains and domain-specific ideal types, these models uproot comparative-historical sociologists from historical narrative and offer means of orientation as well as organizing mechanisms that facilitate the analytic ordering and causal explanation of regular action. The world systems, interpretive historical, and causal analytic schools all fail to offer comparable constructs.

The affinity and antagonism interactions across the life-spheres, universal organizations, and status groups scrutinized here constitute only a segment of the hypothesis-forming analytic relationships evident in Weber's analytic treatise, *E&S*. Furthermore, as in regard to the intra-domain causal models of antagonism, Weber formulates inter-domain models of affinity and antagonism in respect to demarcated *themes*. For example, the status ethics of civil servants, intellectuals, the feudal aristocracy, and patrimonial officials all yield, if examined closely in reference to one another, particular models of "proper" *education*. The civil servant's ideal of specialized training and a "vocation" oriented toward the acquisition of technical knowledge and based upon standardized tests of expertise stands in strict opposition on the one hand to the classical intellectual's humanist, or "gentleman's," education with its emphasis upon philosophy, theology, literature, history, and languages (see *E&S*, pp. 998–1002/576–8), and on the other hand to the aristocracy. The latter's stress upon pride of status and sense of honor indicates a kinship with a playful and artistic notion of education and an "heroic hostility" to all utilitarian ways of life that involve either a means–end rational service to a "mission" or a systematic pursuit of goals (see *E&S*, pp. 1090/639–40, 1106/651, 1108/653). The particular notion of education implied by patrimonialism stands in a relationship of polar antithesis: here a clerical–rational education, often endowed with a strong literary character and an emphasis upon conventions, prevails. Imbued with a distinct utilitarian aspect, this notion of education could merge easily with the

31   This antagonism is particularly severe wherever prophets demand the loyalties of disciples in charismatic communities ("IR," p. 328/542).

professional specialization of civil servants in modern bureaucracies (see *E&S*, pp. 1090/640, 1108/652, 1145/678).

These few examples must suffice to indicate the manner in which Weber's interaction models of affinity and antagonism articulate delimited causal hypotheses. Because they are logical constructs only, he fully expects all hypotheses, just as those formulated by dynamic and contextual models, to be "dislocated" when confronted by empirical realities. Concrete historical circumstances and contexts will invariably strengthen or weaken particular components of an analytic relationship. Whether the dual inclinations of religious intellectuals tended in reality more toward mystic "illumination," contemplation, and a total withdrawal from the world or a theoretical rationalization of religious doctrines depended upon an empirical situation: was an immanent or monotheistic supreme Being dominant (*E&S*, p. 505/307; "I," p. 290/263)? Given other empirical circumstances, the tendency of religious intellectuals on the one hand toward mysticism and withdrawal and on the other toward a theoretical rationalization of doctrines might follow one upon the other (*RofI*, p. 342/377). To Weber, the postulated status ethics of intellectuals were shaped differently in India, China, and ancient Greece, most importantly by empirical "interests . . . and political circumstances" (*RofI*, p. 352, n. 5/139, n. 1) and "different social structures" (*soziale Grundstruktur*) (*RofI*, p. 139/137). The Chinese literati, as a consequence of the religious demands placed upon devout intellectuals in India, could not have become influential in India, despite remarkable similarities among these intellectual strata (see *RofI*, p. 139/137): "It is understandable that an intellectual stratum of officials and aspirants to office in a patrimonial state [in China] could accept neither the individualist quest for salvation nor the broken humility of the [Indian] mystic" (*RofC*, p. 186/471).[32]

Some historical constellations, of course, might *radically* call into question an *E&S* elective affinity or antagonism relationship. Unusual situations, for example, such as the great public excitement that surrounded Teddy Roosevelt's campaign in 1912, can lead to the "triumph of charisma over the organization" (*E&S*, p. 1132/669). Similarly, the case of Calvinism contradicts Weber's postulated relationship of antagonism between salvation religions and the rational economy: in the process of attributing religious significance to a methodical work ethic, Calvinism penetrated deeply into the market economy. Historical forces have even shattered, for example, the typical antagonism of large-scale traders and financiers to religion, as occurred in parts of China where traders cultivated Taoist magic

32 Weber examines the different social settings within which Chinese and Indian intellectuals found themselves in some detail; see e.g. *RofC*, pp. 108–11/396–401, 122/410–11; *RofI*, pp. 137–54/134–57. He also compares the Levite priests of ancient Judaism to the Brahmins in respect to their different social contexts (see *AJ*, pp. 171–4/183–6), as he does Greek philosophers and Confucian literati (see *RofC*, pp. 175–6/460–2). Again, the centrality of empirical contexts for Weber is apparent.

(see *RofC*, pp. 196/481) and in India where a mystical holy-seeking spread throughout the merchant and banker Vallabhachari sect (*RofI*, pp. 314–17/ 346–9). Finally, the analytic relationship between patrimonialism and an immanent view of the supernatural, which held quite nicely for India and China, must be rejected unequivocally in the case of the ancient Near East (see *E&S*, pp. 448/273–4).

Weber sees as well that logical relations of antagonism may be overcome empirically. This may occur as a consequence of a powerful external force, indeed to such an extent that a coalition arises of groups postulated by the *E&S* model to stand in an antagonistic relationship. Despite great disagreements, the priesthood and the urban petty-bourgeoisie, for example, typically cooperate and support one another when threatened by a feudal aristocracy (see *E&S*, p. 1180/704). Similarly, reformist monks and secular rulers are often forced into alliances by feudal rulership.

Many further examples, even *E&S* itself, could be given to illustrate this fundamental tenet: for Weber, because they are models only, analytic relationships of antagonism and elective affinity are seldom transferred into empirical reality. He takes cognizance in principle of the capacity, above all, of power, charismatic leaders, and historical imponderables selectively to skew, weaken, and even contradict *all* affinity and antagonism models, as well as the dynamic and contextual models noted earlier. Such an acknowledgment derives on the one hand from the disjunction at the very core of Weber's sociology – his strict separation of the analytical and empirical levels – and, on the other hand, as will be discussed again in chapter 5, his stress upon social contexts. For these reasons, his affinity and antagonism constructs cannot be understood, as little as the hypotheses formulated by his dynamic and contextual models, as (*a*) unveiling even weak empirical relationships or (*b*) accurately capturing Weber's mode of causal analysis.

As noted, the formulation of affinity and antagonism models results from *logical* relationships across the theoretical framework provided by the *E&S* societal domains and domain-specific ideal types rather than from historical and changing factors, such as power, external constraint, rulership, or particular historical events. Thus, because these limited analytic generalizations fail to inform us in respect to the character of any given empirical reality, the existence of specific historical cases that contradict a postulated relationship does not itself call into question this procedure or the usefulness of these constructs. The great power of these models remains exclusively heuristic and analytic: (*a*) to postulate delimited and empirically-testable causal relationships; (*b*) to isolate and define significant causal action-orientations; (*c*) to provide theoretical frameworks for comparative-historical sociologists seeking to order and conceptualize the interactions of action under investigation; and (*d*) to locate these interactions within a theoretical framework anchored by sociologically significant domains and domain-specific ideal types.[33] Rather than rooting itself in problems and cases alone, as do the interpretive historical and causal analytic schools, the comparative-historical enterprise must recognize, according to Weber, such models as indispensable. *E&S* provides a reservoir of models capable of *orienting* innumerable empirical investigations.

For him, hypothesis-building models can assist significantly the fulfillment of comparative-historical sociology's designated purpose: the causal explanation of unique cases and developments. Yet this is the limit of their service. Under no circumstances should analytic relationships be viewed as themselves constituting empirical causal relationships. Causal relationships can be established only through much more complicated procedures and strategies. They will be reconstructed in chapter 5.

A fourth type of hypothesis-forming model prominent throughout *E&S* must be examined now: the *developmental* model. This model as well contributes decisively to the capacity of Weber's substantive works to draw comparative-historical sociology away from the focus upon problems characteristic of the interpretive historical and causal analytic approaches, and toward the precise theoretical framing of the problem under investigation. These models, as the dynamic, contextual and affinity and antagonism models, further dramatically demonstrate the universal range of his substantive studies: the entire spectrum from the ancient past to the present as well as civilizations of the East and West constitutes his concern rather than simply the rise of the state or Western modernization processes.

Developmental Models

Weber's *E&S* developmental models constitute limited analytic generalizations distinct from his other models. On the one hand, these constructs hypothesize a *course* of action that implies a number of ideal-typical stages through which patterned action-orientations proceed. At each stage, hypotheses are formulated regarding the further path of regular action. On the other hand, these models are distinquished by their incorporation of discrete "driving forces"; that is, the models themselves are anchored in and set into motion by an "internal" force. This driving force is linked indigenously to the *course* of action, or "developmental path" (*Entwicklungsweg*).

The principled distinction in Weber's substantive sociology between the empirical and analytic levels must be kept particularly in mind in respect to

33   Again, only a fraction of *E&S*'s interaction models have been presented here. My purpose has been to provide a sampling capable of conveying Weber's *style* of model-building and the centrality of models in his comparative-historical sociology.

developmental models. Empirically, as was emphasized in chapter 2, Weber's comparative-historical sociology remains radically multicausal. At the analytic level, however, he stands "outside of history" and repeatedly formulates developmental constructs driven by a single set of action-orientations. Thus, when discussing these models, Weber stresses even more than otherwise that they must not be "confused with reality" (see "Obj," pp. 101–3/203–6; R&K, pp. 73–80/22–30). Particular caution must be exercised to insure a clear separation between this "scaffolding" (E&S, p. 116/63) and the historical process. Diverse factors, in each *empirical* case, call forth action-orientations that "intervene" to upset all postulated, or "pure" developmental paths, which are presented in each model in a manner more internally consistent and systematically unified than any given empirical development.[34] In opposition to Schmoller (1900, 1904), Bücher (1894), and Schönberg (1882; see E&S, pp. 118/64–5), Weber emphasized that the stages of each developmental model should never be viewed either as capturing the course of history or as constituting "effective forces"; nor are they designed to chart a universal or evolutionary tendency for all history to pass through each stage ("Obj," pp. 102–3/203–5). For example, although, when viewed from the perspective of a change from substantive to formal rationality, the types of legitimate rulership can be arranged in a developmental model that moves from charismatic and traditional to rational–legal rulership, the researcher should not be led from this mode of conceptualization to conclude that such a transformation actually occurred empirically.[35]

This tenet separates Weber clearly from all evolutionary schools of thought that seek either to identify society's "scientific laws of development" or to view history as a succession of invariable stages.[36] His compara-

34 As "technical aids" prepared with a "rational consistency . . . rarely found in reality" ("IR," p. 323/537), these constructs chart a developmental course that will be taken if certain "irrational" empirical disturbances do not intervene ("Obj," pp. 101–3/203–5).

35 Weber makes this point cogently in an early essay: "It is a serious misunderstanding of the research *goal* of cultural history to consider the construction of 'cultural stages' as *more* than a heuristic means, and the ordering of historical events under such abstractions as the *purpose* of scholarly work . . . ; it is a violation of research methodology to view a 'cultural stage' as anything but a *concept*, to treat it as a *real* entity in the manner of biological organisms, or an Hegelian 'idea,' from which the individual components 'emanate,' and thus to use the 'stage' for arriving at *conclusions* by analogy" (GAzSW, p. 517; emph. orig.). For Weber's rejection of all "logical developments in the manner of Hegel," see *PE II*, pp. 16, 28–9; Honigsheim, 1968, p. 14. Whether the course of history actually followed the analytic path of development laid out by a particular developmental model always remains, for Weber, an issue for detailed empirical investigation by specialists (see "Obj," p. 103/205).

36 I am here in strict disagreement with Parsons, who sees Weber's "thought as basically evolutionary" (e.g. 1963, pp. lx, lxv), as well as the attempts by Tenbruck (1980), Habermas (1979, 1984), and Schluchter (1981, 1989) to place Weber within the evolutionary camp. On Weber's opposition to evolutionism generally, see, in addition to the above references, e.g. "I," pp. 292/264–5; GAzSW, pp. 517, 524 (translated in Roth, 1968, p. xxxviii); Winckelmann (1965), Bendix (1962; 1965, pp. 11–12), Bendix and Roth (1971, pp. 114–28, 209–24, 253–65), Hennis (1983), and Mommsen (1987; 1989, p. 127). English readers may be confused on

tive-historical sociology takes *neither* historical development itself *nor* an overarching evolutionary or teleological model as its level of analysis. Least of all does it seek, as does the world systems school, to understand history in reference to a theoretical scheme (see, for example, *R&K*, pp. 63–6/11–15). Indeed, Weber's formulation and utilization of developmental models can be understood as the natural outcome of his rejection on the one hand of universal evolutionary stages[37] as well as the functionalist conception of societies as "whole" (*E&S*, p. 15/7; see *PE*, pp. 75–7/60–2), and on the other hand of all attempts to establish causality through historical narrative and rich description. Given this point of departure and his endorsement of the ideal type as his fundamental methodological construct, the developmental model emerges as a suitable device for the investigation of the unfolding of patterned action-orientations.

Weber's developmental models serve as constructs that provide the researcher with clear and practical organizational mechanisms. As the dynamic, contextual, and affinity and antagonism models, each construct fulfills, in Weber's view, purposes indispensable to comparative-historical sociology: each can be utilized not only as a "yardstick" to assist the clear definition of the particular empirical development at hand,[38] but also as a theoretical framework that facilitates a conceptual grasp upon and analytic location of empirical developments. Delimited hypotheses regarding causal patterns of action are formulated at each stage, each of which can be assessed by specialists in reference to the empirical development under investigation.

This section examines the major types of developmental models formulated in *E&S*.[39] What are the bases that drive these constructs? Models anchored in and set into motion by interests and formal and theoretical rationalization processes are prominent. Once again, Weber's universal range will become apparent.[40]

---

this matter by the frequent translation in *PE* and *E&S* of *Entwicklung* (development) as "evolution."

37   Indeed, more generally, the ideal type itself can be understood, as Roth has noted (1968, p. xxxii; 1971, pp. 253–65), as Weber's answer to the evolutionary stage theories of his time.

38   To Weber, "even developments can be constructed as ideal types, and these constructs may have quite considerable heuristic value" ("Obj," p. 101/203).

39   *E&S* constitutes the source for all such models in Weber's substantive texts. At times, as above, passages from other texts will complement these reconstructions. Again, these broad-ranging illustrations are presented in some detail in order to convey clearly a sense for the model building component in Weber's comparative-historical sociology, its capacity to confront the problem-focussed schools, and its centrality in Weber's substantive sociology rather than to convince contemporary comparative-historical sociologists that these *particular* constructs should be utilized in their own research. In addition, this detailed presentation may offer guidelines to comparative-historical sociologists inclined to become engaged in such model building.

40   "Developmental model," "processual construct," and "developmental path" are used synonymously.

Developmental models anchored in interests: the closure of social relationships and the routinization of charisma models

Interests, to Weber, are ubiquitous. Depictions of the clash of action oriented to interests can be found on nearly every page of his substantive writings, with the exception of *PE*. Frequently they are simply "random." The developmental models in this section examine a particular way in which interests appear prominently in *E&S*, namely, in regard to their capacity to set into motion and drive developmental processes.[41] Formulated from empirical observations of diverse civilizations, a variety of such delineated analytic processes rooted in interest-oriented action are found in *E&S*. Each construct charts a *course* of patterned action in "pure" form and, at each stage, articulates discrete hypotheses.[42] Only two developmental models can be illustrated here: the closure of social relationships and the routinization of charisma models.[43]

The closure of social relationships and the monopolization of opportunities
To Weber, processes of closure, exclusion, and even monopolization of resources and opportunities reappear throughout history and in all civilizations. They may be driven by interest-oriented action. His developmental model captures such processes.

Closure of a social relationship takes place to the degree that a regulation of interaction with outsiders arises, conditions of participation are articulated, and exclusion is practiced. In Weber's short-hand expression, closure insures the fulfillment of "internal or external" interests (*E&S*, pp. 344–5/203–4). Three interests in particular stand behind thrusts toward closure: action in behalf of prestige, social honor, and profit that attempts to "maintain quality"; action in behalf of a desire to acquire and maintain monopolies of consumption; and action in behalf of an attempt to deal with an increasing scarcity of acquisition opportunities.[44] Such interests regu-

41   It must be emphasized that not all interest-oriented action becomes manifest in *developmental* models, the concern here. For examples of the importance Weber attaches to interests as general causal forces see the discussion above on "orders" (chapter 1, pp. 32–9).

42   The question of whether, in this or that empirical situation, the hypothesized developmental course was followed through to its final stage cannot be addressed in this purely analytical discussion. Moreover, every empirical development depends, of course, for Weber upon a variety of factors, such as the strength of carrier strata, power, historical accident, successful coalitions, etc. The model reconstructed here is rooted *only* in interests. Again, this pivotal analytical/empirical distinction must be kept particularly in mind throughout this section on developmental models.

43   These two models, which are formulated most clearly in *E&S*, are utilized throughout Weber's substantive texts. They constitute the most prominent examples of developmental processes rooted in interests. They are reconstructed here in succinct form. To repeat: the emphasis *in each model* upon interests as driving forces does not deny that other factors may *empirically* be central and even decisive.

44   Weber employs the concept of "interests" (*Interessen, Interessenlage*) frequently, yet he never offers an adequate discussion of the many shadings this term possesses in his compara-

larly congeal in behalf of exclusion (see *E&S*, pp. 43–6/23–5, 341–8/201–7). Weber's models postulate paths toward closure-oriented action rooted in interests most prominently in economic relationships, in status groups, in rulership organizations, and in the life-sphere of religion (*E&S*, p. 344/ 203).[45] Each will be briefly examined. Again, as ideal-typical constructs, these processual models are rooted in empirical histories yet also separate from them. They formulate causal hypotheses regarding *a course* of patterned social action.

Economic relationships tend toward closure. Exclusive control is sought over services and commodities. Frequently posed historically against monopolies rooted in status honor, capitalists, for example, once having benefited from the expansion of the free market[46] and once competition becomes intense, seek, this model hypothesizes, to appropriate productive resources and to monopolize advantages. The external features of competitors – race, language, religion, etc. – may be utilized as a pretext to justify exclusion. "Interest groups" and "cooperative organizations" arise and, if political alliances are secured, monopolistic practices may become protected by laws. In this case, joint action and identifiable associations lead to a "legally privileged group." At each stage in the developmental model, the aim to close economic opportunities to outsiders guides action. An association of engineering graduates, for example, may attempt to acquire a legal right to certain positions; former soldiers may lobby on behalf of laws that allocate a specific number of civil service positions to them; or master-craftsmen may be granted legal privileges that guarantee a steady flow of customers. This construct postulates that the closure of economic relationships must be seen as an ever-recurring process (for further examples, see *E&S*, pp. 342–8/201–7).

An analytic development, anchored in interests, from openness to closure and monopolization typifies as well the movement toward exclusivity that takes place as *status groups* become cohesive. Regular action may be

---

tive-historical sociology. The discussion in his "Basic Sociological Terms" chapter is severely foreshortened (*E&S*, p. 30/15). He occasionally employs the expression "ideal and material interests." Although this phrase does capture Weber's intent to define interests as involving also a non-material dimension, and even values (see Kalberg, 1985a), it does not capture his manifold usage of this concept. The complexity of this theme requires a chapter in itself. An exegetical discussion must be postponed, as well as an examination of the relationship between interests and power. Interests in this section are defined exclusively by reference to their usage in the two developmental models reconstructed here. As will be noted, in each case Weber's usage is broad.

45   Again, no attempt has been made here "exhaustively" to mine *E&S* for all such processes. Rather, in order to illustrate this developmental model rooted in interests, this short section aims only to provide the most prominent examples. As Weber notes: "Any cultural trait, no matter how superficial, can serve as a starting point for the familiar tendency to monopolistic closure" (*E&S*, p. 388/236).

46   For Weber's comments on the manner in which action oriented to an economic interest in the expansion of the market can lead clearly to imperialism, see *E&S*, p. 346/205.

oriented to specific notions of social honor that imply social distance and exclusiveness (see *E&S*, pp. 932–3/534–5). Weber hypothesizes that status groups may, under certain circumstances, crystallize from such action-orientations, and they may be distinguished from competing status groups by the articulation of a particular way of life (*Lebensführung*), rights, and privileges. Individuals "attempt to increase status by making it scarce" (*E&S*, p. 1139/674).[47] Typically, the placing of restrictions upon social intercourse occurs in some cases to such an extent that permission to marry is confined to a delineated status circle. A coherent "status ethic" arises to legitimize status group closure, and it is strengthened whenever exclusionary procedures develop parallel to its formation.[48] Stable status group conventions, this model postulates, may unfold at this developmental stage into legally-sanctioned privileges and employment monopolies over special offices (*E&S*, pp. 932–3/535). In the case of extreme closure, status groups call forth action oriented to castes; religious forces as well as conventions and laws may then guarantee distinctions across status groups (see *E&S*, pp. 933–4/536). More generally: "for all practical purposes, stratification by status goes hand in hand with a monopolization of ideal and material goods or opportunities" (*E&S*, p. 935/537).

Rulership organizations may also follow a typical developmental course in which action-orientations move from ones of openness to ones of closure. This processual model is as well thrust forth by interests, in this case those of ruling groups. Processes of exclusion and the monopolization of resources in the rulership domain have remained strong, even though no longer rooted in blood lineage, the power of tradition, and economic function,[49] and instead based upon the specialized and technical knowledge, standardized examinations, and impersonal norms and rules characteristic of bureaucracies. Exclusion may occur even to the extent that civil servants develop, this model hypothesizes, a belief in a "right to the office." Even a rebirth of "aristocracy" may take place (*E&S*, pp. 1000–1/577, 1080–1/ 632–3).

> The elaboration of the diplomas from universities, business and engineering colleges, and the universal clamor for the creation of further educational certificates in all fields serve the formation of a privileged stratum in bureaus and in offices. Such certificates support their holders' . . . claims for a "status-appropriate" salary instead of a wage according to performance, claims for assured advancement and old-age insurance, and, above all, claims to the monopolization of socially and economically advantageous positions. (*E&S*, pp. 1000–1/577)[50]

47   Weber overstates his case in the example to which this quote refers: the putative move in American life away from a "Puritan mentality that glorified the self-made man" to an emphasis upon descent and membership in an "old wealth" family.

48   For a succinct example, see the discussion of the English *ministeriales* (*E&S*, pp. 1026–7/ 595).

49   On the manner in which feudal conventions and the scarcity of fiefs lead to stages of increasing closure and monopolization, see *E&S*, pp. 1080–1/632–3.

50   For Weber, given this tendency toward closure and monopolization ("'history' continues inexorably to bring forth new 'aristocracies' and 'authorities'" [1905, p. 282/63]), the empiri-

Weber constructs a parallel developmental model anchored in interests from action oriented to openness to action oriented to closure and monopolization in the life-sphere of *religion*. The possessors of religious "goods" seek to proselytize and expand as a means of guaranteeing their survival. Priests have been particularly concerned to defend and protect sacred values against competitors, especially to the extent that struggles between prophets, the laity, and the priesthood subside. Weber's processual construct formulates hypotheses about the activity of this stratum, which typically seeks to defend interests and expand a base of support: it may not only produce canonical scriptures and dogmas, adopt them to the "religious qualifications" of the laity, and seek official sanction for them as a protection against heterodoxy, but also constitute itself as the most significant social carrier in this domain of group closure and monopolization processes. In doing this, priests effectively confront indifference among the laity and place substantial barriers against any inclinations of church members to transfer to another denomination. Priests recognize in particular, this closure model hypothesizes, that all claims to power ultimately depend upon the degree to which the education of youth is monopolized (see "IR," p. 351/565; *E&S*, pp. 457–61/279–81).

Weber formulates a similar processual model pushed forth by interests in respect to *spiritual goods*: churches (and, most forcefully, the church as an hierocratic institution) propound action oriented to closure and the monopolization of religious values (see *E&S*, pp. 560–3/339–40; "I," p. 288/260; *RofI*, p. 6/6). This remains the case despite the church's distinguishing feature as "the trustee of a 'trust fund' of eternal blessings . . . offered to everyone" (*E&S*, pp. 1164/692–3). The action-orientations of this organization's "professional priesthood" do not alone set into motion a concerted attempt to define and monopolize orthodoxy; in addition, the demand of all representatives of this religious body for loyalty above household, sib, tribal, and political ties, Weber's construct postulates, leads in this direction. Indeed, in behalf of their attempts to eliminate competing powers and acquire the complete devotion of believers, their patterned action becomes oriented toward a denigration of all non-religious ties of the laity. This same interest in appropriating the dispensation of religious values and all routes to salvation sets hierocracies strictly in opposition to the challenges of prophets and other charismatic figures. The institutionalization by churches and hierocracies of specific educational paths for their officials and

---

cally realistic posing of the problem of democracy does not involve a search to eliminate rulership (see *E&S*, pp. 987–9/569–71). This is least of all the case in our own epoch: direct democracy is impossible wherever administrative tasks of massive scale make bureaucratic administration indispensable (*E&S*, pp. 223/128, 283–5/567–8, 291–3/171–2). Rather, the question must be confronted on the one hand of how democracies can construct procedures that effectively constrain extreme monopolization of social and economic resources as well as power by rulership organizations (see *E&S*, pp. 289/169, 985/568), and on the other hand of how the "resolute *will* of a nation not to allow itself to be led like a flock of sheep" (1905, p. 282/64) can be developed.

their striving to regulate believers' conduct as well constitute means, in Weber's developmental construct, that guarantee the perpetuation of claims to elite status and a monopoly over all sacred values (see *E&S*, pp. 1163–7/692–4; "IR," pp. 327–8/541; "I," pp. 282–3/254–5).

To Weber, all such developmental models of closure, exclusion, and even the monopolization of resources and opportunities in economic relationships, status groups, rulership organizations, and the domain of religion formulate, at each stage, clear causal hypotheses regarding a route of patterned social action.[51] Each demarcated hypothesis can be tested against an empirical development of interest to the investigator; divergence from the postulated developmental path can be clearly identified and hypotheses regarding motives other than interests (for example, values or traditions) can be formulated. Specific to these models is their *course* toward closure and their driving force: they are set into motion and carried along primarily by interests. As the dynamic, contextual, and affinity and antagonism models, these limited analytic generalizations, as hypothesis-forming constructs, inject a theoretical dimension into the very core of Weber's substantive sociology, in the process again distinguishing it from the problem focus of the interpretive historical and causal analytic schools. These models, on the other hand, avoid the pre-formulated theory of the world systems approach.

Another analytic process rooted in and thrust forth by interests is prominent in *E&S*: the routinization of charisma. Again, causal hypotheses in respect to a course of patterned action-orientations are postulated at each stage.

The routinization of charisma model   The charismatic leader acts in reference to his "inner calling" and endows his "cause" with legitimacy through the sheer force of his personality. For this reason, Weber sees charisma as standing in fundamental and revolutionary opposition to all means–end rational action as well as all existing and stable forces of daily life (see *E&S*, pp. 291/140, 1112–14/655–6, 1119–20/659–60; "I," pp. 295–6/269).[52]

Weber stresses, however, not only the unique powers of charismatic rulership to call forth radically new patterns of action, but also its fragility. As a consequence of its location strictly in the "supernatural qualities" of great leaders and the necessity for the "superhuman" personality repeatedly to demonstrate unusual powers and a "right to rule," "charismatic rulership is naturally unstable" (*E&S*, pp. 1112–14/655–6). Even the great-

---

51   Further illustrations of this developmental model might include e.g. the ways in which *ethnicity* may provide the basis for monopolization processes; see *E&S*, pp. 386–93/234–40. Again, this section has sought to illustrate this construct rather than to discuss all examples found in Weber's texts.

52   "Genuine charismatic rulership knows no abstract laws and regulations and no formal adjudication. Its 'objective' law flows from the highly personal experience of divine grace and god-like heroic strength and rejects all external order.... Hence, in a revolutionary and sovereign manner, charismatic rulership transforms all values and breaks all traditional and rational norms" (*E&S*, p. 1115/657).

est intensity of personal devotion to the charismatic leader and a complete "revolution from within" (see *E&S*, pp. 1116–17/657–8) in the attitudes of followers cannot guarantee the perpetuation of the extraordinary figure's teachings in their pure form. Instead, charisma follows a developmental path characterized by its weakening and "routinization." In this processual model, this "creative aspect" of the human spirit is repeatedly absorbed, in all societal domains, into the permanent institutions of everyday life (see *E&S*, pp. 1131–3/668–70, 1156/687; "EK," p. 470). Indeed, such a transformation of charisma has always been sought in the hope that, in the process, a permanent protection against sickness, disease, and natural catastrophe will be acquired (see, for example, *E&S*, pp. 1146–9/679–81).

Weber's "routinization of charisma" construct postulates that the material and power interests of the charismatic community of followers and disciples constitute the driving force in institutionalizing innovations and the "transitory gift of grace . . . into a permanent possession of everyday life" (*E&S*, p. 1121/661). The regular orientation of followers toward an interest in legitimizing positions of prestige and rulership, as well as in securing lasting economic resources, has been central at each stage of this developmental model. In addition, other persons in possession of economic and social power seek, with the aim of legitimating positions of privilege, to "capture" the charismatic movement and to utilize the charismatic inspiration for their own ends (see *E&S*, pp. 252/146–7, 1121–3/661–2). To Weber, the purity of charisma can be preserved against everyday interests only by the "common danger of military life or a love ethos of an unworldly discipleship" (*E&S*, pp. 1120/660–1).

The search for economic advantage has been especially central at each stage in this routinization of charisma model (see *E&S*, pp. 148/254, 262/ 153, 1120/660, 1146/679, 1156/687). The normal, everyday operation of the marketplace demands predictability and reliability. Thus, those followers in positions to secure economic advantage assert their power to transform the "irrational" charismatic force into a "rational" and orderly mode of exchange. This developmental construct hypothesizes that the weight of a diverse array of vested interests alters "the charismatic message [into] dogma, doctrine, theory . . . law or petrified tradition"; disciples become "professional" magicians (*berufsmässiger Zauberer*) and priests; great warriors become fief-holders, the founders of noble lineage groups, and kings; followers become state and party officials; and the charismatic community becomes a church, hierocracy, sect, academy, or party (*E&S*, pp. 1121–2/ 660–1, 1141–2/676, 1165–6/692; "IR," pp. 327–8/541).[53]

Nonetheless, and even though the revolutionary essence of charisma and its capacity to legitimize rulership through heroism wanes, Weber's

53 Again, this developmental model refers to causal hypotheses, or *possible* empirical outcomes. Weber discusses such limited analytic generalizations on a number of occasions. On the model followed by warrior organizations to status groups and then to permanent political structures, see *E&S*, pp. 906–8/516–18, 1087/637, 1377/("EK")450; on the unfolding of perma-

routinization model does not postulate the demise of the orientation of regular action toward charisma. Here again interests push this developmental construct. Individuals seek to preserve the charismatic inspiration in depersonalized (*versachlichte*) form. They do so not only in the hope of facilitating the transformation of sheer power relationships into legitimated rights, but also as a means of sanctifying extant power and privileges (see, for example, *E&S*, pp. 251/146, 1123/662-3, 1139–41/674–5, 1146–8/679–81; "I," p. 297/270). Even when no longer manifest in its pure form, the charisma attached to the community of disciples of the extraordinary charismatic figure plays, Weber's model hypothesizes, an indispensable role in attracting new followers to its fold, in establishing the legitimacy of new status groups, forms of rulership, and religious doctrines, and in facilitating ascent to positions of dominance in status, rulership, and religious hierarchies. As a part of everyday life and capable, often through ceremonies involving magic, of being transmitted to family members, offices or institutions, "hereditary," "institutionalized," and "office" charisma serve to legitimize "acquired rights." Impersonal and altered into these "routinized forms," charisma is upheld in all these stages, in this model, by persons with an economic interest in doing so, as well by all those in possession of power and property who see their position of advantage as legitimated by its rulership,[54] for example, court officials, priests, parliamentary monarchs, high dignitaries, and party leaders (*E&S*, pp. 1122–3/662, 1126–7/665, 1146–7/679–80; "I," p. 297/270; see Bendix, 1962, pp. 308–18).

Thus, a broad array of patterned social actions oriented to interests[55] sets into motion and pushes this routinization of charisma model,[56] as is typical for the developmental construct that charts the closure of social relation-

---

nent economic structures, see e.g. *E&S*, p. 345/205; on the process from patrimonial to bureaucratic forms of rulership, see *E&S*, pp. 1014–15/586, 1020/590, 1029–31/597–8; and on the rise of priests, churches, and hierocratic authority, see "IR," pp. 327–8/541, *E&S*, pp. 248–9/144, 1166/693–4; *RofI*, pp. 319–20/351–3. Of course, all these permanent structures may appear empirically not only as a consequence of the routinization of charisma and of economic interests, as this model postulates.

54   Indeed, because it implies at this stage a readiness to defend social honor and economic interests vigorously, routinized charisma serves, ironically, as a strong bulwark against genuine charisma. This remains the case regardless of whether it eventually appears in the form of a status ethic or religious doctrine, or as hereditary or office charisma (see e.g. "I," p. 297/269).

55   Of course, again, *empirically* the routinization of charisma, for Weber, may be driven not only by such interests. As a rule, Weber emphasizes, a vast variety of causal forces intertwine. In this developmental model, however, interests constitute the central driving force. A touch of Weber's "sober realism" fully neglected by the American reception until recently (with the exception of Roth and Bendix) is apparent here, as well as in the above model.

56   It should be obvious by now that the revolutionary force of charisma cannot be understood as standing exclusively at the beginning of history and as characterized by an inevitable and slow decline, as Parsons (see 1963), in equating charisma and its routinization to the law of entropy, argues. Rather, Weber's substantive texts depict charismatic rulership as depen-

ships. Each causal model hypothesizes a *course* of patterned action and, thereby, various stages through which regular action passes. These limited analytic generalizations as well, just as the dynamic, contextual, affinity, and antagonism constructs, illustrate Weber's model building procedures and the manner in which his comparative-historical texts emphasizes the framing theoretically of empirical developments. Once again, the capacity of *E&S* to do so distinguishes Weber's substantive sociology clearly on the one hand from the problem focus and tendency to lapse into historical narrative typical of both the interpretive historical and causal analytic approaches, and on the other hand from the theoretical formulations of the world systems approach. Rationalization processes also prominently anchor developmental models in Weber's comparative-historical sociology.[57]

Developmental models anchored in rationalization processes: formal and theoretical rationalization models

Two developmental models rooted in rationalization processes are pivotal in *E&S*: formal rationalization processes based upon means–end rational action, and theoretical rationalization processes based upon a "cognitive need" of intellectuals. In each case, as for the processual constructs anchored in interests, no empirical development is depicted. Rather, and although formulated from empirical observations, the path of patterned action demarcated by these models constitutes an analytic development alone. At each stage, a theoretical framework is provided that assists conceptualization of empirical developments and constructs hypotheses regarding courses of action-orientations.[58] By indicating further the central-

---

dent upon delimited historical contexts and interactions with, mainly, status groups, classes, and various organizations. This remains the case even though Weber does see a general empirical advance in the West away from the situation in early history in which charismatic and traditional forms of rulership "shared the most important types of rulership relations between them" ("I," p. 297/270; transl. alt.; see *E&S*, pp. 245/142, 1131/668) to a situation in which permanent institutional structures became increasingly central (see *E&S*, pp. 1133/670, 1156/606–7; "EK," p. 470). Despite this overall drift, as demarcated social contexts shift, charismatic personalities reappear, their pronouncements repeatedly ring out, and they are heard.

57   A further type of developmental model, one located in the domain of religion and anchored in "psychological processes" – varying "religious qualifications": "virtuoso" and "mass" – is also prominent in *E&S* (see pp. 422–7/257–61, 437–9/267–8, 466–7/284–5, 487–8/296–7) as well as in *EEWR* (see "I," pp. 270/240, 287/259; *RofI*, pp. 176–82/183–91, 236–7/255). For reasons of space it must be omitted here.

58   I have identified two other types of rationality: practical and substantive (see 1980). Practical rationality does not anchor rationalization processes that can be articulated as analytic developments; it implies a boundedness of (means–end rational) action to the flow of daily realities. While substantive rationalities, which are anchored in configurations of values (see Kalberg, 1980, pp. 1155–7; Levine, 1985), quite clearly place strong thrusts into motion, Weber fails to see a *course* that charts development from one set of values to another. Values

ity of hypothesis-formation, delimited model building, and theoretical frameworks in Weber's substantive sociology, these developmental models once again testify to its divergence from all contemporary schools.[59]

Formal rationalization developmental models: the free market and the state
Weber's models of formal rationalization processes imply a predominance of means–end rational action and its orientation to formalized and universally applied rules, laws, and regulations. Decision-making takes place outside a substantively rational framework of values and without regard to the personal qualities of individuals.[60] Formal rationalization processes root and set into motion two developmental models in *E&S*.[61] They chart, as analytic constructs, the unfolding of action-orientations to (*a*) the free market and (*b*) the state. At each stage of its development, each model demarcates delimited causal hypotheses regarding a course of patterned action.

Weber's developmental model of the *free market* charts a path of action in which, at each stage, the formal rationality of the market repeatedly expands against substantive rational restrictions. How does this analytic process occur?

In Weber's ideal type "market economy," economic activity assumes a formally rational character. The orientation of action to associative (*vergesellschaftete*) social relationships, in which a transfer of goods and decision-making take place in accord with the rules of commercial accounting and efficient management, is typical. In essence, means–end rational action in a relatively pure form triumphs in the marketplace over the other types of social action, all of which keep calculation at a low level.[62] To the same degree that all technically possible calculations within the "laws of the

---

remain, for him, far too heterogenous to be plotted, even analytically, along stages of development. However, once a cohesive *constellation* of values has crystallized, then, in reference to these values, a theoretical rationalization process can be charted as an analytic development. See Kalberg, 1979, 1990, and below, pp. 138–40.

59   As will become clear in this section, Weber charts rationalization processes in reference to societal domains rather than as societal-overarching and parallel developing processes (see e.g. *PE*, pp. 74–8/60–2; Kalberg, 1980, 1983; forthcoming c). The secondary literature generally views the rationalization theme in far too global a manner (see Kalberg, 1989). It as well fails to recognize adequately the analytic character of Weber's treatment of this theme.

60   For a more detailed definition of formal rationality, see Kalberg, 1980, pp. 1158–9.

61   These are the two major such models. Weber nowhere discusses them in a succinct manner. In reconstructing both models I have utilized several texts to complement *E&S*. A developmental causal model anchored in formal rationalization processes in bureaucratic rulership could be also reconstructed. An abbreviated model for this process appears near the end of the examination below of formal rationalization processes in the modern state.

62   The exception here is the modern economic ethic of Calvinism. Action in reference to values constitutes the overwhelming motivation in this ideal type. Moreover, these values in Weber's terms are "market-rational," or oriented to the maximization of economic efficiency in the market (see Kalberg, 1983, pp. 274–5, 278–81).

market" are universally carried out and the "struggle of interests" determines the formation of market value rather than personal considerations or substantive rationalities, formal rationality unfolds in reference to sheer market forces (*E&S*, pp. 85/44–5, 636/383): "The growing impersonality of the economy on the basis of association in the marketplace follows its own impersonal lawfulness, disobedience to which entails economic failure and, in the long run, economic ruin" (*E&S*, p. 585/353; transl. alt.).[63]

Many action-orientations have constricted, diverted, or upset the calculation of profit in an exchange and, in the process, introduced "irrational" economic effects that have constrained the market's developmental path toward greater and greater formal rationality. Diverse constellations of "market-irrational" substantive rationalities anchored in the religion (*E&S*, pp. 544/331, 1188–9/710–11)[64] and rulership spheres of life, universal organizations (*E&S*, pp. 636–7/383),[65] and status groups (*E&S*, p. 937/538; "I," pp. 301/274–5)[66] have stood in relationships of strict antagonism to the market's formal rationality and restrained the calculation of profit in exchanges. Action oriented to laws as well might restrict market freedom, particularly market-oriented action of a specific status group. They might also decree rationing in cases of war, famine or other emergencies (*E&S*, pp. 83–4/44, 351/209). Guild regulations allowed sales on the market only

---

63 On the *Sachgesetzlichkeiten* (impersonal lawfulness) of the market, see also *E&S*, pp. 346/205, 600/361, 731/440, 1186–7/709; *R&K*, pp. 193/133, 202/140; *PE*, pp. 54–5/37, 72–3/56; "IR," p. 331/544; *GEH*, pp. 357–8/305.

64 Various religious organizations did so through taboos and magic; churches and sects often did so through ethical values. Weber's most detailed *empirical* analysis of the manner in which salvation religions placed communal relations above the market's impersonal associative relationships relates the history of the Catholic Church's struggle against the expansion of free market capitalism (see *E&S*, pp. 1186–91/708–13, 583–8/352–5; "IR," pp. 331–2/545). The Catholic hierarchy has consistently stood behind the conservative forces of personal patriarchal rulership as well as the traditionalist interests of peasant and petty-bourgeois strata as a consequence, basically, of its incapacity to "bridge the gap between its highest ethical ideals and a rational, methodical orientation toward the capitalist enterprise which treats profit as the ultimate goal of a vocation and – this is the main point – regards it as a measure of personal virtue" (*E&S*, pp. 1190–1/712). The two major moral demands of Catholicism, the prohibition against usury and the commandment to demand and give the "just price," manifest precisely this resistance of ethical religions of brotherhood to the market's formal rational calculation. The rejection of usury, in particular, is, to Weber, evidence of the distinct antagonism of salvation religions to the domain of commercial enterprises and rational profit-making (*E&S*, pp. 582–3/352; *GEH*, pp. 357–8/305; Nelson, 1949).

65 Kinship organizations often did so through the inheritance of property. The resistance of the Chinese household to the market's autonomy provides one of Weber's major empirical examples (see *E&S*, pp. 377/227–8). The market's formal rationality may be also restricted when the management of a business remains in the hands of the members of its founding family rather than in those of individuals technically best qualified from the standpoint of the concern's profitability (*E&S*, p. 138/79).

66 Stratification by status permeated, for example, the communities of Antiquity and the Middle Ages to such an extent that "one can never speak of a genuinely free market competition as we understand it today" (*E&S*, p. 937/538; see also p. 84/44). Such stratification often prohibited specific categories of persons from engaging in trade, such as nobles and peasants, as well as, at times, even artisans.

after goods had been offered to fellow guild members. The developmental path toward greater formal rationality hypothesized by the free market model may be also restricted when free labor is organized in accord with administrative, legal, or taxation expediencies rather than in terms of a calculation of its efficiency in the marketplace (*E&S*, p. 240/139). Such "economically-irrational" regulations have oriented action away from the market situation, thereby restricting and even directly opposing the opportunities of participants in the marketplace for either profit or the sheer provision of needs. Formal rationality in the market is reduced to the same extent that non-market-oriented action significantly influences economically-oriented action.

Weber's developmental model postulates that the formal rationality of the marketplace penetrates into and weakens all these "market-irrational" forces, especially magic and religion, traditional and charismatic forms of rulership, universal organizations, and status groups.[67] Formal rationalization processes, in this construct, carry the "non-ethical" exchange relationship into organizations and groups previously dominated by ethics of brotherliness, in the process lifting the barrier between internal and external ethics and establishing commercial accountability within these groups (see *GEH*, pp. 312–13/269, 356/303–4). This analytic path is characterized by a breaking down and alteration of the economically-irrational substantive rationalities that presented obstacles to free exchange, and their displacement by the "substantive conditions" that allow market freedom and formal rationality to expand and attain its maximum influence (see Kalberg, 1983, pp. 274–81).[68]

With the unrestricted diffusion of regular action oriented to the free market under modern capitalism, the most important substantive condition for the triumph of formal rationality over all economically-irrational substantive rationalities appears.[69] Moreover, because permeated by the impersonal "spirit of calculation" rather than the ethic of brotherhood, the

67   Of course, *empirically*, a variety of additional causal action-orientations must congeal. Again, the developmental model reconstructed here is thrust forth only by formal rationalization processes.

68   The modern bourgeoisie, which stood radically in opposition to all market-irrational substantive rationalities and possessed clear interests in the expansion of formal rationality as well as the unhindered production and marketability of goods, proved indispensable as an empirical carrier in this process. Its rise, however, was greatly facilitated by the completion of the *transition* from the "traditional" to the "rational" economic ethic (see *PE*, pp. 47–63/30–48, 98–128/87–128). The social carriers of the rational economic ethic – the ascetic Protestant churches and sects – were, according to Weber, motivated not by means–end rational action, which was too weak to shatter the traditional economic ethic, but by religious *values* (see chapter 2, pp. 63–4).

69   The substantive conditions that maximize formally rational capital accounting include the presence of a "complete calculability of the technical conditions of the production process; that is, a mechanically rational technology" (*E&S*, pp. 161–2/94; see also pp. 107–8/58–9, 82/43; *GEH*, pp. 276–8/239–40). This type of capitalism implies free labor and its rational organization as well as a systematic aspect to profit-making and capital accounting (see *E&S*, pp. 127–9/70–2; Kalberg, 1983, pp. 271–7).

market now follows its "own laws." Those types of economically-oriented social action generally capable only of low levels of calculation – traditional, value-rational, and affectual action – become subordinate, Weber's model hypothesizes, to means–end rational action. Market freedom, as well as haggling and dickering, now expand unhindered. Unrestrained by personal relations and immune to all ethical claims, the formal rationality of rational capitalism now functions, this model postulates, solely in relation to the laws of the market. Severed from market-irrational restrictions, economic activity becomes exclusively a matter of increasingly refined calculations.

According to Weber's processual construct, this development occurs as patterned action oriented to the free market – or, more precisely, the impersonal market "free" of all restrictions and open to all forms of competition – expands. Once in motion, calculation formally rationalizes larger and larger sectors of the capitalist economy. Within the realms of universal exchange and objectified associative relationships, decisions are made in accord with the rules of commercial accounting and efficient management rather than "in regard to persons": "Wherever the market is left to its own autonomous laws, it recognizes only things and never persons, neither in the form of acknowledging duties of brotherhood and loyalty nor of any of the human relationships traditionally carried by the primeval, person-oriented groups" (*E&S*, p. 636/383; transl. alt.). Furthermore, the "laws of the market" in the rationalized economic cosmos of modern capitalism, Weber's developmental model postulates, severely proscribe non-market oriented action, for the penalty for non-compliance with formally rational procedures is a fatal one: bankruptcy and extinction (*E&S*, p. 1186/709).[70]

Thus, this model postulates a developmental course of regular action, one characterized by distinct stages. A theoretical framework is articulated that assists a conceptual grasp upon empirical patterned action; the case-specific, in-depth investigation of formal rationalization processes in the marketplace is thereby facilitated. Empirically testable hypotheses regarding causal action-orientations are formulated at each stage.

Unlike the market model, which takes developments occurring over perhaps the entire span of written history as its empirical point of departure, the next processual construct – the development of the state – refers to a delineated period as its empirical base: the modern epoch. This model demarcates formal rationalization processes typical for the development of

---

70 Even socialist ideologies, in Weber's view, cannot, in the long run, abolish a predominance in the economic sphere of means–end rational orientations to self-interests. This remains the case despite their command over certain ideal motives (see *E&S*, pp. 110–11/60, 202–4/119–20). For the most part, value-rational motivations for economic activity find their origins, according to Weber, in religious sources or in "the high social esteem in which the particular form of work as such is held" (*E&S*, pp. 151/87, 202/119). Viewed from the vantage point of long-term social change, "all other sources of motivation [for economic activity] directed to values must be viewed as transitional phenomena" (*E&S*, p. 151/87; transl. alt.; see also pp. 69–71/35, 110/60; Kalberg, 1992).

the state. Once again, a theoretical framework is articulated and causal hypotheses are formulated at each stage in respect to courses of patterned action.

The state successfully monopolizes the employment of physical force within a specified area through its control over an elaborate administrative system operated by specialized officials and characterized by abstract rules, regulations, and laws (*E&S*, p. 56/30; "PV," pp. 82–3/510–11). This force can be legitimately employed if in accordance with enacted statutes. As a "compulsory institution" (*Anstalt*), the state claims rulership within a given territory.

All of the universal organizations and traditional forms of rulership were, at times, as the state, "political" organizations, as were certain routinized forms of charismatic rulership, such as clan charisma (see *E&S*, pp. 250/145, 1136/671–2), as well as guilds and religious organizations. Of course, empirically, in some cultures political power remained rooted in the kin group and *ad hoc* in character far longer than in others. Weber cites the example of the Arabs (*E&S*, pp. 909–10/519). He views the modern state as resulting historically from struggles for power between patrimonialism and feudalism and as a unique product of the Occident (see *E&S*, pp. 904–10/516–19, esp. pp. 904–5; "AI," pp. 16/3–4, 25/11; *GEH*, pp. 338–9/289–90). Weber's developmental model traces the analytic route taken by "political action" from the universal organizations to the formal rationality of the modern state (see generally *E&S*, pp. 904–10/516–19).

The state's appropriation of the powers of marauding warriors, feudal lords, and patrimonial monarchs, no less than those of all other autonomous private bearers of financial organization, administrative warfare, and the formation of law, constitute the stages of this processual construct. Similarly, the power of the household, sib group or neighborhood to dispose over the means of violence is also constricted by the state: feuds and blood vengeance become submitted to the arbitration of judges who render decisions and punishment in accordance with enacted procedures. As this occurs, organizations, classes, and status groups acquire influence, power, and the capacity to employ physical force only to the extent permitted by the state. Even private organizations, as well as social, professional, and political clubs, are very often denied the right to regulate fully their own affairs, such as the penalizing of cantankerous members.[71] Policemen act in reference to laws and regulations.[72] The enhancement of the state's coercive apparatus implies, Weber's developmental path postulates, a concomitant

71 In the United States, for example, the courts possessed the power even in Weber's day to regulate political parties and the use of union labels.
72 In this analytic process, a direct road leads from mere modifications of the blood feud, sacerdotally or by means of arbitration, to the present position of the policeman as the "representative of God on earth." The former means still placed the guarantees for the individual's rights and security squarely upon the members of his sib, who were obligated to assist him with oath and vengeance (*E&S*, p. 972/561; see also *E&S*, pp. 318/186, 375/226).

expansion of its "area of jurisdiction" and its "prosecution of an ever widening sphere of injuries to persons and property" (*E&S*, pp. 318/186, 908/518–19). At the foundation of this analytic model stands the growth of formal rationality and formal rationalization processes.

Formal rationality, in the case of the state, implies social action that is continuous rather than *ad hoc* and oriented to impersonal and universal statutes and regulations rather than to traditions or to persons. As in the bureaucratic form of rational–legal rulership, which is as a rule adopted by the state as a result of its formal rationality, the orientation of action to general rules and prescribed jurisdictions of competence prevails over affectual action. Moreover, the exercise of violence is no longer the privileged domain of a specific ruler; rather, it takes place within a "compulsory institution" in which abstract laws are enacted in reference to written documents and applied universally. The exercise of rulership becomes gradually transformed into an institution for the protection of rights (*Rechtsschutzanstalt*).[73]

The predominant orientation of action by the state's civil servants to the fulfillment of abstract laws and regulations, rather than to persons and traditions, provides the fundamental precondition, in Weber's model, that enables this organization to follow a distinct analytic path characterized by increasing formal rationality. In becoming state-oriented, patterned action turns away from the traditional forms of rulership as well as the universal organizations, all of which imply distinct substantive rationalities as well as a strongly personal element. The state elevates the axiom "without regard to persons" to a position of absolute validity, and the *homo politicus*, if integrated fully into the state's mechanisms, and civil servant manage affairs according to the rational rules of the state and in a matter of fact manner (see *GEH*, pp. 338–40/289–90; *E&S*, pp. 54/29, 56/30, 598–601/360–2). These "objective" procedures uphold as well modern notions of justice, which in turn strengthen the state's formal rationality (*E&S*, p. 600/361).

All tasks of the depersonalized and bureaucratic modern state, including the allocation of justice, are "regulated by . . . 'reasons of state'" ("IR," p. 334/547). Just this indigenous problematic constitutes the core of the formal rationality that, according to this developmental model, anchors and sets into motion the unfolding of the constitutional state: "'reasons of state' . . . follow their own internal and external laws" ("IR," p. 334/547). To the same extent that impersonal considerations prevail, ethical restraints against "reasons of state" prove just as ineffective as they do against the

---

73   "[The] modern state is essentially characterized by the following criteria: It is a consociation [*anstaltsmässige Vergesellschaftung*] of bearers of certain defined *imperia*; these bearers are selected according to established rules; their *imperia* are delimited from each other by general rules of separation of powers; and internally each of them finds the legitimacy of its power of command defined by set rules of limitation of power" (*E&S*, pp. 652/393–4; emph. orig.).

sheer calculation of gain typical of market transactions ("IR," p. 334/547; "PV," pp. 118–27/549–59). Wherever logical formal law and bureaucratic rulership arise to support the state and the state "reciprocates" by claiming to be the sole source of "legitimate" law, the "autonomy" of the state's formal rationalization processes, Weber's construct postulates, is strengthened. This occurs simply because trained jurists and a professional and specialized officialdom oriented to statutory regulations and their objective administration intensify the impersonal and universalist character of the state. In the process, it becomes still more formally rational, more calculating, and more estranged from an ethic of brotherhood. According to Weber's developmental model:

> By virtue of its depersonalization, the bureaucratic state . . . is less accessible to ethical demands than were the patriarchal orders of the past. . . . These orders were based upon personal obligations of piety, and the patriarchal rulers considered the merit of the concrete, single case precisely with "regard to the person." In the final analysis . . . the whole course of the state's inner political functions, of justice and administration, is repeatedly and unavoidably regulated by the objective pragmatism of "reasons of state." ("IR," p. 334/547; transl. alt.; see further "IR," p. 335/548)

Weber is quite specific, in this processual construct, regarding the manner in which the bureaucratic form of organization, for example, whenever allied with the modern state, *pushes* the state's formal rationalization. Officials in bureaucracies, according to his ideal type, possess a vested interest in stability, preserving their own position, and maintaining the legitimacy of bureaucratic rulership. However, not simply interests, a bureaucratic "ethic," or the attempt to preserve power characterizes this stratum; rather, it sets into motion as well an indigenous developmental process. Unlike traditional and charismatic forms of rulership, the bureaucracy introduces, with formal rationalization, a driving force. Personal discretion and sentiment fail to govern administration; rather, the subsumption of the particular case under statutes or a weighing of means and ends reigns. In Weber's model, bureaucratic rulership implies this "formalistic impersonality," and technical and "purely objective considerations" prevail; thus, all barriers created by substantive rationalities, individual circumstances, and personally motivated favor are shattered (*E&S*, pp. 979–80/565). In this manner, the bureaucracy acquires a developmental thrust distinctly its own, one rooted not simply in "external" sources such as democratization movements (*E&S*, pp. 979/565, 984–5/568, 990–1/572) and the advance of capitalism (*E&S*, p. 224/129), but in formal rationalization processes carried by the bureaucracy's trained managers and officials. The power interests of this stratum tend merely to accelerate formal rationalization processes (*E&S*, p. 225/129).[74]

---

74 Again, for Weber, whether this formal rationalization thrust of this model proves stronger than opposing economic, political, ethical, and other action-orientations remains an *empirical* question. Also, it should be emphasized that Weber does not look for the *origins* of the

According to Weber's developmental construct, such processes acquire an "autonomy," just as those in the free market, simply as a consequence of their predominantly impersonal character. No orientation of regular action to persons, values, or traditions prevails, but to general rules and statutes; a rule-bound and "cool matter-of-factness" prevails. Decision-making "without hatred or passion" and in terms of the most adequate means for continued adherence to these rules and statutes reigns.

These two developmental models anchored in formal rationalization processes have charted the analytic unfolding of patterned action-orientations to the free market and the state. Although formulated from empirical studies, each ideal-typical developmental construct must be understood as providing a *theoretical framework* that assists the clear conceptualization of diffuse empirical developments as well as the identification of relevant causal action-orientations and their empirical investigation. Thus, these developmental models again testify to the centrality of model building and hypothesis-formation procedures in Weber's comparative-historical sociology. They separate his substantive sociology clearly from the problem focus of both the causal analytic and interpretive historical schools. They stand as well in contrast to the pre-formulated theory of the world systems approach.

Further developmental models anchored by rationalization processes are also prominent in *E&S*. The analytic paths they chart, however, are driven by different causal forces. They derive from a "cognitive need" of intellectuals.

Theoretical rationalization developmental models: religion To Weber: "the rationality, in the sense of the logical or theoretical 'consistency' of an intellectual–theoretical . . . attitude has and always has had power over man, however limited and unstable this power is and always has been in the face of other forces of historical life" ("IR," p. 324/537). According to him, the "intellect's . . . autonomy" ("IR," p. 353/566) anchors and sets into motion a developmental course of action prominently in the domain of religion.[75] Hypotheses regarding paths of patterned action are formulated throughout this theoretical rationalization developmental model.

An "intrinsic intellectual need" for symmetry and internal coherence became manifest among the social carriers of both "primitive" and salvation religions.[76] However much the greater tendency of religious thinkers to

---

bureaucracy in a process specific to the rulership societal domain; rather, he sees these origins as quite diverse (see e.g. *E&S*, pp. 224–5/129, 971–5/560–3) and makes no note, in this regard, of any autonomy process.

75 Theoretical rationalization processes also anchor the development of law (see e.g. *E&S*, pp. 656–7/396, 853–5/491–3) and Western science. Space prohibits a reconstruction of the former model and Weber's texts are simply too incomplete to yield a developmental model in regard to science. See note 83 below and Tenbruck, 1974; Kalberg, 1980, p. 1153.

76 The reconstruction of this model relies also upon Weber's major analytic writings, in addition to chapter 6 in *E&S*, on religion: the "I" and "IR" essays.

concern themselves with the reasons for enduring misery may have been intensified by natural disaster, material need, or inner psychological stress, it did not, according to Weber's processual construct, originate from these factors. The "social situation of the disprivileged and the rationalism of the bourgeoisie" (*E&S*, p. 499/304) also do not alone account for its origin (see "I," p. 277/248; *E&S*, pp. 492–8/300–3). Rather, it originated from the ideal-typical inner compulsion *of intellectuals* to transcend sheer given routine and to supply the random events of everyday life with significance and a pervasive "meaning." It expressed, to Weber, a "metaphysical need" or "irrepressible quest" of the "human mind as it is driven to reflect on ethical and religious questions." A "natural rationalistic need of intellectualism" cognitively to conceive the world as a totality and as a problem of meaning characterized these religious thinkers (*E&S*, p. 499/304).[77] To Weber, the domain of religion stood generally in an "intimate relationship" with "rational intellectualism."

> Religious interpretations of the world and ethics of religions created by intellectuals and meant to be rational have been strongly exposed to the imperative of consistency. The effect of the *ratio*, especially of a teleological deduction of practical postulates, is in some way, and often very strongly, noticeable among all religious ethics. This holds however little the religious interpretations of the world in the individual case have complied with the demand for consistency. ("IR," p. 324/537)

On the basis of his empirical observations, Weber formulates developmental models anchored in theoretical rationalization processes even with respect to the earliest stages of religious history. The cognitive needs of religious thinkers are apparent even in these models. The rationalization of perceptions of metaphysical entities in "primitive" religions by sorcerers and priests continually led to the repudiation of a certain explanation for suffering and the birth of another, rather than an escape from evil, as hoped. The introduction of magic, for example, which was originally perceived as a means to manipulate spirits and thus as a means for the amelioration of misery, led to the recognition, as suffering persisted, that these supersensual entities were not powerful enough to protect early man from evil. This acknowledgment not only weakened the orientation of action to ceremonies dedicated to the performance of magic, but also induced religious thinkers to conclude that they had misunderstood the nature of the epiphenomenal realm (*E&S*, pp. 407–20/250–7). Deities much stronger than spirits and radically separate from terrestrial inhabitants were now believed, according to Weber's processual construct, to populate the supernatural sphere. Accordingly, theocentric dualism made its appearance.[78]

77 See further on the "ideal interests" of intellectuals in respect to religion, *E&S*, pp. 500–18/ 304–14; "I," pp. 280/251–2.
78 Unfortunately, Weber never offers a detailed analysis of the role of rational speculations in the development from monism to theocentric dualism. However, in the passages where this

When these mighty gods appeared as functionally specialized entities able to protect all against evils, yet in turn failed to do so, priests and sorcerers confronted this quandary. Their abstract thinking led to the conclusion that these gods were egoistic beings and that their anger could be calmed only by entreaties and supplications (*E&S*, pp. 432/264, 424/258). Action-orientations of the devout were altered accordingly in the direction of ritual and a variety of worship forms.

Theoretical rationalization processes oriented to religious questions also proved to be pivotal, according to Weber's developmental model, for the rise of ethical gods. The view of the metaphysical arena as inhabited by deities much stronger than spirits brought about another unforeseen consequence: instead of protecting tribal man against misery, these mighty gods with an enduring character seemed, by permitting lasting distress, to reject the best efforts of priests and the laity to appease their egoistic wishes through supplications. If gods were now powerful enough to prevent all evil, yet failed to do so, it was reasoned that the perpetuation of suffering must be attributed to the divinities themselves. Their character had been misunderstood, and deities as well as spirits became feared. When the ritualistic techniques of worship practiced by priesthoods became recognized as unable to offer an escape from suffering, religious thinkers again, through theoretical rationalization processes, formulated a new view of the supernatural realm: the persistence of misery soon became understood, according to Weber's construct, as no longer evidence of a particular spirit's or god's weakness or of a failure to gratify a deity's egoistic wishes through prayer and worship; rather, it testified to a violation of divinely appointed norms under the guardianship of an ethical god and his consequent "ethical displeasure" (*E&S*, pp. 437/267, 1179/703–4).[79] Likewise, in his analysis of the rise of universal gods, Weber calls attention to the theoretical rationalization processes carried out by priests and prophets. In general, for him, "reason favored the primacy of universal gods" (*E&S*, pp. 417–18/256–7).

In Weber's developmental model, the history of the search, through theoretical rationalization processes, for an end to suffering and a satisfactory relationship to the supernatural realm records such reversals and ironies repeatedly. The attainment of every "answer" to unexplained "internal and external" evils gave birth to unforeseen consequences which, in turn,

---

transformation is discussed (*E&S*, pp. 407–20/250–7; "I," pp. 271–3/241–4), theoretical rationalization processes are clear. For example: "Every consistent crystallization of a pantheon followed systematic rational principles to some degree, since it was always influenced by the professional rationalism of priests or by the rational striving for order on the part of secular individuals" (*E&S*, p. 417/256; transl. alt.). He details more thoroughly *organizational* changes (see *E&S*, pp. 407–17/250–6).

79   The diverse developments in the social fabric that also gave rise to the understanding of gods as ethical beings, and which occurred concomitantly with these theoretical rationalization processes and purely religious considerations, cannot, of course, be included in this model (see *E&S*, pp. 430/263, 1179–80/703–4).

called forth further cognitive formulations of the reasons for continued evil. The high expectations that congealed with each new explanation were inevitably disappointed, yet the perpetual alteration of the perspective within which the religious thinker attempted cognitively to unravel the mystery of hardship itself always yielded a further "answer." Weber's developmental construct, which formulates hypotheses regarding patterned action-orientations at each stage, captures this dynamic process.

It results directly from his anthropological assumptions: as rationally acting beings, persons seek relief from internal and external distress. They do so in "primitive" religions by demanding explanations for their hardship from religious thinkers. These virtuosi repeatedly recast the prevalent conception of the metaphysical sphere as well as the action-orientations appropriate for interaction with it. Yet, since misery continues and every explanation is destined to be unsatisfactory, a new "answer" invariably arises to explain the problem of suffering – and, as well, new appropriate action. Such religion-oriented theoretical rationalization processes recur until a rationally consistent explanation for the perennial appearance of evil and injustice appears.

Theoretical rationalization processes became even more apparent at the stage of ethical salvation religions. In offering an "ultimate stand" toward the world based upon a "direct grasp of the world's 'meaning'" ("IR," p. 352/566), these religions result, according to this model, from the intellectual's typical endeavor to systematize and rationalize life's realities on behalf of a liberation from random misery and distress ("IR," pp. 327/540–1, 341/555, 353–4/567; "I," pp. 280–1/252–3).[80] With the appearance of ethical salvation religions, priests, monks, and theologians rationalize the values implicit in the world view of prophets into internally consistent world views and doctrines, all of which offer comprehensive explanations for a problem that repeatedly provides the driving force behind these theoretical rationalization processes: the problem of theodicy. These unified views of the cosmos, and man's place within it, purport to offer exhaustive explanations for suffering and injustice. Religious thinkers accordingly, in the hope of deducing discrete patterns of action that will alleviate misery and insure a state of grace for believers, reorder and systematize the world view's religious values ("I," pp. 280–1/252–3; *E&S*, pp. 578–9/349–50).

Yet, and regardless how finely tuned, unmerited suffering remains. The stubborn persistence of misery and chaos now, however, given the juxtapo-

---

80   Weber stresses again, just as in respect to the rationalization processes that preceded it, that this development cannot be viewed as one that occurred in response to economic changes: "The 'internalization' and rationalization of religiosity – that is, the acquisition by religion of ethical standards and commandments and the transformation of gods to ethical powers – usually develops parallel to a certain degree of handicraft production, most of the time to that of the urban trades. . . . [However], this is not to say that some kind of clear dependency characterizes this development: the rationalization of religion has its own internal dynamic that economic conditions effect only as 'developmental paths' [*Entwicklungswege*]; above all, it is linked to the emergence of a specifically priestly education" (*E&S*, pp. 1179/703–4; transl. alt.; see also e.g. p. 577/349).

sition of a "divine" and unified world view with the "metaphysical need" of religion-oriented intellectuals for ethical salvation, assumes a qualitatively different significance: the "inner quest of intellectualism" for salvation, Weber's developmental model postulates, not only rationalizes the incoherent teachings of the prophet, but also actively attempts further to unify and rationalize the relationship between the devout and God. However divergent the particular intellectualism of priests, monks, and theologians has been in its influence upon specific salvation religions, a delineated status group, in response to the implacable endurance of suffering and misfortune, now repeatedly and independently rationalizes believers' relations to transcendent beings and defines specific actions as capable of insuring salvation. This task constitutes to Weber the "core" of the rational thrust of religious thinking ("I," p. 281/253; *E&S*, pp. 501–3/305–6; "IR," p. 324/537). It takes place, in this model of religious rationalization, specifically in reference to religious values: "Certainly not always and surely even less exclusively, the ultimate values toward which this rationalization has been oriented were nonetheless, to the extent that an *ethical* rationalization was placed into motion and to the extent of its influence, as a rule *also* and frequently fully decisively *religiously* determined" ("I," p. 287/259; transl. alt.; emph. orig.; see also p. 240/270; *RofC*, p. 249/536).

Intellectualism's persistent search, through theoretical rationalization processes,[81] for a rational solution to the problem of suffering carries and drives Weber's "religious rationalism" model. This "rational element . . . namely, the structure of [the] special theodicy" ("IR," p. 358/572), the developmental construct hypothesizes, next leads to a devaluation of worldly endeavors and then to the formulation of other-worldly salvation religions. The teachings and doctrines of these religions call for a rejection of terrestrial life and an orientation of action to inward sacred values. Such action stands in the most consistent opposition to magic and ritual, both of which possess a fragmented and stereotypical character (see *E&S*, pp. 578–9/349–50; "IR," p. 357/571). Radically different orientations of action become appropriate. "Methodologies of sanctification" – asceticism or mysticism – may arise as salvation paths, and these paths place "psychological premiums" upon "methodical rational ways of life" (see Kalberg, 1980, 1990).[82] Precisely in this manner, Weber's model postulates, "the effect of the *ratio* . . . in the sense of logical or teleological 'consistency' has, in

81 Weber does not doubt that occasionally the analytic path charted by this developmental model has had, *empirically*, "extremely strong effects . . . molding important traits of such religions as Hinduism, Zoroastrism, and Judaism and, to a certain extent, Paulinian and later Christianity" ("I," p. 275/247). On ancient Judaism, see *AJ*, pp. 225/239–40. Regarding later Christianity, Weber is quite explicit; see *PE*, pp. 111–12/105–6.

82 Tenbruck's (1980) discussion of the autonomy of religious rationalization fails to construct this process as a developmental *model*. Rather, he argues that Weber views it as an empirical process, one that *itself carries* the entire Western rationalization process. He fails to note even that, for Weber, empirically, in addition to conducive economic and political configurations, a coherent stratum of intellectuals is necessary. For critical commentaries, see Kalberg, 1979; Winckelmann, 1980; Riesebrodt, 1980; Schluchter, 1989, pp. 411–32.

the realm of religion, influenced and transformed action" ("IR," p. 324/537).[83]

In sum, these formal and theoretical rationalization models have charted stages and postulated courses of patterned action in respect to the development of the market and the state on the one hand and religion on the other. All have offered theoretical frameworks that assist conceptualization. Driving forces are indigenous to these constructs. Of course, as is the case for all of Weber's models and as he continuously emphasizes, *empirical* forces repeatedly "intervene" to upset the hypothesized developmental paths.

These developmental models, as those discussed above anchored in interests, (*a*) facilitate the ordering and clear conceptualization of the particular development under investigation and its significant causal action-orientations; and (*b*) postulate delineated, empirically-testable developmental courses of patterned action. In doing so, they, as the dynamic, contextual, affinity, and antagonism models, inject a strongly theoretical dimension into the very core of Weber's comparative-historical sociology. This dimension places it in direct opposition to the problem focus and tendency to lapse into historical narrative of both the interpretive historical and causal analytic approaches. Weber's constructs instead chart analytic processes. Moreover, rather than claiming to unveil empirical developments, as do all contemporary schools, his models serve heuristic purposes only. Whether regular action oriented toward formal and theoretical rationalization processes in fact "captures" the histories of particular social groupings – and if so, to what extent – remains a subject for a case-by-case, in-depth historical, and broadly multicausal investigation. For this reason, Weber's interest in rationalization processes by no means implies an evolutionary understanding of history.

The four types of models from Weber's analytic treatise, *E&S*, discussed in this chapter – the dynamic, contextual, affinity, antagonism, and developmental models – stand at the very center of his comparative-historical sociology and render a pivotal contribution to its rigor, analytic power, and uniqueness. Scarcely examined in a systematic fashion by the secondary literature in terms of their capacity to inject theoretical frameworks into the comparative-historical enterprise, they again reveal Weber's sociology as quite distinct from the causal analytic, interpretive historical, and world

83 Much of the background material for this theoretical rationalization process can be found in Kalberg (1980, 1990). Theoretical rationalization processes were also undertaken by Western scientists dedicated to the systematization of the scientific world view. Motivated in the seventeenth century by the belief that their empirical research would unveil God's laws and thereby offer more precise instructions for the conduct of the religious life ("SV," pp. 142/597), later scientists continued this "disenchantment process." Weber called attention explicitly to the unforeseen and ironic consequence of this entire theoretical rationalization process: the search for a solution to the problem of suffering and to the discovery of God's laws contributed to secularization and the abolition of God (see e.g. "IR," pp. 350–7/564–71). Unfortunately, Weber's texts do not, as noted, yield a theoretical rationalization model for modern science.

systems schools. None of these approaches offers models designed to assist the conceptual framing of cases, relationships, and developments, as does, throughout its 1500 pages, *E&S*. Moreover, because all constructs remain rooted in empirical realities and postulate decidedly delineated generalizations, they demonstrate as well Weber's clear opposition to the pre-formulated theory of the world systems school. Finally, Weber's model building distinguishes his substantive texts in another manner clearly from all contemporary approaches: it indicates again, as the illustrations in this section have revealed, the universal range of his comparative-historical sociology.

Weber views the various models formulated in *E&S* as heuristic tools. They are *useful* to comparative-historical sociologists as organizing mechanisms. They facilitate, on the one hand, a purchase upon and comprehension of amorphous empirical realities and patterns of action-orientations and, on the other hand, the clear conceptualization and theoretical framing of particular cases, relationships, and developments. They offer "analytic locations" for these cases, relationships, and developments. In doing so, they enable the identification of significant causal action-orientations and provide procedures that assist the research process in general. All models do so by formulating, as this chapter has sought to demonstrate, delimited and empirically-testable hypotheses regarding the interactions of their indigenous component patterns of action (dynamic models), the impact of specific social contexts (contextual models), interactions of regular action across models (affinity and antagonism models), and developmental courses of action (developmental models). In performing these tasks, all models further assist the attainment of the overall goal of Weber's comparative-historical sociology: the causal explanation of cases and developments. An in-depth investigation of salient causal action-orientations, undertaken by specialists, can then proceed.

Emphatically, as this chapter has sought to demonstrate, the task of comparative-historical sociology, according to Weber, cannot be fulfilled without a precise and forceful theoretical framing of the problem at hand. Indeed, the prominence of model building in Weber's sociology indicates an explicit attempt on his part to draw comparative-historical sociology *away* from attempts to establish causality alone through narrative procedures and a problem focus. Instead, by constructing a comparative-historical sociology that takes models and model building as not only indispensable but also central, he injects a theoretical dimension into the core of the comparative-historical enterprise.[84] An understanding of ideal types exclusively as "yardsticks" neglects this accomplishment.

84   This is, of course, the real message of this detailed chapter on Weber's hypothesis-forming causal models. Rather than seeking to persuade contemporary comparative-historical sociologists of the utility for their own research of the *particular* models discussed above, or others from *E&S*, this chapter has sought above all, through illustrations of Weber's model building procedures, to demonstrate the indispensability to comparative-historical sociology of the precise theoretical framing of problems through models.

However pivotal in Weber's substantive texts, model building should not be viewed as the final stage in his causal sociology. Rather, his "mode of causal analysis," which is radically multicausal as well as contextual and conjunctural, constitutes its high point. It must be thoroughly reconstructed.

5

The Mode of Causal Analysis Reconstructed: Causal Methodology and Theoretical Framework

Weber's overall aim to offer causal explanations of specific cases and developments is far from fulfilled by an examination of his ideal types, model building, and multicausality. His substantive texts move beyond these themes. The practiced modes – his strategies and procedures – by which he actually ascertains causality constitute, in many ways, the culmination of his entire comparative-historical sociology. They remain, however, among its most obscure and least well-defined aspects.

Take *The Protestant Ethic and the Spirit of Capitalism*, for example. While providing a superb illustration of the methodology of *Verstehen*, the intentional "one-sided" emphasis upon "ideal" configurations disqualifies this study as an example of the mode of causal analysis Weber practices in his substantive texts (see *PE*, pp. 183/205–6).[1] Nor are his actual procedures clarified in his methodological essays or the "Basic Sociological Terms" chapter in *E&S*. At times Weber even contradicts himself and allocates the task of causal analysis not to sociologists but to historians (*E&S*, pp. 19/9, 29/15). On other occasions he limits the task of sociology to the formation of "type concepts and generalized uniformities of empirical process" and the "search for empirical regularities and types" (see *E&S*, pp. 19/9, 331–2/ 195).[2] At still other times he discusses causality solely in respect to the

1 Many commentators on the issue of causality have focussed their efforts alone upon a close scrutiny of the causal logic implied in "the Protestant ethic thesis" (see Eisenstadt, 1968a; Green, 1973).
2 Such very modest statements regarding the task of sociology can be understood in part as a consequence of Weber's delimited aims in *E&S*, in part as a result of his desire to avoid contributing to a polarization of history and sociology (see e.g. *E&S*, p. 13/6), and in part as his overly cautious answer to the many skeptics of sociology in his time, all of whom faulted this discipline as lacking a firm theoretical foundation. His substantive texts, however, simply do not fit this narrow definition of sociology. To understand Weber as viewing sociology as nothing more than a discipline auxiliary to history, which alone carries out causal analyses (see Burger, 1976, p. 138; Roth, 1968, p. xxxi; 1976, p. 307), overly constricts, as this chapter will demonstrate, his comparative-historical sociology. Roth has moderated his position in later writings; see 1979, pp. 121, 205; 1981, p. xxiii.

manner in which subjective meaning, as captured by ideal types, orients action and, thereby, causally explains it (for example, *E&S*, p. 4/1; "EK," p. 437; see chapter 1, pp. 48–9).

Despite the orientation of his substantive texts to the issue of causality, Weber failed to discuss his practiced mode of causal analysis in any systematic fashion. The reader searches in vain for a clear articulation of the procedures and strategies that guide Weber's attempts to draw inferences systematically. Indeed, he fails to apply them himself in a sustained and consistent manner. However, a rigorous approach does exist in his comparative-historical writings.[3] A reconstruction of this mode of causal analysis is undertaken in this chapter.[4] Its focus will be upon his practiced causal methodology on the one hand and the theoretical framework provided by *E&S* – its societal domains and domain-specific ideal types – on the other hand. This chapter concludes with an illustration of this mode of causal analysis: a reconstruction of Weber on the rise to dominance of the caste system in India.

The Mode of Causal Analysis: an Overview and Comparison to Recent Schools

Weber's rejection of single factors as alone capable of the sustained influence necessary to call forth new cases and developments, his resolute antagonism to all "needs for a world formula" (*Weltformelbedürfnis*) that would embrace all macrocausal analysis, and his historicist scorn for all evolutionary formulations of necessary causality that discover a "lawful" sweep in historical developments fail to lead him to an understanding of social life as fundamentally chaotic. Despite his repeated stress as well upon the significance of conflict and sheer power, and his insistence that historical accident can upset even deeply entrenched tendencies, he opposes all nihilist conclusions. While cognizant of the infinite complexity of history's pulsating motion, Weber keeps his sights focussed upon an empirically-based level of analysis and charts the fine line that juxtaposes the unexpected event with patterned social action.

3   Attempts to extract his mode of causal analysis from his substantive writings and to render it in concise form have only rarely been undertaken in the secondary literature (see Eisenstadt, 1968a; Roth, 1968, 1971c, 1976; Smelser, 1976; Warner, 1972; Fulbrook, 1978; and Collins, 1981). Although they advance beyond those studies that understand Weber's texts primarily by reference to the charisma/tradition and charisma/bureaucratization–rationalization dichotomies (see e.g. Salomon, 1945, pp. 597–600; Mommsen, 1974a, 1987, pp. 47–51, and 1989), these investigations remain incomplete in various ways. A commentary upon this literature is provided in notes 38 and 42.
4   I have referred generally to my interpretation thus far as involving a "systematization" (with the exception of the developmental models section in the last chapter). However, because the major procedures and strategies of Weber's mode of causal analysis are buried deeply in his substantive texts, a qualitatively greater degree of interpretation is now required. Thus, this chapter will be referred to as a "reconstruction."

His stated goal for sociology – to offer causal explanations of unique cases and developments – combined with his opposition to laws might appear to bring Weber's mode of causal analysis dangerously close to the problem focus of both the interpretive historical and causal analytic schools. Indeed, as opposed to the discussion of his hypothesis-forming models in the last chapter, which took *E&S* as its focus, any reconstruction of his mode of causal analysis must be based also upon the other substantive texts, particularly *EEWR*. *GEH*, *AG*, and *EEWR* are far more "historical" and descriptive than Weber's analytic treatise. Nonetheless, his mode of causal analysis avoids the problem focus of these approaches. He undertakes causal analyses on a regular basis, even in *E&S*, throughout his substantive texts, albeit in most cases in a quite incomplete, even fragmentary manner.

The procedures and strategies of Weber's practiced mode of causal analysis can be articulated most clearly if examined first in an overview fashion. Its two major components will remain central: its causal methodology and theoretical framework. Once reconstructed, a mode of causal analysis quite distinct from the world systems, interpretive historical, and causal analytic schools will be apparent.

The causal methodology

The prominence of *Verstehen* in Weber's comparative-historical sociology should not lead to the conclusion that it alone constitutes his causal methodology. As noted (see chapters 3 and 4), all investigations of subjective meaning must be supplemented by causal procedures and strategies that capture empirically observed action-orientations: "In every case and as much as possible, the 'understanding' of a relationship must, before a seemingly evident meaningful interpretation can be viewed as a valid 'interpretive explanation,' be checked using the normal methods of causal assessment" ("EK," p. 428).[5]

However, and despite this call for rigorous experimental and comparative procedures, Weber refuses to embrace "strong causality": "It is not . . . possible to prove a strictly inevitable causal relationship in [historical] cases, any more than it is possible in any other case of strictly individual events" (*E&S*, p. 200/118; see also, for example, pp. 10/4–5 and "Logic," p. 169/271). This position conveys Weber's skepticism regarding determinism as well as his selection of a middle road in opposition to the dichotomy prominent in his time: chance or necessity. The opposite of "chance," for him, is not "necessity," but "adequacy." He contrasts "adequate causation" to "chance causation" and defines the former as "understandable in light of

5   Along these same lines: "By no means is the actual likelihood of the occurrence of a given course of overt action *always* directly proportional to the clarity of subjective interpretation" (*E&S*, p. 12/6; emph. orig.; see also *R&K*, pp. 160/102, 197/136).

general empirical rules as the 'adequate' effect of certain prior events" ("Logic," p. 185/287). On another occasion Weber defines this notion more precisely:

> The interpretation of a sequence of events will . . . be called *causally* adequate insofar as, according to established generalizations from experience, there is a probability that it will always actually occur in the same way. . . . Thus, causal explanation depends on being able to determine that there is a probability, which in the rare ideal case can be numerically stated, but is always in some sense calculable, that a given observable event (overt or subjective) will be accompanied by another event. (*E&S*, pp. 11–12/5).[6]

Weber offers, however, remarkably few clues regarding his practiced causal methodology. Because never articulated, it must be reconstructed from his various substantive texts. Several patterns emerge from a close reading of *AG*, *GEH*, *E&S*, and, especially, *EEWR*. Two stages stand at the foundation of this methodology: a distinction between "facilitating" and "necessary" orientations of patterned action on the one hand and synchronic (within the present) and diachronic (between past and present) interactions of patterned action on the other. Though unstated, both of these distinctions are pivotal and run throughout Weber's empirical texts. They must, however, be seen as preliminary stages in his causal methodology. His substantive writings testify that entire constellations of regular action-orientations alone constitute effective causal forces. Finally, because a particular effect may arise not only from an array of action-orientations but also from their variable ordering, the importance of the *context* of patterned action must be acknowledged. Within demarcated contexts *conjunctural* interactions of diverse action-orientations occur, and these interactions imply causation. Weber is convinced that new regularities of action may, in a reverberating fashion, recast an entire multitude of action-orientations.

Thus, Weber's causal methodology does not involve simply the identification of positive or favoring orientations of action and their "weighing" against other patterned actions that impede and obstruct. Moreover, his attention to delineated historical factors does not lead him to formulate a methodology based only upon "causal chain" models of multiple forces.[7] Both of these procedures imply a linearity fundamentally foreign to his substantive as well as his methodological writings. For Weber, regular

6 On these concepts, see further *E&S*, pp. 11–12/5–6; "Logic," pp. 164–6/266–8, 174–5/276–7, 184–5/286–7; "Obj," pp. 80/179–80. In these passages, as well as the quotation above, Weber's awareness of the difficulties involved in all attempts to establish causation is apparent. See especially *E&S*, pp. 9–11/4–5.

7 In order to avoid stylistic awkwardness, I will at times employ standard terminology: "causal forces," "causal factors," and "causal variables." However, it should once again be kept in mind that each such "variable," to Weber, implies nothing more than orientations of action in a patterned manner by delimited groupings of people.

orientations of action never stand alone; rather, they exist in constellations and interact continuously, indeed to such a degree that the creation of a single effect is extremely unlikely. A *contextual* mode of explanation endowed with the analytic power to conceptualize *hosts* of patterned action-orientations and the *conjunctural* relationships between them is required.[8]

In sum, if adequate causality, according to Weber's practiced causal methodology, is to be achieved, (*a*) facilitating and necessary orientations of action and (*b*) synchronic and diachronic interaction must be present. Moreover, (*c*) the conjunctural interactions of patterned action that occur within a context of regular action-orientations must be identified. By acknowledging the causal importance of both the present and the past and integrating single facilitating and necessary action-orientations into a fabric of multiple action-orientations, such dynamic interactions alone,[9] in Weber's texts, provide adequate causal explanations of cases and developments.

That Weber actually practices such a three-stage causal methodology in the developed causal analyses in his substantive texts can be demonstrated only through a close scrutiny of these writings. This is the task of pp. 151–77 of this chapter. Before doing so, a few comparisons to the world systems, interpretive historical, and causal analytic schools will serve to isolate further the distinct contours of Weber's methodology.

It diverges sharply from the world systems approach. This school understands social change by reference to an overriding principle: as the world economy changes, an alteration of the domestic economies and politics of countries located in the "semi-periphery" and "periphery" will take place. The laws and operation of the international economy and the location of states remain central. An array of standard structural variables – for example, urbanization, capital accumulation, and the development of the state – serve to assess such changes.

These premises enable the world systems school to avoid acknowledgment of a complex and broad multicausality involving values, traditions, and interests. Indigenous traditions and cultural variation in the periphery and semi-periphery areas are scrutinized primarily by reference to economic and political interests located at the core of the world system; they are generally downplayed as viable causal factors. Although highly historical, descriptive, contextual, and even conjunctural in their many case studies, proponents of this approach typically conclude their causal analyses by emphasizing the force of the world economy. The conjunctural impact of a

8   Precisely Weber's emphasis upon conjunctural interaction implies that he would by no means be satisfied with the attempt, typical among American-trained methodologists, to identify simply necessary and sufficient causes. Weber rejects the entire notion of "sufficient causality." See below, pp. 168–77.
9   I am using the terms "conjunctural" and "dynamic" synonymously.

full spectrum of causal variables one upon another, especially ones not emanating in the end from the world system, is given less attention. In general, such causal complexity is not acknowledged. Indeed, basic agreement among world systems theorists regarding the direction of the causal flow, as well as the nature of the central causal variables, renders a causal methodology superfluous. The interpretive historical and causal analytic schools,[10] on the other hand, aim, to a qualitatively greater degree, to capture and explain the uniqueness and specificity of the given case, set of cases, or development. The particular outcome remains central. Events and developments are examined repeatedly, each time from a slightly different perspective. In this manner, varying combinations of factors and their contextual "arrangement," as well as dynamic interactions, are attended to.

Despite this common ground, the interpretive historical and causal analytic schools soon part ways. The former tends to view its detailed description of the individual case as of greatest importance and often leaves comparisons across cases to the reader. Moreover, beyond its derivation of common frameworks from a few concepts, general questions, and common themes, and its aim to provide a "thick description," the interpretive historical school offers few guidelines or procedures to assess causality. Studies indebted to this approach rely upon rich detail itself to express causality. No methodology is evident. Indeed, narrative procedures and individual cases constitute the exclusive focus to such a degree that the formulation of causal propositions is renounced. Just in this respect the contours of the causal analytic approach become clear: it attempts to construct explanatory theories and offers a clear methodology in this behalf. Rigorous procedures oriented explicitly toward the controlling of variation and the establishment of causality guide these investigations. Typical is the case-specific formulation of hypotheses and their testing, generally through the controlling of variables and a manifest dependence upon Mill's methods of "difference" and "agreement" (see Mill, 1843; Skocpol, 1979). Systematic and controlled comparisons serve the purpose of isolating likely causal forces (see Introduction, pp. 7–9).

While siding clearly with the interpretive historical and causal analytic schools against the theory-centered world systems approach, Weber departs fundamentally from both of these schools as well. In opposition to the attempt by the interpretive historical approach to establish causality through "the detailed richness of descriptions," his comparative-historical investigations proceed, although normally without explicit explanation, by reference to clear strategies, procedures, and stages. Nonetheless, his practiced methodology retains the unique strength of this school: its radical multicausality. Just this feature of his methodology sets Weber in opposi-

10   It will be recalled that Tilly and Bendix on the one hand and Skocpol and Moore on the other hand are representative figures respectively for the interpretive historical and causal analytic approaches.

tion to the causal analytic approach. Even though he welcomes comparative analysis and research design procedures to infer causality, he criticizes this school's failure to retain a commitment to a broad multicausality. A dominant structuralism that downplays cultural forces and an overriding emphasis upon the economy and the state repeatedly appears among proponents of this perspective.

Weber's three-stage causal methodology will be reconstructed in detail shortly. The second major component of his mode of causal analysis must be first briefly outlined: its *theoretical framework*.

The theoretical framework: domains and domain-specific ideal types

As noted, Weber's mode of causal analysis reveals a more "historical" Weber than was apparent in the models of *E&S* (see chapter 4), none of which, by his standards, yields causally adequate explanations. Nonetheless, the more historical Weber of *AG*, *GEH*, and *EEWR* must not be viewed as a sociologist engaged in problem-centered research alone, as are adherents of the interpretive historical and causal analytic schools. This is the case not only because ideal types constitute the level of analysis in these texts, but also because they are guided by a theoretical framework, namely, one that Weber made explicit in *E&S*. This framework precludes a convergence with these approaches.

Far from random in respect to causal action-orientations, the various causal analyses scattered throughout *AG*, *GEH*, and especially *EEWR* are guided by the societal domains – religion, law, the economy, rulership, the universal organizations, and status groups – and the domain-specific ideal types constructed in *E&S*. They constitute, in effect, an organizational frame of reference for these texts:[11] the paths to salvation in the sphere of religion (through a savior, an institution, ritual, good works, mysticism, and asceticism), the types of law ("primitive," traditional, natural, and logical formal), the stages of development in the economy (the agricultural and industrial organization of work; the natural, money, planned, market and capitalist types of economies), the types of authority (charismatic, patriarchal, feudal, patrimonial, and bureaucratic), the types of universal organizations (the family, clan, and neighborhood), classes, and major status groups (such as intellectuals, peasants, civil servants, and feudal nobles).[12] As noted, each ideal type implies patterned orientations of meaningful action.

11 On the selection of these domains and ideal types, see chapter 4, pp. 104–5.
12 Action-orientations in Weber's sociology always take place in reference to ideal types rather than societal domains. Nonetheless, I will generally employ the entire phrase – societal

In respect to Weber's mode of causal analysis, all domains and domain-specific ideal types can be best understood as constructing a theoretical framework, one employed in order to isolate and define clearly causal action-orientations.[13] They are not intended to be exhaustive in respect to causal forces as such. Because unique, every case or development involves case-specific and development-specific causes. Weber is adamant in this regard. Thus, the "incomplete" and "open-ended" theoretical framework never *encompasses* all sociologically-significant patterns of action. Indeed, in some empirical cases, action-orientations that fall outside the domain-based frame of reference, such as orientations toward technological or geographical forces, may constitute the central causal forces. Nonetheless, a close reading of the diverse causal analyses undertaken in *E&S*, *AG*, *GEH*, and *EEWR* reveals that reference to a delimited array of domain-specific action-orientations *guides* Weber's attempts to establish adequate causality.[14]

He utilizes this heuristic construct, in conjunction with standard research design comparisons, in order to isolate and identify, above all, patterned action-orientations at the level of *necessary* causality. The domain-specific ideal types, in effect, indicate to Weber *strong possibilities* in respect to causal action-orientations. He keeps them in mind whenever he undertakes a causal analysis; they orient his investigations. In this manner, and although the unique sets of action-orientations causally-significant for specific cases and developments comprise his subject of research, he refuses to proceed in a purely problem-focussed manner. Rather, a continuous back and forth movement between the patterned action of the case or development under investigation and the means of orientation provided by domains and domain-specific ideal types characterizes, in addition to his adherence to a three-stage causal methodology, Weber's mode of causal analysis.[15]

---

domains and domain-specific ideal types – in order to emphasize that these ideal types, rather than being random, are linked analytically by Weber to prominent domains.

13   Of course this usage of the phrase "theoretical framework" varies from its usage in reference to models (see chapter 4). Whereas all models imply hypotheses regarding patterned action, the domains and domain-specific ideal types constitute a theoretical framework more in the sense of a conceptual analytic; owing to its internally logical and consistent character, this analytic provides a standard in reference to which fragmented regular action can be ordered and better understood. Thus, the usage of "theoretical framework" in this chapter parallels the "yardstick" usage of ideal types discussed in chapter 3. "Frame of reference," "orientational mechanism," "heuristic construct," and "means of orientation" are used synonymously.

14   This occurs more in *EEWR* and *E&S* and less in *AG* and *GEH*. The latter texts move farther in the direction of empirical studies. Perhaps this is the case because (*a*) *AG* was written before *E&S* and before Weber became interested in the development of sociology as a discipline, whereas *EEWR* was written roughly simultaneously with *E&S*; and (*b*) *GEH* is a compilation of students' notes from a lecture course on economic history. This being said, it must also be recalled that many empirical analyses are found throughout *EEWR* and *E&S*.

15   Owing to the centrality of these domains and domain-specific ideal types in *E&S* and Weber's other substantive texts, his comparative-historical sociology opposes all diffusionist

Once the societal domains and domain-specific ideal types emphasized in *E&S* have been acknowledged as the orientational mechanism that "uproots" Weber's investigations from an exclusive focus upon empirical reality, it becomes evident that his practiced mode of causal analysis diverges sharply from the world systems, interpretive historical, and causal analytic schools. None of these contemporary approaches formulates constructs that offer a theoretical framework for causal analysis comparable to the domains and domain-specific ideal types of *E&S*. Both the interpretive historical and causal analytic schools remain problem-focussed. According to proponents of the interpretive historical approach, causality can be established through a thick description and detailed narrative. The guidelines provided by the causal analytic school, on the other hand, remain limited to research design procedures; no pluralistic orientational mechanism is offered. Moreover, Weber's theoretical framework itself *ensures* that causal analysis will take place by reference to a broad *multiplicity* of patterned action-orientations. In this manner purely structural causal arguments, whether those of the world systems or causal analytic schools, are guarded against.

Unarticulated in either his substantive or methodological texts, Weber's practiced mode of causal analysis must be reconstructed. Only an overview has been offered thus far. Its two major components – its causal methodology and theoretical framework – guide his questioning whenever he undertakes a causal analysis; they will be examined in detail and interwoven in the next section. The final section of this chapter offers an illustration of Weber's mode of causal analysis.

The Mode of Causal Analysis Reconstructed: Causal Methodology and Theoretical Framework

Two distinctions are apparent throughout Weber's causal analyses: between "facilitating" and "necessary" action-orientations on the one hand and synchronic (within the present) and diachronic (between past and present) interactions of action on the other. Once we have defined and illustrated these preliminary stages of his causal methodology, the context-based, conjunctural interactions of regular action also prominent throughout his texts can then be examined.[16] The orientational capacity of domains

---

schools. Diffusionists generally assume that change typically originates from without. As a consequence of Weber's focus upon endogenous patterns of action-orientations, as captured mainly by the domain-specific ideal types, the manner in which the borrowed phenomenon is shaped and changed is stressed. For Weber, moreover, the mere demonstration of commonality by no means constitutes evidence of inter-cultural contact, let alone influence. This remains an empirical question. See e.g. *AJ*, pp. 7/9, 13/16, 262/279; *RofC*, pp. 205/489–90.

16 As noted, model building is not the only focus of *E&S*. Dozens of delimited causal analyses – always incomplete by the standards of Weber's mode of causal analysis recon-

and domain-specific ideal types will become evident when necessary action-orientations are scrutinized.

Degrees of causality: the separation of facilitating from necessary action-orientations through comparisons

Weber employs the tools of comparative analysis in order to isolate a single factor's degree of causality. He notes his straightforward, experimental procedure, which conforms to the Millian "method of difference" utilized by the causal analytic school, in the *E&S* "Basic Sociological Terms" chapter: "There remains only the possibility of comparing the largest possible number of historical or contemporary occurrences which, while otherwise similar, differ in the *one* decisive point of their relation to the particular "motive" or "factor" the role of which is being investigated. This is an important task of comparative sociology" (*E&S*, p. 10/5).[17] Weber utilizes such research design procedures in order to assess whether, in respect to the case or development under investigation, a specific pattern of action (*a*) is without causal significance and should be ruled out, or accorded (*b*) facilitating or (*c*) necessary causal status.[18]

His substantive texts repeatedly distinguish between facilitating and necessary orientations of action. Facilitating, or "favorable," orientations of action are indirect and less powerful background factors, whereas necessary patterned action is crucial, directly relevant, and decisive if the specific case or development under investigation is to be explained.[19] Because they often exist universally, facilitating forces are incapable of causally explaining specific cases or developments. The role of guilds in the development of independent cities in the medieval West provides an example:

> Occupational unions [were not] initial stages or forerunners of *coniurationes*, for they appear throughout the world, even where no burgher commune has arisen. The effect of all these associations was essentially indirect. They facilitated the city union by habituating the burghers to the formation of coalitions in the pursuit of common interests, and by providing models for the cumulation of leadership positions in the hands of persons who had gained

---

structed in this chapter – are offered throughout *E&S*, especially in Part II (pp. 311–1374/181–814). Thus, the illustrations in this section are drawn from *E&S* as well as *EEWR*, *GEH*, and *AG*.

17 Weber concedes that in many cases this rigorous approach may not be feasible and the comparative-historical sociologist must be content to utilize the "uncertain procedure" of the "mental experiment" (*gedankliches Experiment*). This procedure "consists in thinking away certain elements of a chain of motivation and working out the course of action which would then probably ensue, thus arriving at a causal judgment" (*E&S*, p. 10/5). See also *E&S*, pp. 10–11/5; "Logic," pp. 171–5/273–8; Smelser, 1976, pp. 67–9, 147–8; Schelting, 1934, pp. 255–308; and Roth, 1968, p. xliii; 1971c, p. 81.

18 With respect to (*a*), see the excellent discussion by Smelser, 1976, pp. 141–9.

19 For facilitating factors Weber uses terms such as *günstig* (favorable) and *sehr günstig* (very favorable). *Bedingung* (condition) is generally employed to refer to necessary forces.

experience and social influence in the direction of such associations. (*E&S*, p. 1258/754)

At this foundational stage of his practiced causal methodology Weber attends to a broad array of case-specific empirical action-orientations. Only marginal guidance is provided by the *E&S* societal domains and domain-specific frame of reference. Because of its general familiarity, the examples used to illustrate his procedures will be taken largely from his analysis of the rise of modern capitalism.

Since the economic pressures that derive from the requirements of military conflict exist universally, yet modern capitalism arose only in one civilization and one epoch, actions oriented toward the preparation for war are best understood as facilitating rather than necessary (see *RofC*, p. 249/535; *GEH*, pp. 170/155–6, 307–9/265–6). Similarly, a rapid growth in population undoubtedly assisted the development of "economic rationalism" in the sixteenth and seventeenth centuries in the West, yet, because an equally strong increase in population occurred in China in the seventeenth century without leading to modern capitalism, Weber concluded that this factor must also be viewed as favorable rather than crucial (see *RofC*, p. 55/341; *GEH*, p. 352/360). Likewise, an expansion in the supply of precious metals and a concomitant intensification of the money economy may be also perceived as important for the development of modern capitalism. However, once Weber discovered that this factor existed in China as well as in the West, he felt confident in assigning to it facilitating rather than necessary status (*RofC*, pp. 12/289–90, 248–9/535). Utilizing the same comparative procedures and taking India as his point of reference he defines a number of additional patterned action-orientations as favorable to the unfolding of modern capitalism rather than as necessary: urban development, extensive trade, a number system that allowed strict calculability, and a general acquisitiveness and ruthless search for profit (see *RofI*, p. 4/4; "AI," pp. 20–4/6–10; *GEH*, p. 232/205). Through comparisons to Ancient civilizations he rejects the advantages offered by the Mediterranean sea and inland waterways as well as coastal trade and luxury demand as direct causal variables (see *GEH*, pp. 354/301–2, 170–1/155–6, 309–10/266–7).

This comparative mode of analysis enables Weber to identify these regular action-orientations as relevant. However, by calling attention to their widespread and even universal character, it also allows an accurate assessment of their strength: none was a necessary causal factor. Necessary orientations of action convey a far more direct notion of causality. Whereas facilitating action-orientations appear both where the case or development to be explained exists (modern capitalism) as well as in its absence, and must be viewed more as background orientations of action, necessary patterned action is powerful and crucial for a causal explanation of the case or development under investigation. In effect, facilitating action-orientations serve merely to narrow down the number of potentially critical patterns of action and to point the investigation to the necessary factors, each of which can be viewed as a valid cause. Weber now attempts to identify patterned action that exhibits a *direct* association with the case or development to be explained. He seeks to isolate orientations of action *unique* to the situation through comparisons to similar situations where the patterned action-orientations are absent. Having done so, he then infers that the unique action-orientations are not only causally related to the case or development under investigation, but also necessary for its origin.

The *E&S* societal domains and domain-specific ideal types enter more conspicuously at this point into his assessments regarding potential causes. While never capable of identifying *all* crucial causes, they offer a frame of reference that guides the researcher toward significant causal action-orientations. In doing so, his mode of causal analysis avoids an exclusive reliance on the one hand upon "thick description" and on the other hand upon a research design methodology. In respect to the rise of modern capitalism, for example, Weber isolated, through comparisons and by reference to his guiding framework, a series of patterned action-orientations intimately related to its occurrence that existed *only* in the West. Because modern capitalism appeared only in Western civilization he concluded that these action-orientations constitute causal factors indispensable for an explanation of this unique economy: toward a rational law and form of rulership, a monetary system capable of sustaining a maximum degree of formal rationality of capital accounting, the growth of bourgeois and consumer classes, production for markets, and a "rationalistic economic ethic."[20] Of course, because his investigation proceeded empirically, Weber discovered further factors indigenous to this particular development not identified by his domains and domain-specific ideal types orientational framework: the rational permanent enterprise (*Betrieb*), rational technology, rational science, and citizenship (see *GEH*, pp. 313–14/270, 354/302; *E&S*, pp. 161–4/94–5; *RofC*, pp. 249/535–6; "AI"). All constitute, for him, necessary action-orientations.

The identification of facilitating and necessary patterns of action stands out as a core strategy in Weber's various causal analyses. Nonetheless, regardless how "exhaustive" they are when in combinations and "added up" into causal chains, even multiple necessary factors never provide an adequate causal explanation.[21] Only the first stage of his practiced causal methodology has been reconstructed. However, the distinction between

20 The last factor implies a systematic approach to profit and labor and its organization as well as, in particular, an overcoming of the traditional dualistic ethic in which an "internal ethic" of honesty and fair play applied to "insiders" while one of calculation, cheating, and a means–end rational pursuit of gain applied to "outsiders" (see *GEH*, pp. 355–61/302–7, 312–13/269; *PE*, pp. 48–50/31–2; "Sects").

21 It is above all for this reason that Weber's "facilitating" and "necessary" degrees of causality should not be equated with the common "necessary and sufficient" usage today. Weber's methodology, on the contrary, is non-linear and requires a further distinct ingredient: conjunctural interaction. See below.

facilitating and necessary action-orientations already separates Weber from the world systems, interpretive historical, and causal analytic schools.

Societal domains and synchronic and diachronic interactions of action

A close reading of the causal analyses in Weber's substantive texts reveals that two basic types of interaction of action-orientations are attended to on a regular basis: synchronic and diachronic interactions. Diachronic interactions appear as either "legacies" or "antecedent conditions." An assessment of the "penetration range" of synchronic and diachronic interactions is as well a typical procedure in these texts. Of most importance to Weber, in order to establish adequate causality, are those interactions at the level of necessary causality. They must be isolated, defined, and their causal impact assessed. The means of orientation provided by the societal domains and domain-specific ideal types of *E&S*, in conjunction with comparative and experimental procedures, assist Weber just in this regard.

Synchronic interaction   The identification of significant synchronic interactions constitutes a major task in Weber's causal analyses. Because it offers a purchase upon diffuse reality that facilitates the identification of empirical action-orientations, the *E&S* theoretical framework is utilized continuously in these analyses. The illustrations to follow are drawn from a variety of his analyses.

The precise identification of the manner in which action oriented to *religion* may interact with, for example, the *universal organizations*, altering action-orientations in the process, is facilitated by the *E&S* frame of reference. In other words, with this heuristic construct in mind, Weber assesses whether, in respect to the case or development under investigation, regular action oriented to religion penetrates deeply into action oriented to the family, clan, or traditional neighborhood. Magical forces, for example, in some empirical situations, may be seen to intensify the family's values, customs, and conventions. This occurred especially in Asia (and above all in China), in fact to such an extent that changes of any sort threatened to call forth the wrath of evil spirits. Weber then assesses the consequences of such a domain-based interaction, and sees its relevance even in respect to the rise of modern capitalism: the Chinese and Japanese family and clan, once strengthened in this manner, succeeded in maintaining a rigidly patriarchal structure even against all thrusts toward development of the economy (*E&S*, p. 412/253).

Similarly, the *E&S* analytic, by providing means of orientation, enables the isolation and clear identification of the interaction of empirical patterned action oriented on the one hand to *religion* and on the other hand to *rulership*. In China, for example, patrimonial, or monarchical, rulership (see

E&S, p. 1050/610) is seen to have become tightly interwoven with action oriented to magic. Weber again emphasizes the consequences: action became stereotyped to such an extent that it blocked, even more effectively than material interests, attempts to introduce more rational trade practices and routes of transportation (*GEH*, p. 303/355). That action oriented to religion penetrated deeply into the rulership domain can be clearly seen as well, with the assistance of the *E&S* orientational construct, in respect to a further empirical case: in Germany Pietism and Lutheranism permeated both patrimonial and bureaucratic types of rulership. The "ideological halo" provided by these religions called forth the "bureaucratic ethos" – disciplined and regular work, the reliable performance of tasks, and punctuality (see *E&S*, pp. 476/290, 959/553, 1108/652).

Finally, the *E&S* heuristic construct also helps to identify, for example, the empirical expansion of patterned action oriented to *religious teachings* beyond the sphere of religion and into the *status ethics* of various strata. The teachings of Hinduism and Confucianism prevented craftsmen and small merchants from serving as the carriers of a "rational religious ethic," as postulated by the *E&S* ideal type for such civic strata (see *E&S*, pp. 477–84/ 291–5; "I," pp. 284–5/256–7). In India specific empirical forces intervened: caste taboos, ritual, and the belief in reincarnation altered and even stereotyped the "typical" ethic of craftsmen and merchants (*E&S*, p. 484/295). In China the general tendency of small businessmen and craftsmen to lead "practical rational" lives based upon financial and other calculations of advantage, as articulated also in the *E&S* ideal type for civic strata, could be seen to be dislocated as a consequence of the deep permeation of magic into these strata (see *GEH*, p. 161/148).

In this manner, by utilizing the *E&S* societal domains and domain-specific ideal types as heuristic yardsticks, Weber can conceptually grasp otherwise amorphous empirical realities and, on behalf of a causal analysis of a specific case or development, define "mixtures" of patterned action-orientations. However, his causal analyses not only commonly identify the interaction of a single set of action-orientations; they also isolate repeatedly the ways in which action-orientations indigenous to a particular domain permeate into and influence an *entire cluster* of action-orientations in a *variety* of domains. In doing so, the "penetration range" of patterned action is assessed. Because the world systems, interpretive historical, and causal analytic schools all fail to offer an orientational framework, all remain incapable of ascertaining precisely and consistently the penetration range of sociologically-significant action.

Penetration range   Weber's domain-based framework assists the identification of empirical patterns of action that are influential far and wide. Some action-orientations indigenous to specific *strata*, for example, are seen to penetrate, in a variety of cases, widely into an array of societal domains: the priesthood in Egypt, the literati in China, the Brahmins in India, the Junkers in Prussia, and the business classes in the United States all cast a

broad influence. The empirical expansion of action oriented to "economically-irrational" status monopolies ("stratification by status") into various
domains, including the economy, becomes as well visible (*E&S*, p. 937/538;
"I," pp. 301/274–5; Kalberg, 1983, pp. 274–6). The caste system, for example, which constitutes an extreme accentuation of status stratification, is
seen to penetrate into the most remote interstices of Indian society. Weber
then, as usual, undertakes to evaluate the wide-ranging consequences: in
denying any "natural" equality of persons before an authority, least of all
before a "super-worldly god" (*RofI*, pp. 144/142–3), the caste system stands
strongly in opposition to all notions of natural law and human rights. Caste
ritual, or *dharma*, acknowledges only the rights and duties of particular
castes and prevents the appearance of more universal concepts, such as
"state," "citizen," and "subject" (*RofI*, pp. 144–7/143–8). Only a status-
compartmentalized positive law could survive in India.

The theoretical framework of domains and domain-specific ideal types
also enables the isolation and clear identification of empirical cases in
which action-orientations indigenous to the *types of rulership* (see *E&S*,
pp. 212–66/122–55, 941–1157/541–687) spread broadly. Guided by this
orientational mechanism, Weber can see that some empirical cases –
manorial–feudal rulership in the medieval Occident, for example – became
so firmly entrenched that patterns of action indigenous to them extended
deeply into the *economy and religion* domains, indeed with a clear consequence: the traditions, values, and interests of feudal lords placed a strong
barrier against the development of the economy and religion (*E&S*, p. 1181/
705). The hegemonic and encompassing influence in Japan of feudal
rulership and the Samurai ruling stratum can, as well, be identified in this
manner: the ethic of this form of rulership, rather than a religious belief
system, can be seen to have "carried" the dominant Japanese value constellation (*RofI*, pp. 270–82/295–308). In our own epoch, action oriented to
bureaucratic rulership, formal rationality, and the ethos of the civil servant
can be seen, with the assistance of the *E&S* analytic (see pp. 956–1005/551–
78), to have permeated, Weber repeatedly notes, broadly into the economy,
law, and political domains.[22]

The domain-based frame of reference formulated in *E&S* and utilized
throughout Weber's comparative-historical texts facilitates the precise
identification as well of the empirical influence of *religion* in different
civilizations and epochs. It often penetrated far and wide. The overwhelming centrality of Islam, Hinduism, Confucianism, and Judaism in their respective classical eras implied not only a thorough expansion of religious
teachings into the law, rulership, and universal organizations domains, but
also their deep extension into the economy. Even daily life conventions and
customs became shaped by religion-based action-orientations (see, for example, *E&S*, p. 577/348). In effect, the domain of religion acquired such a

22   On the latter influence, see *E&S*, pp. 998–1002/576–8.

position of hegemony in these cases that it imprinted and stereotyped with ritual all societal domains. A broad empirical penetration of religion as well in the Western Middle Ages becomes apparent. The influence in a comprehensive manner of action-orientations toward religion also becomes clear in the case of Colonial America: ascetic Protestantism and its distinctly inner-worldly work ethic. More concretely, the encompassing range of the religious realm in these civilizations implied that, for example, rulership had to acquire, if to be perceived as legitimate, a religious cast.[23]

These few examples have aimed merely to demonstrate the centrality throughout Weber's causal analyses of a particular mode of procedure, one that constitutes a major stage in his causal methodology: the identification of sociologically-significant synchronic interactions of patterned action. Reference to the limited array of societal domains and domain-specific ideal types of *E&S*, which offers an indispensable means of orientation to fragmented realities, enables the requisite conceptual purchase. Although practitioners of the world systems, interpretive historical, and causal analytic approaches remain far more cognizant of synchronic interactions than the structural–functional theories of modernization and political development of the 1950s, these recent approaches fail to construct an heuristic means of orientation that facilitates their clear isolation and definition. Nor do these schools articulate a strategy of any sort to assess penetration range. The centrality of domains and domain-specific ideal types distinguishes Weber's mode of causal analysis clearly from the problem focus of the interpretive historical and causal analytic schools. Furthermore, by designating *multiple* domain-specific ideal types as endowed with causal status, *E&S* proclaims that a pluralism of action-orientations must be taken into consideration in every causal analysis. In this manner, Weber's comparative-historical sociology erects a strong barrier against the practice, common among adherents of the world systems and causal analytic approaches, of elevating a limited number of – or even single – factors to positions of general causal priority.

  However, Weber's causal methodology not only identifies empirical synchronic interactions of patterned action-orientations; the identification of past and present – or *diachronic* – interactions is also pivotal. The causal analysis of the origins of a specific case or development requires that both types of interaction be charted rigorously and their consequences assessed.

Diachronic interaction: legacies and antecedent conditions   Weber's understanding of "societies" as only loosely held together and as constituted from numerous competing and reciprocally interacting patterns of action-orien-

23   On the American colonies, in this respect, see e.g. Bellah's description of Governor John Winthrop (1985, pp. 28–9).

tations by persons in delineated groupings persuades him of the extreme importance, for any explanation of the present, of past developments. It convinces him as well that patterned action-orientations permeate in multiple, often clandestine, ways deeply into the present. He would reject as far too global all analyses that view societies as either "traditional" or "modern," as did the structural functionalism school of modernization and political development. Weber also opposes the view that past action-orientations, if influential in the present at all, remain circumscribed in their impact and endowed with little long-term, significant consequence. Instead, for him, the past may live on for millennia within the interstices of the present and even within its central core. Indeed, despite the advent of drastic contextual metamorphoses, patterned social action may play a distinct and influential causal role in epochs far removed from its origin. Even the abrupt appearance of "the new" – even the "supernatural" power of charisma – never fully ruptures ties to the past. To Weber: "That which has been handed down from the past becomes everywhere the immediate precursor of that taken in the present as valid" (*E&S*, p. 29/15; transl. alt.). Far from being banished, history interacts with the present to such an extent that, unless its influence is acknowledged, any attempt to explain the uniqueness of present-day regular social action remains a hopeless undertaking.

These fundamental premises undergird Weber's substantive texts. They are shared by the world systems, interpretive historical, and causal analytic approaches. However, a set of regularly employed concepts or procedures that capture the empirical impact of the past upon the present is never constructed by proponents of these schools. Two distinct modes of diachronic interaction, each of which charts the manner in which past patterned social action influences present regular action, reappear throughout Weber's causal analyses, as well as his comparative-historical texts in general: "legacy" and "antecedent condition" interactions.[24] As with synchronic interactions, the *E&S* societal domains and domain-specific ideal types, while never "exhaustive," provide a frame of reference that assists their clear identification. Once this occurs, an assessment of causal significance can occur. A few illustrations of intra-domain, inter-domain, and penetration range interactions will testify to the centrality of these modes of diachronic interaction in Weber's practiced causal methodology.

Although originating in a particular epoch, certain patterns of social action endure as *legacies* and cast their shadows across subsequent epochs, indeed

---

24   Neither in his methodological essays nor in the "Basic Sociological Terms" chapter (*E&S*, pp. 3–62/1–30) does Weber inform us regarding the significance of these concepts in his substantive writings. He offers no definitions of them. I have extracted them from these substantive texts. I am not aware of discussions in the secondary literature that have addressed these modes of diachronic interaction in a systematic fashion.

to such an extent that a significant and permanent influence upon action in the later period is apparent. Weber's causal analyses call attention repeatedly, and frequently in an ironic fashion, to the ways in which such regularities of action "survive."[25]

Intra-domain interactions The *E&S* frame of reference, which Weber keeps in mind whenever he undertakes empirical investigations,[26] facilitates the clear identification of prominent intra-domain empirical legacies in the domains, for example, of *religion and law*. Legacies in the realm of religion in the West can be seen to have been left by ancient Judaism to Catholicism and Protestantism: to both the notion of a monotheistic God and, to Protestantism in particular, a deeply anti-magical strain (*AJ*, pp. 3–5/5–7; "I," p. 286/258). Thus, the scriptural prophets not only left a clear legacy to early Christianity – "the entire interpretation of the mission of the Nazarene was primarily determined by the old promises to Israel" – but also "cast their shadows through the millennia into the present" (*AJ*, p. 334/350). The legalistic ethic of Jewish law, for example, "was absorbed by the Puritan ethic and thus put into the context of modern bourgeois economic morality" (*E&S*, p. 1204/721).

In the law sphere as well, empirical legacies become, with the assistance of the *E&S* analytic, visible. The oath, or "self-curse," for example, endured until logical formal law, and charismatic law-creation, in the figures of Lenin and Mao, survived into our own century. As Weber states:

> Characteristics of the charismatic epoch of lawmaking and lawfinding have persisted to a considerable extent in many of the institutions of the period of rational enactment and application of the law. Remnants still survive even at the present day. As late a writer as Blackstone called the English judge a sort of living oracle; and, as a matter of fact, the role played by decision as the indispensable and specific form in which the common law is embodied corresponds to the role of the oracle in ancient law. (*E&S*, p. 767/450)

Moreover, the "rational traditions of the Roman law" influenced not only Canon law (*E&S*, p. 828/480), but also modern formal law (*E&S*, pp. 853–5/491–3), and Canon law "became . . . one of the guides for secular law on the road to rationality" (*E&S*, p. 829/481).

Inter-domain interactions Weber's many causal analyses also chart regularly the expansion of patterned action in one societal domain in one epoch into a different domain in a subsequent era. This is, Weber's texts testify, an empirically widespread occurrence. Just how this occurs becomes apparent with the assistance of the *E&S* framework. Again, only a few

---

25 Weber's terms are *Reste*, *Überbleibsel*, *verbliebener Rest*.

26 In other words, as noted, *E&S*, as Weber's analytic treatise, *most* vividly articulates his domain-based frame of reference. It is, however, also apparent when he conducts causal investigations in *AG*, *GEH*, and *EEWR*. Many of the examples in this section and the next, all of which aim merely to indicate the centrality of legacies and antecedent conditions for Weber, are from these investigations.

examples can be noted.

The *household's* principle of communism of property and consumption, as well as solidarity against the outside world, implied a joint responsibility toward creditors. In the form of the concept of joint liability, this notion left a legacy that became a pivotal source for the legal forms of modern capitalism (*E&S*, p. 359/214). Faithfulness, originally located in the *clan*, reappeared in all the world religions (*E&S*, pp. 361–3/216–18). In ancient Israel the prohibition against taking interest from "a poor Israelite," which constituted the source of Judaism's distinction between in-group and out-group morality, was originally a purely legal expression of the ethic of brotherliness among *neighbors* (see *AJ*, pp. 63–4/69, 70/76–7, 342/357).

Weber's causal analyses also emphasize that regular action oriented to *rulership organizations* survived empirically far beyond the epoch of its origin and penetrated into new domains. Feudalism, for example, left several legacies. Most notably, its high sense of dignity rooted in personal honor and the basic attitudes of knighthood survived and influenced, in later epochs, the Occidental *ministerales*, the English gentleman ideal, and even the ideal of the Puritan gentleman. For all these strata, "feudal knighthood was the original, specifically medieval center of orientation" (*E&S*, pp. 1068–9/623).[27] The ancient "political feudalism" in China also cast a broad shadow, crucially assisting the development of the status ethic of Confucianism in the classical and post-classical epochs (*RofC*, pp. 46/329–30). Even our own era is permeated by the various types of rulership specific to past epochs which "extend as survivals into the present" ("I," p. 295/268).[28]

The *E&S* frame of reference provides as well the means of orientation to diffuse reality that identifies the expansion of patterned action originating in one societal domain in one epoch across an *entire cluster* of domains in a subsequent era. Even though the interpretive historical, world systems, and causal analytic schools attend to the impact of past action-orientations upon present patterned action, none of these approaches articulates concepts and strategies that assist the identification of the penetration range of legacies, let alone a theoretical framework for doing so.

Penetration range   Weber's causal analyses repeatedly note the staying power of regularities of action originating in the *universal organizations*. They remain extremely durable over the centuries and influential across a variety of societal domains. Piety and respect for the elderly, which found

---

27   Weber notes further the influence of the Puritan's cool reserve and quiet self-control upon the American and English gentleman of the present (see *PE*, p. 119/117). He views this same self-control as one root of modern military discipline (see *PE*, pp. 235–6, n. 81/117, n. 4).

28   For several examples that demonstrate the extension of personal rulership into industrialized countries, see Roth, 1971a, pp. 160–2; 1989. Weber notes, in an ironic fashion, that the necessity to participate in a dueling fraternity in turn-of-the-century German universities can be seen as a "surviving remnant" of "the old requirement of a knightly style of life" (*E&S*, p. 1000/577; see also Weber, 1917, p. 389).

their origin in the household, resurfaced as reverence toward ancestors in several world religions and as piety and loyalty toward the ruler and prince in patrimonial and feudal forms of rulership (*E&S*, pp. 359/214, 1070/625). Action oriented to a "neighborhood ethic" also survived as a causally effective force beyond its period of origin and penetrated far and wide beyond the boundaries of its original carrier organization. This occurred above all in respect to the domains of *religion and the economy*.

Whether initially found within a community of villagers, a guild, or partners in seafaring, hunting, or warring expeditions, the typical action-orientations in "associations of neighbors" survived among the brethren in the faith in many religions. This ethic's idea of reciprocity was manifest under the mottos "as you do unto me, I shall do unto you" and "your want of today may be mine of tomorrow." Reciprocity implied, wherever it intermingled with the realm of religion, above all a religiously-rooted obligation to assist all fellow believers whenever emergencies arose. Not only blood brothers and members of a clan or tribe now deserved help in times of need, but also brethren in the faith. This in-group ethos of assistance meant, for example, that widows and orphans in distress would be aided, that children would be cared for when necessary, that a liberal hospitality and support would be extended without compensation, and that the poor and sick might expect the generosity of the well-to-do. The neighborhood ethic also became a major source of the commandment to provide the "just price" for products and labor and for the prohibition against usury in the West, while in India it survived in Hinduism's creed of veracity and its "prohibition against the laying of hands on other people's property" (*E&S*, pp. 361–3/216–18, 365–6/219–20, 577–81/350–1, 583–4/352, 1188–9/710; *GEH*, pp. 43–6/54–7; *RofI*, pp. 150/151–2; "IR," pp. 329–30/543).

On the other hand, the assistance of the *E&S* theoretical framework reveals that some legacies *prevent*, across an array of societal domains, patterned action-orientations from arising. In India, "the prestige of magical power was firmly established" for the thought of the Brahmin literati (*RofI*, p. 171/177). This prestige became fully visible in the virtuoso's salvation goal: gnostic knowledge was viewed as possessing a magical *significance* and the ecstatic rapture of mystical illumination was understood to be a magical state that endowed the *sramana* with magical powers (*RofI*, pp. 166/170, 170/176, 177/185).[29] Magic, having acquired a strong carrier stratum, remained powerful across an expanse of domains for millennia in India. An effective de-magification was precluded.

In certain empirical cases, two or more established and powerful domains have coalesced and attained such a strong hegemony that their interlocking, patterned action-orientations influenced an entire civilization

29 "According to undoubted doctrines, right knowledge supplied magical power.... The holy gnosis enabled [the Brahmin] to perform miracles" (*RofI*, p. 156/159).

across centuries and even millennia. Weber's domain and domain-specific ideal types framework allows the identification of such cases precisely. This occurred, for example, in China when patrimonial rulers formed an alliance with Confucianism and the values of the sib group, in India when Hindu Brahmins coalesced with the Kshatriya princes and kings, and in the United States when the Calvinist work ethic combined with a strong business class and modern capitalism.[30]

However, legacies alone fail to capture fully the manner in which past action-orientations in Weber's causal analyses assert a direct influence upon regular social action in the present. A further, frequently utilized concept – *antecedent conditions* – testifies as well to the manner in which, throughout his comparative-historical texts, past action-orientations regularly influence action-orientations in the present. The world systems, interpretive historical, and causal analytic schools all fail to construct a comparable concept, even though all acknowledge the causal importance of the past. Once again, the societal domains and domain-specific ideal types articulated in *E&S* serve as a theoretical framework that assists the identification of empirical antecedent conditions.

Antecedent conditions, for Weber, may become significant causal action-

30 Of course, empirically, legacies do not always fall, for Weber, within the societal domains and domain-specific ideal types. Again, this theoretical framework is not intended to be "comprehensive," but to serve as an heuristic frame of reference that assists in the identification of causally significant patterns of action. His texts provide many examples. He notes that a "sober practical rationalism" of *Roman times*, in casting the framework for the dogmatic and ethical systematization of belief, constituted "the most important legacy of Rome to the Christian Church" (*E&S*, pp. 554–5/336). Similarly, an extremely militaristic *era* in pre-Classical China left such a strong legacy of pride, stoicism, and a rejection of "the beyond" that Chinese balladeers, even as late as the seventh century BC, sang "praises of warriors in preference to sages and literati" (*RofC*, p. 41/323). Weber sees that legacies from the religion domain expanded empirically *in the United States* not simply into a societal domain or several domains, but generally. Central values in Protestant asceticism – disciplined and routine work in a "calling," the regular giving to charity organizations, the formation of impersonal and abstract goals, the orientation to the future and world mastery, an optimism regarding the capacity to shape personal destinies, and a strong intolerance of "evil" – remain integral in American life generally despite the fact that many who uphold these values do not perceive them as religious virtues or as even linked intimately to a religious heritage. The Protestant notion of duty in one's calling "prowls about in our lives like the ghost of dead religious beliefs" (*PE*, p. 182/204; see also pp. 72/55–6; 181/203; 282, n.108/200–1, n.4; *GEH*, pp. 368–9/ 313–14; *E&S*, p. 1187/709; Kalberg, 1991). (Weber refers to this situation as a *caput mortuum* legacy, a term found with some regularity throughout his comparative-historical texts; see e.g. *E&S*, pp. 1150/682, 1154/685 [here translated as "remnant"]; *PE*, pp. 181–2/203–4.) The "direct democratic administration" by the congregation in the Protestant sects in the United States, as well as the hostility of sect members to the charisma of office, left a legacy crucial for the establishment of democratic forms of government. The Quakers in particular, in advocating freedom of conscience for others as well as for themselves, paved the way for political tolerance (see *E&S*, pp. 1204–10/721–6). On the other hand, given his dominant focus upon societal domains rather than "societies," Weber would reject Parsons's construct of "seedbed societies" as too amorphous (see Parsons, 1966, 1971).

orientations.[31] Several examples will demonstrate the centrality of this mode of diachronic interaction.[32]

Intra-domain interactions   A concern to identify antecedent conditions characterizes Weber's entire comparative-historical analysis of *religion*. The means utilized by sorcerers magically to coerce spirits very often formed clear precursors to the various soteriological methods of salvation (*E&S*, p. 537/326). Similarly, the magician in "primitive" religions can be viewed as the "developmental-historical predecessor" of prophecy, both scriptural and exemplary ("IR," p. 327/540).

This attention to antecedent conditions, and their clear identification, is apparent as well in Weber's studies of the world religions. His elaborate discussion of Vedic religion and its causal influence in the classical period upon the formation of Hinduism and Buddhism offers an example (see *RofI*, pp. 25–9/27–31). It is apparent likewise in his examination of the diverse ways in which the ritual laws that represented the interests of small proprietors and the poor laid down in the Book of Covenant, as well as the sacred *berith* with Yahwe, established fixed precedents that shaped the speeches of the scriptural prophets. Rather than claiming to announce new commandments in the form utilized by Jesus – "It is written, but I say unto you" – the prophets identified ancient customs, Levitical teaching (Amos 2:4; Isa. 24:5), and legal verdicts as the sources of their morality. The Levitical practice of confession and expiation, for example, formed the basis for the prophets' pronouncements that Yahwe would inflict enormous suffering whenever moral and social-ethical commandments had been violated (*AJ*, pp. 295/310, 304–5/319, 235/251; see also pp. 332–5/348–50, 316/331). Similarly, the pattern of other-worldly asceticism and monasticism that originated in medieval Catholicism, on the basis of a notion of collectivity far more developed than that which existed in their counterparts in India (see also Silber, 1985), set a clear precedent for the particular inner-worldly asceticism that emerged with the Protestant sects.[33]

In the domain of *rulership* the charisma of the great warrior and the legendary knight, both of whom promised success despite risk and hardship as well as relief from extraordinary distress, served as a precursor to kingship: "Kingship grows out [*wächst*] of charismatic heroism" (*E&S*, pp. 1141–2/676, 1134/670). Patterned action oriented to charisma formed an

31   "Antecedent condition" (*Voraussetzung*), "precedent" (*Vorbedingung*), and "precursor" (*Vorläufer*) will be used synonymously. The German terms are often, unfortunately, translated as "prerequisite." Because it implies a stronger and more direct causal link than Weber wishes to convey, this translation will not be employed here. Weber's notion of antecedent condition should not be confused with the structural-functional notion of "functional prerequisite."
32   It is quite difficult to separate the two modes of diachronic interaction – legacies and antecedent conditions – in Weber's texts. I have distinguished them analytically and illustrated them separately in order to demonstrate the full expanse of Weber's attention to the influence of the past upon the present.
33   Weber notes more precedents for the development of the Protestant ethic as well. See *PE*, pp. 170/189, 276, n.78/189, n.4; *RofI*, pp. 337–8/372; and Weber, 1889.

antecedent condition for another form of charisma in the cases of the Nabi ecstatics, who presaged the classical scriptural prophets in ancient Palestine.[34] As well, the educational system in patrimonial rulership, because of its stress upon administrative training, accounting, clerical work, and the training in law, formulated a precedent for the modern bureaucracy's ideal of "vocation" (*E&S*, p. 1108/653).

Inter-domain interactions The identification of causally-significant antecedent action-orientations by reference to inter-domain interactions constitutes a common undertaking as well throughout Weber's substantive texts. His *sociology of law* offers vivid empirical examples. The formal qualities of Roman law and legal training provided precursors for patrimonial justice as well as, in combination with values associated with natural law, the development of a legitimizing framework of universalism for the modern epoch's bureaucratic rulership (*E&S*, pp. 853/491–2). Logical formal law, in articulating firmly the basic Rights of Man and providing fixed rules and legal techniques (for example, the law of agency and the principle of free negotiability) for business transactions as well as procedures for the enforcement of contracts, paved the way for "the capitalist to use things and men freely," thereby assisting the rise of modern capitalism (*E&S*, pp. 667/398, 681–3/407–8, 706/424, 1209/725–6). On the other hand, Weber cites the Enlightenment, carried by a *status group* of intellectuals. Its juxtaposition of the Rights of Man with a belief in individual reason established not only its opposition to patrimonial and feudal law, but also a precursor for the institutionalization of abstract norms in the legal sphere (*E&S*, pp. 1209/725–6).[35] One very important constellation of action patterns in the development of modern capitalism – "a rational and innerworldly ethic" – itself in turn depends upon the appearance of *civic* strata: "The establishment of a rational and innerworldly ethic was bound up in the Occident with the appearance of thinkers and prophets who developed a social structure [*Gebilde*] on the basis of *political* problems which were very foreign to Asiatic culture; these were the political problems of civic status groups of the city without which neither Judaism nor Christianity nor the development of Hellenic thought is conceivable" (*RofI*, pp. 337–8/372; emph. orig.).

Perhaps the most important precedent related to the *universal organizations* concerns their destruction: the obliteration of house and clan industry in the Middle Ages was necessary for the development of guilds and production for the market (*GEH*, pp. 146–7/135–6). The crystallization of

34 Even though this early prophecy was only partially politically oriented, the scriptural prophets were vividly aware of its message. Through comparisons of events in their own period to the "good old times" and the "good old law," they acquired strength and confidence from this message (see *AJ*, pp. 101–3/110–12, 268/282).

35 In his political writings Weber is less cautious in expressing the importance of the precedent set by the Enlightenment for the modern epoch: "It is a gross self-deception to believe that without the achievements of the age of the Rights of Man any one of us, including the most conservative, can go on living" (*E&S*, p. 1403/(*PS*), p. 333).

certain *strata* as well required certain antecedent conditions: "In East Asia and India, pariah intellectualism is practically non-existent, as is petty-bourgeois intellectualism. This results from the fact that both types of intellectualism require the communal feeling of an urban citizenry, which is absent. Absent also is a further antecedent condition: emancipation from magic" (*E&S*, p. 508/309; transl. alt.). Finally, a *fusion* of domains may lay down an antecedent condition: for example, in the form of "clan charisma" an interesting combination of universal (the clan) and rulership (patriarchal) organizations arose in India. This fusing formed a decisive precursor for the development of the Brahmin caste as well as the caste system as a whole (*RofI*, pp. 49–50/51–2; see below, pp. 180–1).[36]

However, the concern so prominent throughout Weber's causal analyses as well as his substantive texts in general to identify diachronic interactions of regular action,[37] and indeed entire arrays of antecedent conditions, should not lead to the conclusion that simple reference to "causal chains" – once all relevant factors appear together, then a causal explanation of the case or development under investigation is established – accurately captures Weber's practiced causal methodology. All such "static" approaches remain, to him, both unilinear and drastically incomplete.

36   Again (see note 30), although the domains and domain-specific ideal types prominent in *E&S* constitute the theoretical framework for Weber that assists the identification of causally significant antecedent conditions, he offers many empirical examples not grasped by this framework. Because it is open-ended, the heuristic construct does not imply an "exhaustive" ordering of all empirical patterns of action. For example, he sees the development of *mass democracy* as a precursor for the growth of bureaucracies. A societal democratization, characterized by a leveling of economic and social differences on the one hand and of plutocratic privileges on the other, calls forth bureaucracies. (Although, as Weber is quick to point out, democratization is not the only possible foundation for bureaucratization [see *E&S*, pp. 990–1/572]; when he examines its sources, he refers as well to the "major role" played by capitalism and to developments in the fields of communication and transportation [see e.g. *E&S*, p. 224/129].) Simply the "necessities" of mass democracy here come into play: "Bureaucracy inevitably accompanies modern *mass democracy*, in contrast to the democratic self-government of small homogeneous units. This results from its characteristic principle: the abstract regularity of the exercise of rulership, which is a result of the demand for 'equality before the law' in the personal and functional sense – hence of the horror of 'privilege' – and the principled rejection of doing business 'from case to case'" (*E&S*, p. 983/567, emph. orig.; transl. alt.; see also pp. 225/129–30). Weber also notes the *Occidental city* as forming antecedent conditions: the "communal feeling of an urban citizenry," together with an emancipation from magic in these cities, constituted an antecedent condition for the development of citizenship and democracy (see *GEH*, pp. 315–31/270–83; *E&S*, pp. 1236–65/741–57; and Bendix's summary [1962, pp. 77–8]), as well as both pariah and petty-bourgeois intellectualism (see *E&S*, p. 508/309).
37   In light of this emphasis upon diachronic interaction, Weber would reject Parsons's well-known criticism. Ideal types imply, Parsons aruges, that social change takes place only in an abrupt, even revolutionary fashion; they inadequately attend to gradual, cumulative, and interrelated changes (see 1963, pp. lxiv–lxv). However, Weber's perpetual references to the modes – legacies and antecedent conditions – by which the past permanently penetrates into the present call into question the very occurrence of abrupt and qualitative change. Even the advent of ethical salvation religions, for example, which were everywhere initially carried by charismatic prophets, did not imply an immediate and severe break with the past: "The promises of the religions of salvation at first remained tied to ritualist rather than to ethical preconditions" ("I," p. 273/245; see also e.g. *E&S*, p. 577/349).

First, they neglect an assessment of the capacity of stable action-orienta-tions to defend themselves and impede the transformation of social action. They simply assume, once the causal chain has been formed, that such patterned action will be overcome. The emphasis in Weber's sociology upon the ways in which the four types of social action may call forth regular action, his formulation of a vast range of orders, legitimate orders, and sociological loci, and his stress upon the manner in which individuals at-tribute legitimation to rulership all express the great stability of action (see chapter 1, pp. 32–47).[38]

Second, causal chains offer no means of ascertaining the relative strength of particular causal forces. In separating "facilitating" from "necessary" factors, Weber practices a research strategy that in principle distinguishes degrees of causal centrality.

A final weakness of the causal chain approach calls attention to a general weakness in all approaches that attend only to interaction, whether synchronic or diachronic: the obliviousness to the embeddedness of single factors in discrete social contexts and the ways in which varying contexts may assert diverse influences upon these single factors. This occurs even to such a degree that the same factor will often, depending upon its context, have a different effect. The causal chain approach neglects just this consid-eration. Weber, on the other hand, isolates and notes as causally significant in itself, first, the *interaction* of significant action-orientations in discrete social contexts and, second, the possible crystallization, as a result of this interaction, of significant causal forces.[39] This is the subject of the following section.

However pivotal they are throughout Weber's substantive texts and how-ever vividly they convey the importance he attributes to the past in all analyses of the present, the "legacy" and "antecedent conditions" modes of diachronic interaction never establish, for him, adequate causality. They do so as little as his distinction between facilitating and necessary action-orientations or his emphasis upon synchronic interactions of action. This remains the case even when the theoretical framework provided by the *E&S* societal domains and domain-specific ideal types is kept in mind. One further stage of his practiced causal methodology must be reconstructed:

38   Weber ponders: "There arises the question of how anything could ever change in this inert mass of canonized custom which, just because it is considered as binding, seems as though it could never give birth to anything new" (*E&S*, p. 754/442; transl. alt.). Collins's reconstruction of Weber's "last theory of capitalism" (1981), which constitutes a strong contribution, depends too heavily upon the causal chain concept and neglects the ways in which, for Weber, configu-rations of forces interact in a dynamic fashion. Weber's central notions of "context" and "conjunction" (see below) are entirely absent. Furthermore, Collins is unable to offer criteria that distinguish the stages in his causal chain (intermediate, background, and ultimate condi-tions) clearly from one another.
39   Schluchter's analysis of "the rise of Western rationalism" (1981) fails to address these three problems.

the *conjunctural* interaction of patterned action. Because this interaction takes place in reference to a *full* spectrum of causal action-orientations, Weber must be again distinguished from the world systems and causal analytic schools.

Conjunctural interaction and the context of patterned action

The causal analyses in Weber's substantive texts repeatedly chart the manner in which patterned action takes place within a delineated *context* of multiple action-orientations.[40] When this occurs, regular action interacts in a manner qualitatively different from the linear synchronic and diachronic interactions identified thus far; a conjunctural, or dynamic, interaction takes place. This interaction itself places a significant causal thrust into motion. If adequate causality is to be established, the isolation and clear identification of these interactions are, according to Weber, crucial. Before defining conjunctural interaction, the manner in which his comparative-historical texts attend to contexts of multiple action-orientations must be briefly examined.

However closely regular action may appear bound into linear causal chains, it is always, Weber's empirical texts testify, in principle influenced by a context of action-orientations. Paul's announcement of universal participation in the Eucharist, for example, clearly enunciated the notion of citizenship, yet the cluster of action-orientations implied by this notion became sociologically significant only when a new context of action-orientations – one dominated by cities and strong urban guilds – arose nearly a thousand years later (*RofI*, pp. 37–8/39–40). Similarly, Weber saw that a unique feature of early Christianity's organization – "the fact that the church's functionaries were holders of rationally defined bureaucratic offices" – disappeared temporarily as the feudalism of the early Middle Ages became dominant, only to become, once the context of patterned action had changed, "revived and . . . all-powerful in the eleventh century" (*E&S*, pp. 828–9/480). Weber notes as well specific action-orientations in respect to contexts of regular action: sheer compulsion as a basis for discipline remains latent as long as ethical action dominates, yet becomes overt and "emerges as an irreducible *caput mortuum* in all situations in which the ethical qualities of duty and conscientiousness have failed" (*E&S*, p. 1150/682, transl. alt.). The rise of charismatic leaders also depends upon a context of action-orientations.[41] Even ethical prophecy, which Weber sees as a great charismatic force capable of shattering stereotyped ritual norms and revolutionizing daily life (see, for example, E&S, pp. 577/349, 1116–17/657–8),

---

40   This remains the case even though Weber never discusses succinctly the importance of the social context of regular action-orientations for the establishment of adequate causality.
41   Such leaders are often viewed in the secondary literature on Weber as appearing solely on the basis of personal features.

is normally dependent for its development upon the existence of a "certain minimum of intellectual culture" (*E&S*, p. 486/296).[42]

This concern in Weber's causal analyses with the context of patterned action is manifest as well in his repeated attention to the question of what *can* become sociologically significant in a specific milieu. His magisterial "IR" essay, for example, takes as one of its major threads a vast comparative and historical attempt to demarcate the social, economic, rulership, and religious setting within which a brotherhood ethic can become viable (see "IR," for example, pp. 329–40/542–54; "SV," p. 155/612). Moreover, Weber's focus upon the question of "what can become sociologically significant," given contextual constraints, turns his analyses to conditions that *prevent* a particular development from becoming significant. In light of the withdrawal of "the most sublime values" from all public realms into the private domain of intimacy and brotherliness, it is not surprising that "our greatest art is intimate and not monumental" ("SV," p. 155/612). Nor is it accidental that, within this milieu, a monumental style cannot be simply "invented."[43] Similarly, within a context of intellectualization, disenchantment, and a withdrawal of sublime values into the private realm, great prophets can no longer, by the force of their personalities, weld communities together and give birth to new religions ("SV," p. 155/612). Such an acknowledgment of contexts extends even to a quite specific level. For example, Weber argues that the revisions of the Book of the Covenant that were incorporated into Deuteronomy could have occurred only in the

42 The central importance throughout Weber's comparative-historical sociology of the embeddedness of regular social action in contexts of action constellations has never been acknowledged in the secondary literature. Most commentators upon his substantive texts – e.g. Parsons (1937, 1963), Schluchter (1981, 1989), Bendix (1962, p. 271, n.23), Mommsen (1989, p. 153), Ragin and Zaret (1980), and Alexander (1983) – have neglected his contextual emphasis in respect to causality. All have identified, in this respect, just the starting points. A passage from Smelser, which emphasizes the "yardstick" usage of ideal types, tends to be typical: "For Weber, the principal source of sociological explanation lies in the generation of one or more ideal-type constructions of the subjective meaning complex of actors and the comparison of these expectations with the best available data" (1976, p. 67). Roth's various discussions focus only upon the model character of the ideal type (1971c, pp. 85–93; Roth and Schluchter, 1979, pp. 125–7, 198). He otherwise notes Weber's "structural approach to history" (Roth and Schluchter, 1979, pp. 177–8), his developmental history (1981, 1987, pp. 80–90), and very preliminary "comparative devices": the "negative comparison," the "illustrative analogy," the "metaphorical analogy" (see 1968, p. xliii; 1971c, p. 81) and the "ideal-typical approach" (1971c, pp. 82–4). Weber's emphasis upon the social context of action is nowhere to be found. Even Warner, who otherwise identifies important procedures utilized throughout the comparative-historical texts, ignores this aspect (1972). Collins, as noted, focusses heavily upon "prerequisites" and "causal chains" (1981, pp. 934–6; 1986). Actually, Smelser tends to be most aware of the contextual level in Weber's comparative-historical writings (see 1976, pp. 123, 139–141, 144–5). Yet he remains unsystematic in this respect and falls back on the one hand to a focus upon an "autonomous logic . . . which programs action" and on the other hand upon "conditions" (Smelser, 1976, pp. 126–8, 135).
43 These phrases – "it is no accident that" and "it is not surprising" – frequently conclude Weber's analyses.

period "when the realm of Judah was in fact almost identical with the polis of Jerusalem with its small satellite towns and villages" (*AJ*, pp. 65–6/71).[44] The centrality of this question – what factors can become sociologically significant? – is apparent as well throughout Weber's comparative-historical texts in a number of analyses that pay close attention to the setting within which innovation takes place.[45]

Each milieu[46] of regular action-orientations places a particular imprint upon patterned action. In the process, its impact as well as its substance is shaped. The action-orientations themselves, or the fact of their appearance, fail to capture Weber's attention; rather, the social setting within which they occur remains central.[47] Because the "beginnings" of nearly all conceivable developments have occurred universally,[48] he argues frequently that a focus upon questions of origins alone is relatively unimportant (see, for example, *E&S*, pp. 1050/709, 1087/638; "I," p. 295/268; "AI," pp. 13–17/1–4, 20–3/6–9). The *context* of patterned action remains decisive if new action-orientations are to expand and attain sociological significance. Weber seeks, throughout his comparative-historical writings, to integrate "the 'particular fact' . . . as a real causal factor into a real, hence concrete context" ("Logic," p. 135/237).[49]

This emphasis throughout Weber's substantive texts upon the ways in which regular action is embedded in demarcated contexts of action prevents him from upholding a crucial assumption of Durkheimian sociology: a single cause always produces a single effect.[50] For the same reason, he rejects as well the position that the factors necessary to explain causally the development of certain patterned action must be present in all similar cases. For example: "We have no intention whatever of maintaining such a foolish and doctrinaire thesis as that the 'spirit of capitalism' *could only* have arisen as the result of certain effects of the Reformation" (*PE*, p. 91/83; emph.

44   Weber provides a "sociology of knowledge" of the Book of the Covenant generally at *AJ*, pp. 61–89/66–98.
45   Weber does see a great deal of inter-cultural "borrowing." However, he opposes all diffusionist views. See note 15 above.
46   I am using the terms "context," "milieu," and "setting" synonymously.
47   This strong emphasis upon the context within which action takes place, rather than the nature of the action itself, further separates Weber, in addition to his attention to *four* types of social action and the varying intensity of action (see chapters 1 and 2), sharply from all rational choice theories.
48   For example, in respect to philosophical thought and Asia: "It can here be certified . . . that, in the area of thought concerning the 'meaning' of the world and life, there is actually nothing which has not, in *some* form, already been thought about in Asia" (*RofI*, p. 331/365; transl. alt.).
49   Thus, Weber's attention to the context of patterned action is apparent not only in respect to his linking of agency and structure through sociological loci (see chapter 1, pp. 39–46) and in respect to model-building (see chapter 4, pp. 98–102); it plays a pivotal part in his causal methodology as well. In his methodological writings the clearest example of this emphasis is provided by his discussion of Goethe's letters to Frau von Stein (see "Logic," pp. 138–49/241–51) and by his notion of "cultural significance" (see "Obj," pp. 77–81/176–81).
50   Abbott refers to this axiom as the "univocal meaning" principle (see 1988, pp. 175–6).

orig.).[51] Similarly, Weber notes that the praise by sages of "obedience, silence and an absence of hybris" found its source in Egypt in "bureaucratic subordination," while in Israel "it sprang from the plebeian nature of the patronage" (see *AJ*, pp. 218/232–3).

Weber's attention to the context of action-orientations follows from a specific position: his empirical investigations led him to conclude that the interaction of patterned action within a milieu of multiple regularities of action occurs in a *conjunctural* fashion. A distinct *dynamic* may occur as a consequence of the juxtaposition of two sets of recurring action-orientations, and a further dynamic may be set into motion by the presence of additional patterned action. Conjunctural interactions take place in both cases, and such interactions call forth qualitatively new action-orientations of sociological significance. Indeed, a distinct strengthening or weakening of regular action may occur as a result of conjunctural interactions; degrees of causal centrality – whether unimportant, facilitating or necessary – may change. No unfluctuating, fixed entities independent of the influence of other factors; no "monotonic causal flow" in which causality moves in only one direction; no assumption of a "constant relevance" in which a "given cause is equally relevant at all times"; and no "unity of time and horizon" in which the large causes the small, the enduring the fleeting, characterize the causal analyses in Weber's comparative-historical texts (see Abbott, 1988, pp. 172–5; Coser, 1975).[52] Weber's substantive writings testify that even the ordering of forces, or "sequence effects," is crucial in respect to a specific outcome (see also Abbott, 1983; 1984; 1988, pp. 177–8; 1989; Abbott and Forrest, 1986). Indeed, at times kaleidoscopic alterations take place that lead to a dynamic fusing of heretofore separately unfolding patterns of action-orientations. Often fully unforeseen developments are called forth.[53]

However heuristically helpful it may be to conceptualize patterned action as in isolation or as clustered in hypothesis-forming models on the one hand, as Weber asserts, and as interacting synchronically and diachronically on the other hand, as he also asserts, empirical reality always implies a complex interaction of multiple past and present recurring action-orienta-

51 In searching for "value equivalents" of "the Protestant ethic," the modernization literature of the 1960s implicitly downplayed the contextuality of Weber's thesis.
52 These are all Abbott's terms. He has, among contemporary sociologists, most forcefully argued these points. He sees a widespread assumption of "general linear reality" in contemporary sociology (1988, pp. 169–81, esp. pp. 180–1; see also 1983, 1984, 1989), although this is less so the case in regard to the world systems, interpretive historical, and causal analytic approaches, all of which – albeit to varying degrees in respect to a pluralism of causal forces – stress contextuality and conjunctural interactions. Coser undertakes a parallel critique (1975), though one less differentiated conceptually than Abbott's. See especially Coser's commentary upon the missing "relational" dimension in the occupational stratification and social class literature.
53 An entire chapter could be written on the subject of unforeseen consequences in Weber's sociology. This notion, which reappears throughout his substantive texts, is often rooted in the centrality of conjunctural interactions in his works.

tions and the alteration of each as a consequence of this interaction. This position is clear throughout Weber's substantive texts. The prominence of conjunctural interaction in his comparative-historical sociology requires a fundamental acknowledgment: if the presence of regular action is to be explained at the level of adequate causality, necessary synchronic and diachronic forces must not only be present and even not only present simultaneously; they must also interact in a "correct" dynamic. To Weber: "The totality of *all* the conditions . . . [must] 'act jointly' [*zusammenwirken*] in a certain way and in no other if the concrete effect and no other is to be allowed to appear" ("Logic," p. 187/289; transl. alt.; emph. orig.). His practiced causal methodology insists that *broad* conjunctural interactions must be identified if an explanation is to reach the level of adequate causality. While they also acknowledge conjunctural interactions, the causal analytic and world systems schools fail to do so, as Weber's theoretical framework requires, by reference to a radical pluralism of causal action-orientations.

The manner in which conjunctural interactions play a central part in the causal methodology hidden between the lines of Weber's comparative-historical writings can be demonstrated by three reconstructed examples: the rise of monotheism, the impersonal view of the supernatural in India, and Confucianism. These brief illustrations will include reference to synchronic and diachronic interactions as well. Nearly all regularities of action noted imply necessary causality. Reference to the societal domains and domain-specific ideal types of *E&S* repeatedly assists identification of such causally direct patterns of action; others are acknowledged as specific to the particular empirical development under investigation. Weber's analysis proceeds in a back and forth movement between the *E&S* theoretical framework and the specific empirical case under investigation.

The rise of monotheism   A dynamic interaction of past and present action-orientations proved critical in allowing the traditions set forth by the early prophets in ancient Palestine to become causally effective in the transformation of Yahwe from a regional and warrior deity to a monotheistic God. The old seers and auditory prophets, although powerful among the "plain people," could not become too outspoken under the United Monarchy (*c.* 1004–928 BC). Just as centralized regimes everywhere circumscribed charisma, Solomon's patrimonial bureaucracy and the priesthood stratum silenced these heroic opponents whenever possible (*AJ*, p. 112/121). As the old free prophecy declined in importance, oracle-giving and auditory prophecy became "kingly prophecy" (*AJ*, pp. 98/107, 104/113, 268/282–3).[54] Nonetheless, the charismatic seers and early prophets were not totally stifled. The legacy they had established (the memory of Moses, the Cov-

54   That is, a class of ritually-trained royal priests arose in the period of peace brought by the United Monarchy. Totally controlled by the kings, these "cult priests of the kingly temples" were treated as royal officials and played no noteworthy independent political or religious role (*AJ*, pp. 163/175, 169/181).

enant [*berith*] idea, and the importance of upholding Yahwe's command-ments) reasserted itself when the context of action-orientations changed: when kingship declined and warfare broke out between Israel and its neigh-boring kingdoms.

The decline of patrimonial–bureaucratic kingship, with its hierarchical command, officials, rent masters, army officers, specialized administrators, and royal "strategists" and scribes, indicated a general demise of central-ized control. Within this new, more open milieu, the "classical scriptural prophets" could more freely voice their warnings and appeals to the Israel-ites (*E&S*, p. 418/257). Indeed, because of warfare, these charismatic figures found good reason to intensify their pleas for obedience to Yahwe's com-mandments and a forsaking of false gods, if only because evil and warfare, according to the sacred Covenant, indicated Yahwe's dissatisfaction with his chosen people. The constant threat of warfare over several centuries and the declining prestige of the worldly monarchy brought about not only an aggrandizement in the power of these prophets, but also an ascendance of their god Yahwe to a newfound stature. Moreover, as their appeals grew more shrill, the memory of Moses and the Covenant, in part forgotten under the rulership of the kings, emerged and became paramount. Amidst warfare, decline, and even social chaos, the image voiced by the classical prophets acquired a newfound urgency and credibility: the hallowed figure became the peaceful and devout peasant or shepherd of the Old Confed-eracy (*c.* 1180–1004 BC) (*AJ*, p. 224/239). Not surprisingly, the patrimonial-bureaucratic kingdom of the United Monarchy became perceived as a "defection from Yahwe, the real ruler of the people" (*E&S*, p. 450/274).

The advocacy of the old ideals and a return to the "good old times" found a receptive hearing, namely in that stratum severed from magical beliefs and practices and now less strictly dominated by patrimonial rulership: the urban plebeians. Increasingly, a knowledge of Yahwe's com-mandments became "decisive for the worth and authority of the individual" (*AJ*, p. 224/239). Indeed, a situation arose in which a plebeian stratum became the carrier of a religious ethic that emphasized ethical action. Even among intellectuals, the "nomadic ideal," Yahwe's commandments, and ethical action became central (*AJ*, pp. 224/238–9). To Weber: "One of the secrets of the development of Yahwism lies . . . in the interaction between an enthused stratum of intellectuals and this public composed of demilita-rized and socially declassed strata under the impact of social change dur-ing the time of the kings" (*AJ*, p. 206/220). Past and present action-orientations within a conducive context of patterned action now interacted conjuncturally; a dynamic of forces occurred in such a fashion that all isolated thrusts toward monotheism became intensified. A god of the universe arose, all-mighty above all other deities, omniscient and omnipotent, ubiquitous and majestic: "The ancient warrior god of the Confederacy, who had become the local god of the city of Jerusalem, took on the prophetic and universalistic traits of transcendently sacred omnipotence and inscrutability" (*E&S*, pp. 418–19/257; see also *AJ*, p. 245/261).[55]

The rise of the impersonal view of the supernatural in India   Weber's causal analysis of the rise of the impersonal view of the supernatural realm in the Classical (*c.* 600 BC–700 AD) and Middle Ages (*c.* 700–1200 AD) epochs in India provides another example of his attention in his substantive texts to *conjunctural*, as well as synchronic and diachronic, interaction.

He viewed the predominance of magic in Vedic, or pre-Classical (*c.* 1200–600 BC), India as of extreme intensity (*RofI*, pp. 26–7/28–9). Its omnipresence among both the Vedic priesthood and the Kshatriya princes had the effect of accustoming these status groups to a specific conception of the supernatural. Unlike the constriction of the transcendental realm in historic Israel to the special relationship of the Israelites to Yahwe, the dominance of magic in India led to a conception of the supernatural as impersonal, abstract, and amorphous. This view of "the beyond" remained suppressed, however, as long as charismatic heroes, a feudal ethic, and mighty anthropomorphic, warrior gods were ascendant (see, for example, *RofI*, p. 124/124). Yet this "political feudalism" in India's pre-Classical epoch was anchored mainly in the charisma and feudal ethic of noble sibs rather than, as in the Occidental Middle Ages, in legal and economic structures (see *RofI*, pp. 63–6/64–8; *RofC*, pp. 33–4/314–15). As a consequence, Brahmin and Buddhist intellectuals, once constituted as cohesive status groups in the Classical and Middle Ages periods and allied with various strata and organizations, acquired the power to confront feudalism and slowly to introduce patrimonial rulership and pacification (*RofI*, pp. 57–63/59–64, 125–33/125–33).

As this transformation took place, the individualized hero gods specific to feudalism and warfare faded. In their place, the amorphous and diffuse conception of the transcendent compatible with magic, mysticism, pacification, patrimonialism, and the intellectual strata began its ascent. The impersonal view of "the beyond" resonated in particular with the religious inclinations of intellectuals (see *E&S*, pp. 500–17/304–14; "I," p. 282/254) and the impersonal functioning of the patrimonial bureaucracy (see *E&S*, p. 431/263). The power of this status group and form of rulership became dramatically enhanced in Classical India. Eventually, unification and pacification combined with the protest against Vedic ritual by charismatic magicians, cultured Brahmin intellectuals, and the educated sons of the Kshatriya knights, amidst a conjunctural interaction of action-orientations, to revive the impersonal view of the supernatural realm (*RofI*, p. 183/175). It ascended to a position of absolute supremacy in the Middle Ages and became the cornerstone for the mystical and contemplative elements in Hinduism and Buddhism.

55   For a complete reconstruction of Weber's analysis of the rise of monotheism, see Kalberg, forthcoming b.

The rise of Confucianism   Weber emphasizes as well, in his analysis of the rise of Confucianism, a unique context of action-orientations. Within this context separate patterns of action crucial to the development of Confucianism and its entrenchment conjuncturally interacted in the post-Classical era in China (*c.* 200–800 AD).

Purely historical factors in late Classical China (*c.* 100 BC–200 AD) brought about social changes that led to an altered context within which long-term and recent developments fused. This occurred to such an extent that old and new action-orientations interacted in a "correct" dynamic. Some of these multiple forces became powerful simply as a consequence of the new context of action-orientations called forth by such historical changes. The (*a*) final victory of patrimonial rulership over feudal rulership, (*b*) pacification of the empire, and (*c*) crystallization of the literati as a cohesive stratum proved critical for the surmounting of the major obstacles to the rise of Confucianism and the setting into motion of a strong and unique dynamic of action-orientations that carried the expansion of this world religion.

The eventual defeat of feudal rulership and its replacement by patrimonialism occurred, according to Weber, in part as a consequence of the necessity for princes competing for power to introduce more rational economic policies (*RofC*, pp. 41/322–3), and in part as a result of the ever-present requirement to regulate mighty rivers more systematically. This latter factor, more than any other, crushed the universal tendency of specially-trained armored knights to bring forth an "individualist" social order (see *RofC*, pp. 24–5/303; *E&S*, pp. 1105/650, 1154/685). Moreover, in contrast to feudalism in the West, which was rooted in the economic and legal structures of its age through landlordism, Chinese "political feudalism," as its counterpart in India, remained based solely upon the charisma of distinguished sibs and their legitimating status ethic (see *RofC*, pp. 34–6/314–17, 42/324–5). Consequently, this form of rulership was destined to collapse once a patrimonial bureaucracy, anchored securely by the constant necessity to regulate great rivers and supported by the Confucian ethic, began to thread its way through this civilization.

The gradual pacification of the empire, especially after the completion of the Great Wall, and its unification hastened the decline of "the really sacred order of the fathers" and strengthened patrimonial rulership (*E&S*, p. 1050/611). Moreover, with pacification and the hegemony of patrimonialism, the strongest personal gods known to Chinese history – those that arose as warrior deities during the pre-Confucian Warring States period – faded and eventually became transformed into the impersonal "Heaven." The simultaneous crystallization of the literati into a cohesive stratum and the alliance of members of this stratum, as ritualist advisers and administrators, with patrimonial princes also played a central part in bringing about the demise of the feudal age of "great families," individualist heroes, warrior deities, and firm status prescriptions. As Weber notes: "Feudal elements in the social order receded further and further and patrimonialism became, in all essential respects, the structural form fundamental to the spirit of Confucianism" (*RofC*, p. 47/330; transl. alt.; see also *E&S*, pp. 1048–9/ 609–10).

The separate major forces in the cluster of action-orientations decisive for the development of Confucianism – the clan, patrimonial rulership, the literati stratum, magic, and the examination system – could now crystallize into a configuration of dynamically interweaving and reinforcing, necessary patterns of action in the post-Classical epoch. This took place as the empire became united and pacified and even though the competition between various philosophical schools continued, especially in those periods when imperial power declined. "The literati and their disciples . . . came to compete for the existing offices," as unification and pacification proceeded, "and this development could not fail to result in a unified orthodox doctrine adjusted to the situation.This doctrine was to be *Confucianism*" (*RofC*, p. 112/401; emph. orig.).

Instead of, in any sense, a deviation from the worldly values dominant in China in the sib group, the literati stratum, and patrimonial rulership, Confucianism remained a captive of these mundane values. In this religion the values of the sib group, the literati, and patrimonial rulership interacted conjuncturally and become articulated as a coherent body of teachings (see *RofC*, pp. 164–5/453). According to Weber, this world religion is unique in the degree to which it can be viewed as a "bureaucratic philosophy" and as a "status" religion (*E&S*, p. 1049/610; *RofC*, pp. 226–49/512–36; "I," pp. 268/239, 293/266). Further and deeper conjunctural interactions occurred with the development of the literati into a firm status group, their elevation to the position of this world religion's dominant carrier, and their transformation from wandering intellectuals into officials of patrimonial rulers. Confucianism became entrenched. Moreover, the emperor became fully dependent upon the mandarins: "'Constitutionally' . . . the emperor could rule only by using certified literati as officials; 'classically' he could rule only by using orthodox Confucian officials" (*RofC*, p. 141/430).[56] Anchored by a profound animism that viewed every innovation as capable of conjuring up evil spirits, a rigidity and enduring unchangeableness became characteristic of this world religion (*RofC*, p. 233/519). It attained a full victory over its competitors in the eighth century AD.[57]

These brief examples must suffice to demonstrate the importance of conjunctural interactions of patterned action in Weber's causal analyses. Such interactions alone, by capturing the manner in which present and past action-orientations are integrated into a context of multiple and dynamically interacting action-orientations, provide adequate causal explanations.

56 In 690 AD the T'ang dynasty formulated statutes that protected the literati's high social position, regulated their duties, and established colleges for their education (see *RofC*, pp. 116–17/405–6).
57 For a detailed analysis, see Kalberg, forthcoming a.

Because Weber downplays the origin and mere appearance of regular action and stresses instead the social setting within which patterned action expands and becomes causally significant, the entire vocabulary of all monocausal schools of thought – idealist, materialist, structuralist, instrumentalist, utilitarian, decisionist – must be abandoned at the outset if his practiced causal methodology is to be accurately comprehended. This vocabulary, as well as all causal chain procedures and rational choice theories, neglects the manner in which contexts of multiple action-orientations create *new* interactions. Nor does this vocabulary do justice to the Weberian view of "society" as constituted from multiple interacting, as well as potentially independent, action patterns and unrepeatable configurations. Again, to Weber: "the totality of *all* the conditions ... [must] 'act jointly' in a certain way and in no other if the concrete effect and no other is to be allowed to appear" ("Logic," p. 187/289; emph. orig.).

A detailed illustration will define more precisely the major components of Weber's mode of causal analysis: the three stages of his practiced causal methodology (facilitating and necessary action-orientations, synchronic and diachronic interactions of action, and contextual-conjunctural interactions of action) and the means of orientation provided by the societal domains and domain-specific ideal types articulated in Weber's analytic treatise, *E&S*. Such an illustration will also delineate more sharply his causal procedures and strategies vis-à-vis the world systems, interpretive historical, and causal analytic schools and demonstrate their usefulness.

An Illustration: the Dominance of the Caste System in India

This section reconstructs one of Weber's own causal analyses: the rise to a position of preeminence of the caste system in India.[58] Together, the three stages of his causal methodology and the *E&S* theoretical framework guide his questioning as he approaches unfamiliar terrain.[59]

58 It is no coincidence that this example is taken from *EEWR* rather than *E&S*. The latter, as an analytic treatise, simply does not yield, even through reconstruction, complete analyses at the level of causal adequacy. This remains the case despite Weber's interjection of causal statements and short causal analyses throughout *E&S*. Even *EEWR*, however, frequently violates Weber's mode of causal analysis. For example, Weber often treats action-orientations to the economy and religion in isolation rather than addressing the complicated ways in which they intermix and interact. For this reason, this illustration constitutes a reconstruction. Furthermore, it must be emphasized that Weber's *mode of causal analysis* remains the focus rather than e.g. the accuracy of Weber's historical scholarship. Contemporary scholars have disputed Weber's dating and historical facts on a number of occasions (see Zingerle, 1972, 1981; Rösel, 1986; Kantowsky, 1986; Schluchter, 1983, 1984).
59 The usage of ideal types in this illustration conforms almost entirely to the "yardstick usage" (see chapter 3, pp. 87–91). This results from the focus in this chapter upon Weber's mode of causal analysis rather than upon his models (the dynamic, contextual, elective affinity, relations of antagonism, and developmental) as such. Again, the formation of such models

The modest fashion in which Weber employs this orientational mechanism must be emphasized. Reference to the domains and domain-specific ideal types of *E&S* assists the identification of causally-significant patterns of action. In this manner, it provides a helpful frame of reference for research. It must, however, always be acknowledged as incomplete in respect to the case or development under investigation: it never "encompasses" complex empirical reality. Rather, it serves to "uproot" comparative-historical sociologists from an exclusive focus upon empirical reality by engaging them in a continuous back and forth movement between the particular situation and the heuristic construct. Thus, although reference to the societal domains and domain-specific ideal types assists identification of many significant factors specific to the case under investigation, others – in India, for example, the Hindu Restoration, changes in Hinduism's organizational form, the alliance of the Kshatriya princes and the Hindu Brahmins, and a technological innovation that strengthened the Kshatriya ruling caste – will always fall outside the *E&S* theoretical framework. In sum, the reconstructed analysis to follow proceeds by reference to (*a*) the central stages of Weber's causal methodology;[60] (*b*) the means of orientation provided by the societal domains and domain-specific ideal types of *E&S*; and (*c*) empirical patterned action-orientations unique to the case under investigation.

To Weber, the ubiquitous hegemony of the caste system appeared as the distinguishing aspect of the civilization of India. Its dominance proved so strong that all protesting groups were simply assimilated, and its advance proceeded along an irresistible course of continuing expansion from the third century AD until the beginning of Islamic rule a millennium later. Weber asks: "From whence is this caste order, found nowhere or only incipiently elsewhere, and why, of all things in India?" (*RofI*, p. 123/122).

At the outset, he rejects, by reference to comparative examples, the hypothesis that liturgical guild organizations or the progression of occupational differentiation could have stood at the beginning of its deep segregations. He also opposes the biological theories popular in his time that accounted for culture and class differences by a peculiar "race psychology," "blood," "soul," or "gifts" (*RofI*, pp. 123–4/123; see also "AI," pp. 30–1/15–16). Weber instead scrutinizes the Classical (*c.* 600 BC–700 AD) and Middle Ages (*c.* 700–1200 AD) epochs for clues regarding the caste system's origins. He is convinced that "All factors important for the development of the caste system operated singly also elsewhere in the world. Only in India, however, did they operate conjointly under particular Indian conditions"

---

constitutes, for Weber, an important *preliminary* stage prior to causal investigation: they assist conceptualization and the analytic ordering of the particular empirical case or development.
60   For reasons of space, only one of the two diachronic interaction concepts ("legacy") has been employed.

(RofI, p. 131/131; transl. alt.). An array of patterned action-orientations congealed to firmly entrench the caste order.[61]

Degrees of causal centrality

Facilitating factors   Facilitating action-orientations, as noted, constitute widespread background forces relevant to the rise and spread of specific patterns of action. Rather than being powerful and directly causal, they serve as "favoring" forces. Weber surveys broadly the empirical terrain at this foundational stage of his methodology, and thus the social domains and domain-specific ideal types of *E&S* provide only marginal guidance.

A highly diverse ethnic composition in India contributed to a social landscape within which a caste order could unfold. The fact that each of India's innumerable guest peoples and pariah tribes possessed a particular historical heritage, specialized ritual, and, in many cases, practiced only a specific occupation, prohibited social mixing from the earliest times. Often, interaction between certain tribes was magically tabooed. These differences in respect to style of life were often made socially visible and reaffirmed by contrasts of skin color (*RofI*, pp. 123–5/123–5, 130/130). A configuration of "building blocks" also facilitated the development of the caste system:

> Ancient Indian conditions ... provided the building blocks [*Bausteine*] for the caste system: the interethnic specialization of labor, the development of innumerable guest and pariah peoples, the organization of village crafts on the basis of hereditary artisan cotters, the monopoly of internal trade by guest traders, the small extent of urban development, and the flow of occupational specialization into channels of hereditary status segregation and monopolization of patronage. (*RofI*, p. 130/130)

This ritually-sanctioned, mutual segregation of guest peoples, as well as sib and village endogamy, could never, Weber asserts, support action-orientations powerful enough to allow a free participation in the marketplace and the development of an independent citizenry, nor could it call forth religious groups based in congregations. The consequent estrangement of the various ethnic groupings had the effect of enhancing the possibility that a prestigeful and unified caste could order the ethnic groups and economic classes into a social hierarchy.

All these forces favored the development of the caste system. However, through a series of straightforward comparisons, Weber concluded that these action-orientations existed widely in a variety of civilizations, none of which developed a caste order. Thus, none constituted powerful causal

61 Weber offers a short discussion in *RofI* (pp. 123–33/121–33). This analysis, however, constitutes only an incomplete outline of the analysis contained in *RofI* as a whole and, sporadically, in *E&S*.

patterned action and none could be elevated above the status of a facilitating cause. Nonetheless, assessment of these action-orientations did assist Weber to identify more direct, or necessary, factors.

Necessary action-orientations: clan charisma, the Brahmins, Classical Hinduism, the Hindu Restoration, and changes in Hinduism's organizational form   The *E&S* societal domains and domain-specific ideal types enter more forcefully as a theoretical framework at this stage of Weber's causal methodology. They guide his attempts to isolate and define crucial causal forces. At the same time, Weber refuses to view this frame of reference as encompassing empirical reality to such an extent that it might be relied upon to offer an "exhaustive" inventory of necessary causal action-orientations. Rather, patterned action endogenous to the particular empirical case is in principle recognized. Neither "completely theoretical" nor "completely inductive," Weber's search for causally necessary forces proceeds in a back and forth movement between the *E&S* orientational mechanism and the specific empirical terrain. Thus, the *E&S* heuristic construct assists the identification of clan charisma, a status group (the Brahmins), and a world religion (Hinduism) as necessary causal forces, while his empirical investigation also reveals that two developments fully beyond the *E&S* conceptual framework constitute as well powerful and direct causal patterns of action: the Hindu Restoration and changes in Hinduism's organizational form.[62]

Clan charisma   The unrestricted development of "political feudalism" in pre-Classical times in India not only introduced mighty hero gods and a more differentiated "individualism" than arose in China, but also greatly strengthened the orientations of action toward clan charisma, or the belief that the supernatural quality of charisma adheres not only to a unique person but also to his sibs.[63] The European notion of the "divine right of kings" rests upon such a belief in the extraordinary qualities of the clan, as does the esteem claimed by the Boston "blue blood." When distributed throughout clans, charisma had the effect of stereotyping clan differences, thus contributing to estrangement and strengthening taboos against fraternization. To Weber, clan charisma ordered Indian civilization more than any other form of social organization and became "the decisive underpinning of the Brahmin caste" in the Classical epoch (*RofI*, pp. 49–50/51–2, 54/56–7, 107/105, 125–6/124–6).

Originally charisma, as a magical and extraordinary power of rare individuals, fully opposed the notion of its hereditary transfer (see *E&S*, pp. 241–9/140–4, 1111–48/654–81), yet this route of succession eventually became predominant in India (see *RofI*, p. 53/56). At the time of the early

---

62   Necessary, as facilitative, action-orientations are identified in Weber's texts as well through comparative analysis.

63   Clan charisma can be analytically located by reference to the *E&S* societal domains: it constitutes a fusion of charismatic rulership and the clan universal organization. See *E&S*, pp. 1135–9/671–3.

Vedas (*c.* 1200–1000 BC), when the "priestly nobility divided according to hereditary function and appropriate clan charisma into hereditary 'schools'" (*RofI*, p. 54/57), each clan claimed to possess a magical charisma. Clan charisma expanded its influence throughout India as orientations of action toward magical charisma became attached to all positions of rulership. Eventually, the principle of clan charisma assumed an all-encompassing place (see *RofI*, pp. 50–1/52–3, 107/105; *E&S*, p. 223/147), indeed: "No matter how often individual charismatic upstarts and their freely recruited followings shattered the firm structure of the sibs, the social process always resumed its firm course of charismatic clan organization of tribes, phratries, and sibs" (*RofI*, pp. 54/56–7).

Because it ritually closed positions and professions, Weber asserts that the hereditary transmission of rulership and position through clan charisma accounted for the "nucleus of the caste formation" (*RofI*, p. 126/125). Regular action oriented to clan charisma was stronger in India than in any other country (*RofI*, pp. 50/52, 126/125).

The carrier stratum: the Brahmins   Weber's discussion of the caste order's earliest generation in the late Vedic and early Classical period (*c.* 800–500 BC) of Indian history mainly focusses upon the evolution of the Brahmins into a cohesive group of intellectuals and their subsequent slow and uneven ascent to a position of status and power superiority over the traditional Vedic priesthood. Without the pervasive influence of the Brahmins, the birth and endurance of the caste system would have been inconceivable (*RofI*, p. 131/131). The Brahmins were the earliest caste and the social carriers of Hinduism as well as Indian culture as a whole. By the sixth century BC they had consolidated their powers as the acknowledged and single possessors of spiritual authority. They achieved an even higher level of prestige by the fifth century BC: "The Brahmins who have learned the Vedas and teach them are human gods" (*RofI*, p. 142/140).

Because it transcended the boundaries of the separate pariah tribes and ethnic groups, the influence of the Brahmins was unrivaled. They utilized their monopoly over instruction in magical practices and their sacred knowledge of scriptures to regulate ritualistic economic differentiation as well as the grouping of pariah tribes and guest peoples, each estranged from the others. The Brahmins alone were empowered to assign caste rank for every ethnic and occupational group; they did so for the most part by a determination of the social distance between a given group and themselves (*RofI*, pp. 48/49, 129/129). By virtue of these powers, this status group became the single most important stratum in the establishment of the Indian social hierarchy and the caste system. They also defined authoritatively each caste's ritualistic *dharma*, or the particularistic responsibilities and indispensable tasks "desired by God" (*RofI*, pp. 29–30/31–2, 132/132).

The position and power of the Brahmins, however, failed to account for the long-term endurance and uncompromising rigidity of the caste system, nor for the general acceptance of it as legitimate.

Religion: Classical Hinduism's karma *and* samsara *doctrines*   In explaining the ordering of divine, human, and animal beings into castes, the "organic social ethic" rooted in the *karma* doctrine of ethical compensation and the *samsara* belief in the transmigration of souls laid the foundation for a coexistence of widely varying ethical codes that often stood in sharp conflict with one another (see *RofI*, p. 144/142). The diverse castes were viewed as constituent parts of an organism. A more favorable rebirth could be expected only by those persons who fulfilled the *dharma* incumbent upon their providentially-ordained caste within the organic order (*E&S*, p. 598/360). This remained the case for princes, warriors, judges, artisans, and peasants, as well as intellectuals, kings, robbers, and thieves.

To the extent that action oriented to the *karma* and *samsara* doctrines became entrenched in India, a perfect harmony between religious doctrine and caste particularism arose. The *karma* doctrine of compensation taught the perfunctory performance of caste ritual as the supreme loyalty, thereby justifying the coexistence of diverse ethical codes for different status groups and the ordering of all into castes of varying ranks (*RofI*, pp. 144/142–3). At the same time, the *karma* teaching provided lower castes with a consistent justification for acquiescence to the existing social order, while Hinduism's highest promise, the attainment of *gnosis*, valued absolute flight from this world and a mystic contemplation rather than inner-worldly conduct or, least of all, revolution.[64]

By knitting each individual into a harmonious cosmos of duties believed to be legitimate, castes and the *karma* and *samsara* doctrines provided Hindus with a thoroughly rational and metaphysically satisfying conception of the universe, one that offered hope for a higher rebirth to even the lowest pariah. For Weber, this "ethically-determined cosmos" was the "most consistent theodicy ever produced by history" (*E&S*, p. 599/361; *RofI*, p. 121/120): "Only the wedding of this thought product with the empirical social order through the promise of rebirth gave this order the irresistible power over thought and hope of members and furnished the fixed scheme for the religious and social integration of the various professional groups and pariah peoples" (*RofI*, p. 131/131). As a result of the belief that action-orientations toward the correct performance of caste ritual would lead to a favorable rebirth, the caste system received from this world religion a legitimating "spirit" and theodicy of inestimable power (*RofI*, p. 131/132).

The Hindu Restoration   The classical Hindu teachings fell into disfavor in the period from c. 200 BC to c. 200 AD when Buddhism prevailed across

---

64   Weber argues that the failure of the Hindu laity to develop any revolutionary ethics can be understood only in relation to the internalization by members of the lower castes of the belief that evil magic and unfavorable incarnation would result from any attempt to elevate one's status. Pious low-caste Hindus knew that faithful action-orientations toward caste *dharma* could transform them into a Kshatriya or a Brahmin – if only in the next life. Since the order and rank of the castes were eternal, they need only scrupulously adhere to *dharma* and wait patiently (see *E&S*, pp. 436/266, 493/300, 598/360; *RofI*, pp. 122/121–2).

the religious landscape and Jainism attained its maximum strength.[65] The competition with these youthful salvation religions, however, eventually led to the strengthening of Hinduism in the Indian Middle Ages: in order to gain and retain mass patronage, it became necessary to compromise the ancient soteriology and to "popularize" Hinduism's salvation paths. Because an abyss separated the "masses" immersed in magic and irrational orgiasticism from the Classical soteriology, a qualitative alteration of Hinduism became necessary. By successfully accommodating its teaching to the "religious qualifications" of disprivileged strata and terminating the situation in which Brahminhood took consideration of the plebeian and aliterary strata only as clients, the Hindu Restoration re-established the clear dominance of Hinduism against Buddhism and Jainism (*RofI*, pp. 330/364, 295/322, 153/155; "I," p. 289/262; *E&S*, p. 487/296).

The metamorphosis of the classical, impersonal All-One into personalized gods delineated the metaphysical framework for further changes. Magic and even, to some extent, orgiasticism began to permeate Hinduism, thereby compromising the classical salvation path of adherence to ritual. In addition, the founders of sects, as well as heroes, became deified; redeemer-saviors surfaced to aid the suffering masses, salvation through faith in these redeemers became widespread, and gurus arose as indispensable spiritual counselors. They, eventually, became worshipped themselves.[66] Thus, Hinduism transformed itself into a salvation religion characterized by the worship of deified, this-worldly, and personalized redeemers: "Not new doctrines but the universality of the guru authority symbolized the Restoration of Hinduism. . . . It was a "redeemer" religiosity in a special sense. It offered the masses the corporal living savior, the helper-in-need, confession, magical therapy, and, above all, an object of worship in the form of a dignity-bearing guru or *gossin* – be it through the designation of successors, be it hereditary" (*RofI*, p. 319/351; see also pp. 334–5/367–8, 323–5/356–8). With the devaluation of the traditional elite position of the Brahmin, neo-Brahminism of the Middle Ages generally accepted guruhood to the masses as the Brahmin's legitimate role.

No Classical Brahmin welcomed the popularization of his religion. Instead, changes in Hinduism's salvation paths and goals, as well as in its view of the supernatural realm, originated out of absolute necessity: given the threatening expansion of Jainism, Buddhism, and various Hindu sects, concrete material interests and matters of survival convinced these intellectuals of the necessity for an alteration of their salvation religion's soteriology:[67] "The religious virtuosi saw themselves compelled to adjust their demands to the possibilities of the religiosity of everyday life in order to gain and

65 On Jainism, see *RofI*, pp. 193–204/203–17.
66 For a summary of Weber's more general discussion of popular Hinduism, see Bendix, 1962, pp. 177–99.
67 Rather than, for example, as Tenbruck (1980) would assert, speculations upon the problem of theodicy.

maintain ideal and material mass patronage" ("I," p. 288/261; see also *RofI*, p. 297/325; *E&S*, p. 466/284).

Despite these changes, the organic social ethic as well as the *karma* and *samsara* doctrines remained central to this world religion. In promising a deliverance from suffering, both the guru and the redeemer-savior demanded action-orientations strictly obedient to the particularism of caste *dharma*, for only in this manner could the believer hope for a favorable rebirth. Legitimated with Hinduism's popularization, the particularism of caste ritual could now spread far and wide.

Changes in Hinduism's organizational form   Hinduism's competition in the later Classical era (*c.* 200 BC–700 AD) with the youthful salvation religions – Buddhism and Jainism – led in this period and in the Indian Middle Ages to drastic alterations in the internal organization of this world religion. These changes enhanced the power of the Brahmins and contributed directly to the solidification of the caste order on Indian soil.

A transformation of Hinduism's organizational form accompanied changes in the Classical Brahmin soteriology with the Hindu Restoration and popularization, especially in the era of the Middle Ages. Weber notes that the means of Hinduism's extension throughout India were parallel in form to those that earlier accounted for the success of its challengers, particularly Buddhism: the development of an organized professional monkdom (*RofI*, pp. 293/319–20, 295/322–3).

Hinduism originated as a free community of independent teachers and pupils without fixed rules; it was supported by gifts from the laity. The early Brahmins based their cohesiveness solely upon purely personal relations (*RofI*, p. 156/159). With the recognition of this stratum of cultured intellectuals by Kshatriya princes and kings, many Brahmins moved into the homes of the secular nobility and became the performers of all necessary ritual, as well as royalty's trusted spiritual advisors. Brahmins of lower status, many lacking in knowledge of the Vedas, took up the wandering life as magicians and sophists, practicing an itinerant mendicancy. These transient believers gradually gave birth to Hindu monkdom during Hinduism's renascence.

Cognizant of Hinduism's greater potential to quell the tempers of the masses, princes and kings assisted the Hindu monks in the "external organization of the monastic and temple service" (*RofI*, p. 301/329). The ancient free community of teachers and pupils gradually evolved into a formal organization with positions and prestige, and the hierarchically-organized cloister – as well as "professional monks" – appeared by the Middle Ages period of innumerable competing sects (*RofI*, pp. 292/318, 156/158–9). Hindu professional monks in their monasteries extended their influence among the masses.

The evolution of an organized professional monkdom and the development of hierocracies were not the only aspects of Hinduism's organizational metamorphosis that took place as its "virtuoso" origins became routinized with popularization.[68] As the Hindu Restoration spread across the breadth of India, the position of the Brahmin as house chaplain for royalty could not escape transformation. A usurpation of the heretofore prestigious Brahmin position by fundamentally plebeian mystagogues and less literary gurus resulted from a constellation of factors, including the power the gurus derived from immense incomes collected from their mass sects and their position as indispensable helpers of the masses (*RofI*, pp. 318–20/351–3).

Weber stressed that the popularization of the Brahmin teachers and gurus brought an essential increase in their powers: it allowed Hinduism to extend its influence (*RofI*, pp. 320/352–3). The authority of the guru reached its zenith with the development of a firm organization of his sect and diocese: "The leading guru in a territory is similar to a bishop of a Western church, visiting his diocese accompanied by his following. He had power to excommunicate individuals in the case of the grosser sins. He bestowed absolution for penitence and placed a tax on believers. In all and every consideration the guru was the most decisive advisor and father-confessor authority" (*RofI*, p. 319/352).

Each of these developments in Hinduism's organizational form – the establishment of the hierarchical cloister, the advent of the professional monk, and the legitimation of the Brahmin guru with his diocese – shared the common effect of increasing the grip of the Brahmins and Hinduism over the Indian populace. In combination with the accommodation of the classical Brahmin soteriology to the religious demands of the laity, these organizational transformations assured the suppression of Buddhism and Jainism as well as the success of the Hindu Restoration. Hinduism's extension always signified the blanketing of India's landscape with castes.[69]

Attention to degrees of causal centrality – facilitating and necessary patterns of action-orientations – cannot be found in the world systems, interpretive historical, and causal analytic approaches. This distinction must be viewed as a core feature of Weber's practiced causal methodology. Nonetheless, even multiple necessary factors, regardless how "exhaustive" when in combinations, never comprise an adequate causal explanation. Their identification, which is always undertaken with the assistance of the societal domains and domain-specific ideal types of *E&S*, constitutes, for Weber, only a preliminary stage. The synchronic and diachronic *interaction* of necessary action-orientations must now be addressed. Again, the *E&S* theoretical framework facilitates the identification of these interactions.

68 Weber addresses "routinization" analytically in *E&S*. See pp. 246–54/142–8, 1121–48/661–81; see also above (chapter 4, pp. 124–6).
69 On the organizational weaknesses of Buddhism, see *E&S*, pp. 1123–4/663; *RofI*, pp. 244–56/264–79.

Synchronic and diachronic interactions of action

An identification of the manner in which the various necessary patterns of action Weber identifies interacted with one another is crucial for an adequate causal explanation of the rise to dominance of the caste system in India. Synchronic and diachronic interaction procedures must first be addressed.

Synchronic interaction   An array of patterned action-orientations conducive to the development of the caste order interacted with one another synchronically in India in the Classical and Middle Ages epochs. In the process, they strengthened one another. The coalition of the Brahmin *stratum* with the Hindu salvation *religion* in the Classical era and the alliance of the Kshatriya *rulers* with the Brahmins in late Classical times were of central causal significance.

Unlike Buddhism, no charismatic prophet founded Hinduism. Rather, a loosely-knit group of intellectuals gave birth to this world religion in the sixth century BC. Educated in the pre-Classical Vedas, these men of knowledge eventually developed into the Brahmin hereditary caste of cultured literati, monks, and priests. As a consequence of their capacity to transcend the boundaries of the separate tribes and ethnic groups as well as their support of the *karma* doctrine, the Brahmins served as Hinduism's major carrier stratum and the driving power behind this world religion ("I," pp. 268–9/239). These cultivated and genteel intellectuals found Hinduism attractive as a result of the pure cognitive consistency offered by the *karma* doctrine, its unequivocal solution to the problem of theodicy, and its axiom that only Brahminical authority could provide knowledge of correct ritual action. Hinduism's definition of the Brahmin caste as highest in the status order also enhanced its appeal. The Brahmins, in turn, influenced Hinduism to an "extraordinary degree," especially in its "institutional and social components" (*E&S*, p. 501/305).

Decisive also for the development of the caste order was the manner in which the coalition in the late Classical era between the Kshatriya nobles "engaged in . . . political rule [and] knightly feats of valor" (*RofI*, p. 56/57; see pp. 63–76/64–77) and the Brahmins formulated a powerful constellation. Unlike the Chinese emperor as well as the feudal patricians and kings of ancient Israel's United Monarchy, the Kshatriya rulers could not enter the societal domain of religion. They were thus prohibited from performing ritual sacrifices to the gods. Consequently, they remained dependent upon the magical powers of the Vedic and then the Brahmin priests, all the more so to the extent that the gods of war became indomitable and frightening deities. They also needed the Brahmins to serve as political counselors, house chaplains, and spiritual directors, for, without such persons to legitimize their claims to royalty and high social status, rule over the masses would become difficult, if not impossible. Moreover, owing to their writing skills, the Brahmins became more and more indispensable to the extent that princes consolidated their powers and established patrimonial bureaucracies in the Middle Ages to rule over their expanding kingdoms. Indeed, the Kshatriya rulers perceived their "primary duty," aside from fulfillment of caste *dharma*, as involving support for the Brahmins, especially "by sustaining their authoritarian regulation of the social order according to holy right" (*RofI*, p. 147/147).[70]

For their part, the Brahmins increasingly needed the princes. As members of royal households, they were very often materially dependent upon them. Furthermore, because the necessary supplement to the charismatic powers conferred upon them by their sacred learning – an economic and political base – could be provided only by the Kshatriya princes, the Brahmins viewed these rulers as indispensable for maintenance of their high status and power. As Weber notes: "the political and social power of the [Brahmin] caste" was derived from its position as the "spiritual director of the prince in personal and political affairs" (*RofI*, p. 61/62).[71]

The Brahmins' gradual ascent to a dominating position was marked by a perpetual struggle with the empirical "craft" and stress upon tradition of the Vedic priesthood. The burgeoning coalition of the Brahmins with the Kshatriya rulers constituted a pivotal factor in the eventual subjugation of this priesthood. It also provided the Brahmins with the base of power that enabled them to define caste *dharma*, to order the civilization of India into a hierarchy of castes, and to become decisive proponents of the caste system as a whole.

Diachronic interaction: legacies   The sheer power of the Brahmins in the Classical era left legacies pivotal for the firm entrenchment of the caste order in the Indian landscape in the Middle Ages. Legitimated by their unmediated link with Hinduism's *karma* and *samsara* doctrines and ensconced securely in positions of power by the late Classical era as a consequence of their alliance with the Kshatriya princes, the Brahmins would cast their influence far and wide, even into subsequent epochs. The towering prestige and worldly power of this carrier stratum of Hinduism implied the expansion of castes, for as Hinduism expanded, so also did the caste system. Pivotal, however, in the late Classical era was the suppression of the urban guilds. Once this occurred, a configuration of patterned action-orientations – including orientations toward clan charisma – became secure, indeed to such an extent that they left powerful legacies. The coalition of the Kshatriya nobles with the Brahmins proved crucial, yet instrumental as well was a purely technological innovation: the discovery by the Kshatriya rulers of a new means of monetary support for their administrations.

70   See also *RofI*, pp. 130/131, 125/125, 141/139, 145/145. Louis Dumont confirms the importance of this alliance, its implications for India's history, and its uniqueness (see 1980).
71   Severe conflicts between the Brahmins and the princes, of course, arose permanently. Nonetheless, their alliance remained in the long run intact.

By the seventh century BC, city traders had achieved remarkable successes. The elders in the merchant guilds and confederations stood on an equal social footing with both the Brahmins and the princes, often even marrying the daughters of the nobility. Since they had organized themselves into a solidary association and because kings and princes depended upon merchants to underwrite their wars and loans, the noble rulers were forced to recognize the power of the guilds. Weber notes that the resulting pluralistic competition for political and social superiority among traders, nobles, and Brahmins yielded heretofore unknown social privileges to the trader class. It also largely accounted for the creation of an egalitarian social milieu that offered the opportunity to all peoples to wield political power, even the lowly Shudra class of craftsmen and workers without rights to own property. Wealthy artisans frequently socialized with the nobles. The Brahmins no longer alone advised the princes; city elders also did so (see *RofI*, p. 88/87).

However, decisively, the princes – and they alone – maintained disciplined armies. As their rulership and patrimonial bureaucracies became more and more powerful, the financial dependence of princes upon the urban merchants became less and less acceptable, particularly in the Middle Ages. As soon as they devised an alternative means of monetary support for their administrations – the "substitution of tax liturgies for capitalistic tax farming" and the reliance "upon rural organizations as sources for armies and taxes" – their steady accumulation of power over the guilds became assured (*RofI*, p. 130/130; see also p. 128/128). Eventually, with the stabilization of economic conditions, the success of any surviving, freely mobile merchants and craftsmen became dependent upon their conformity to traditional ritualistic practices. Vocational associations became closed.

With the subjugation of the urban guilds in the late Classical period, all possibilities for the evolution of a solidary and organized independent citizenry, as well as for the extension of a politically cohesive fraternization across a broad cross-section of the citizenry, were eliminated (*RofI*, pp. 33–4/35–6, 131/131). As a consequence, the various guest peoples generally responsible for the growth of urban industries remained estranged and segregated from one another. The victory over the guilds of the kings and their allies, the Brahmins, not only banished a force highly antagonistic to the caste system and greatly strengthened the Brahmins, but also paved the way for a rejuvenation of clan charisma. Once again skilled labor became organized hereditarily, status distinctions accorded certain groups only guest or pariah status, and ritual became increasingly specialized according to ethnic group. This force highly conducive to castes, clan charisma, then remained strong. Indeed, it established a legacy that, in the Middle Ages, would become of pivotal importance in affirming the caste order.

The expansion of clan charisma throughout India occurred with the ascendance to social superiority of the Brahmins. Before long, however, hopeful that Brahmin prestige would accrue to them and motivated by the purely pragmatic desire to insure privileged positions for sibs and descendants, all occupants of positions of religious authority imitated Brahmin magical practices. Further, the adoption of clan charisma as a means of transferring authority was also facilitated by prevailing animistic beliefs that generally associated an appropriately defined magical charisma with certain social positions and especially to positions of authority, whether sacerdotal or secular (*RofI*, pp. 126/125–6). As Weber notes: "More strongly than anywhere else, magical as well as social rejection of communion with strangers was called forth. This helped preserve the charisma of distinguished sibs and established insurmountable barriers between ethnic subject tribes" (*RofI*, p. 131/131). Together with "racial" antagonisms, which provided a particularly effective support (*RofI*, p. 127/127), clan charisma – "the nucleus of caste formation" (*RofI*, p. 126/125) – upheld strongly the rise of the caste order in the Classical era and, after the guilds had been abolished, established a legacy that fostered its entrenchment in the subsequent era.

However, and despite widespread clan charisma, the power and prestige of the Brahmins, their firm alliance with Hinduism on the one hand and the Kshatriya princes on the other hand, and the expanse of the *karma* and *samsara* doctrines, these factors alone cannot, according to Weber, provide an explanation at the level of adequate causality for the universal diffusion of the caste order as it occurred in the period from 700 to 1200 AD on the Indian sub-continent. The entrenchment of the caste system cannot be explained simply by conducive synchronic and diachronic interactions of necessary action-orientations. Indeed, despite such patterned action, Brahmin power and Hinduism were challenged severely in the later Classical era by religions opposed to the caste system: Buddhism and Jainism.

A variety of single forces prominent in the Classical epoch and favorable to the rise and expansion of the caste order crystallized in the Indian Middle Ages not only into a *context* conducive to the rise of the caste order, but also into a configuration of forces that interacted in a *conjunctural* manner.

Conjunctural interactions of action

Long-term *historical* developments finally called forth an altered context within which old and new patterns of action-orientations intermixed and dynamically interacted in a different and "correct" manner, insuring the unshakeability of the caste order. In the process each single factor was strengthened. Castes became entrenched and developed into a caste *order*.

Mahayana, or "lay," Buddhism (see *RofI*, pp. 244–56/265–79) continued to expand across Asian lands until the seventh century AD, yet its influence in India began to wane in the fifth century with the slow and steady revival of Hinduism. Though the first of the great polemicists against Buddhism,

Kumerila Bhatta, appeared in the seventh century, the earliest founder of Hinduism's renascence "in the sense of a joining of the ancient philosophical tradition of intellectual soteriology with the propaganda needs" of the masses, Sankarachrya, lived in the eighth or ninth century (*RofI*, p. 299/327).[72]

Once the Kshatriya/Brahmin alliance fully reasserted itself against Buddhism, this world religion, as well as Jainism, was suppressed. With pacification, the process of re-establishing Brahmin power and prestige could ensue. This situation provided the basic precedent for the Hindu Restoration that saw the devaluation of the elite position of the Brahmin and the worship of deified, this-worldly, and personalized redeemers. Massive popularization and the rise of gurus and monks untrained in the Classical scriptures took place. Hinduism's basic tenets – the *karma* and *samsara* doctrines and the organic social ethic – remained, however, intact and spread widely, for neo-Brahmin gurus and heterodox redeemers demanded strict obedience to caste *dharma*. Simultaneously, Hinduism's drastic *organizational* alteration undertaken in response to the challenge presented by Buddhism and Jainism, which included the rise of hierarchically-organized monasteries and dioceses and the development of a professional monkdom, became complete. These transformations all enhanced the power of the Brahmins and, as well, anchored this religion securely in the social fabric of India. They did so all the more because of their dynamic interaction with prominent legacies, such as clan charisma.

These developments in the Middle Ages provided a context conducive to the unfolding of the caste order, one in which facilitating and necessary action-orientations crystallized into a constellation of forces that reciprocally intensified one another. Some of these forces became powerful as a result alone of the altered context within which they now existed. As a result of the conjunctural interaction, above all of clan charisma, the Brahmin/Kshatriya coalition, and Hinduism, even the extensive development in India of patrimonial kingdoms failed to call forth, as Weber's *E&S* model of patrimonialism hypothesizes (see e.g. *E&S*, pp. 1102–8/648–53), strong civic strata capable of confronting the growth of the caste order. On the contrary, the *karma* and *samsara* doctrines penetrated deeply into even these strata. The supremacy of the Brahmins enabled them to solidify the dominance of Hinduism and to perform their tasks in a manner more effective than ever before: to define the *dharma* for the separate castes and to order them into a social hierarchy. Again: "[In India] . . . all factors important for the development of the caste system operated . . . conjointly" (*RofI*, p. 131/131). One important indicator of the caste system's expansion and entrenchment can be seen in the transformation of the notion of *dharma* from taboos, magical norms, and witchcraft in pre-Classical and

72   According to Weber's calculations, most of which predate the estimates of today's scholarship by about a century.

Classical times into a "binding path" of social-ethical duty in the late Classical and Middle Ages periods (*RofI*, p. 180/188).

This examination of the rise to dominance of the caste order has sought to illustrate the actual *mode of causal analysis* practiced in Weber's substantive texts. Because he failed to present his analysis in systematic form, it has had to be reconstructed. The three stages of his causal methodology have served as guideposts, as has the theoretical framework – societal domains and domain-specific ideal types – articulated in his analytic treatise, *E&S*. All have offered means of orientation for this investigation of the diffuse empirical realities surrounding the rise and expansion of the caste system. In seeking to establish adequate causality, Weber's causal methodology has been seen to emphasize a radical array of causal action-orientations and a distinction between facilitating and necessary patterns of action. Synchronic and diachronic interactions of regular action-orientations have also been crucial, yet Weber stresses as well (*a*) the manner in which *contexts*, within which recurring action crystallizes, are created; and (*b*) the way in which intermixtures of action-orientations lead to *conjunctural* interactions that imply an intensification of the causal role of single factors.

How does Weber's mode of causal analysis contrast with that of the world systems, interpretive historical, and causal analytic schools? This reconstruction of his analysis of the rise to dominance of the caste order in India has illustrated his broad multicausality. In this respect Weber is allied closely with the interpretive historical school. However, his insistence upon a causal methodology and unwillingness to establish causality on the basis of a few major concepts in combination with a richly detailed narrative separates Weber from this approach. Furthermore, the interpretive historical school, as well as the world systems and causal analytic approaches, fails to distinguish between facilitating and necessary action-orientations, nor do these perspectives offer a theoretical framework comparable to the societal domains and domain-specific ideal types of *E&S*, all of which assist above all the clear identification of necessary causal forces on the one hand and synchronic and diachronic interactions on the other. This frame of reference itself separates Weber's mode of causal analysis from the exclusive focus upon problems of the causal analytic and interpretive historical schools. This heuristic construct, in effect, constrains the researcher to become engaged in a continuous back and forth movement between an orientational framework and the diffuse empirical reality under investigation. Yet it fails to push Weber's comparative-historical sociology toward the pre-formulated theory of the world systems approach.

In addition, and even though Weber would appreciate the efforts of causal analytic practitioners to proceed in a systematic and rigorous fashion in respect to the establishment of causality, he would view the methodology they offer as incomplete. This approach, similar to the world systems school, awards special attention to class relations, the economy, and the state, normally at the expense of cultural forces. The very *multiplicity* of the *E&S* societal domains and domain-specific ideal types serves as a barrier to the bestowal of "decisive status" upon single causal variables. Precisely in this regard this theoretical framework accounts for a further distinction between Weber and the causal analytic, as well as the world systems, approaches: its emphasis upon a radical pluralism of causal forces requires that "context" and "conjunctural interactions" be understood far more broadly than do adherents of these schools. While also acknowledging social contexts and the conjunctural interaction of forces, the causal analytic and world systems approaches both fail to do so by reference to a full spectrum of causal factors.

The illustration above of the rise to dominance of the caste order has sought to clarify on the one hand the causal methodology Weber actually employs in his substantive texts and on the other hand the manner in which a theoretical framework is provided for his investigations by the societal domains and domain-specific ideal types of *E&S*. In doing so, it has aimed to demonstrate how Weber's *mode of causal analysis* can be utilized by contemporary comparative-historical researchers.[73] Several other fairly complete analyses that include sustained attention to facilitating and necessary causal patterns of action, synchronic, diachronic, and conjunctural interactions, the contextual dependence of action-orientations, and the theoretical framework of *E&S* are buried deeply within Weber's comparative-historical writings: the rise to dominance of monotheism in ancient Israel (see Kalberg, forthcoming b), Confucianism (see Kalberg, forthcoming a) and patrimonialism in China, mysticism in ancient Buddhism, and modern capitalism in the West.[74] All could be reconstructed by reference to the components of Weber's mode of causal analysis as they have been discussed in this chapter.

---

73   I have attempted, albeit less stringently, two *applications* of Weber's practiced mode of causal analysis. Both studies seek to demonstrate its rigor and uniqueness. One presents an analysis of the rise and expansion of "cultural pessimism" (*Kulturpessimismus*) in turn-of-the-century Germany (1987), the other offers a causal explanation of the diverging loci of work in two advanced industrial nations: the United States and Germany (1992). See also Kalberg, 1993a.

74   The latter reconstruction, which would constitute a substantial book in itself, could not have been undertaken here. Such a reconstruction would utilize, in conjunction with *E&S* and *PE*, the *GEH* study.

Conclusion

Max Weber's Comparative-Historical Sociology and Recent Schools

The strategies and procedures of Max Weber's comparative-historical sociology cannot be adequately comprehended if the memorable phrases frequently associated with his substantive texts are taken as representative: "increasing bureaucratization," "universal rationalization," and the "routinization of charisma." The analytic power and uniqueness of his empirical sociology will also remain occluded if great emphasis is placed upon his most famous phrases, such as "disenchantment [*Entzauberung*] of the world" and "a polar night of icy darkness [lies ahead]" ("PV," p. 128/559). On the other hand, Weber's comparative-historical sociology cannot be understood as simply a series of fragmented, delimited, and problem-based case studies on, for example, charisma, status groups, the "spirit" of capitalism, and the bureaucracy. Nor is it accurately depicted as a vast inventory of ideal types.

Case studies, concept formation, and demarcated problems stand simply at the foundation of his substantive sociology. Concealed within Weber's empirical texts are arrays of strategies and procedures, indeed even a rigorous comparative-historical sociology. Some of its basic orientations (such as the "yardstick" purpose of ideal types) are more familiar today, others less so (such as model building); some have remained unknown. This has been seen particularly to be the case with respect to his mode of causal analysis.

Through a synthetic reading of his empirical texts, this study has systematized and, at some points, reconstructed the major underlying axes of Weber's substantive writings. His comparative-historical sociology is constituted from *interlocking* strategies and procedures, all of which serve an overall purpose: to provide causal explanations of unique cases and developments. Far from devoid of internal coherence, as many have argued, his disparate strategies and procedures are united by this purpose. This study, however, has had a further central purpose: through comparisons between Weber and recent schools of comparative-historical sociology, it has sought to overcome dilemmas and problems confronted by contemporary practitioners and to demonstrate the utility of his strategies and procedures for research today.

The basic orientations of Weber's empirical texts and his contributions to comparative-historical sociology today must now be recapitulated. Comparisons and contrasts to contemporary schools will be undertaken at each step along the way.

An Overview

Chapter 1 examined the manner in which Weber's substantive texts link agency and structure. They pay much greater attention to this issue than the world systems, causal analytic, and interpretive historical schools. The comparative-historical endeavor, according to Weber, requires an explicit elaboration of this linkage. Foundational aspects of his sociology are central in this regard: his methodological individualism, his notion of *Verstehen*, and his analysis of the multiple ways in which action can be oriented by subjective meaning. Unlike rational choice theorists, Weber contends that the *verstehende* investigator must "understand" the action-orientations of persons in reference to the pluralism of motives expressed by four types of social action. He argues that the unequal motivational *intensity* of action remains of utmost significance to comparative-historical sociologists, even in respect to questions such as the origins of modern capitalism.

The discussion of these foundational components of Weber's sociology paved the way for an examination of the manner in which individual action is tied in his texts to social structure. This linkage occurs through three *modes of patterning action*: the orientation of action to "orders" and "legitimate orders" on the one hand and its embeddedness in discrete social contexts, or "sociological loci," on the other. Instead of simply evolving and flourishing as a consequence of the rational choices of individuals, patterned action-orientations acquire an imprint and shape by milieus, or the "social conditions of existence." By calling attention directly to the emphasis upon contexts found throughout Weber's substantive texts, sociological loci models reveal the capacity of his comparative-historical sociology to postulate *likelihoods* regarding the crystallization of certain patterns of social action, and the circumscription of others, in given settings.

This patterning of action – Weber's structural dimension – never implies, however, a loss of the subjective meaning of individuals as the basic unit of analysis, nor of the multivocal ways in which action is oriented. Status groups, conventions, laws, and even bureaucratic organizations will vanish unless individuals orient meaningful action to them in regular ways. Weber's structuralism refers simply to these three modes of patterning action: through orders, legitimate orders, and sociological loci. He asks, throughout his substantive writings, how action is uprooted from its natural, diffuse flow and, despite unceasing conflict, transformed into *regularities* of action.

The world systems, causal analytic, and interpretive historical approaches all fail to offer these or other explicit procedures, strategies, and concepts to tie individual action to social structures. Indeed, these schools generally abandon agency. In defining Weber's foundational "micro" components clearly – his methodological individualism, notion of *Verstehen*, four types of action, and emphasis upon a pluralism of motives – and then discussing them in reference to the order, legitimate order, and sociological loci bridging mechanisms, chapter 1 as well disclosed a larger, *verstehende* purpose behind Weber's comparative-historical sociology: to *assist* macrosociologists in quite practical ways to "understand" putatively irrational action-orientations. To the extent that meaningful action becomes identified as located within orders, legitimate orders, and social contexts and thereby "understood," it becomes "transformed" from "foreign" and "strange" action into "plausible," subjectively meaningful, and perhaps even "altogether logical" action.

The multicausality of Weber's comparative-historical sociology was the subject of chapter 2. His insistence that causal analysis must acknowledge a full spectrum of patterned action-orientations places him in opposition to the world systems and causal analytic approaches. These schools stress structural forces – such as class relations, the state, the interests of ruling classes, urbanization, and capital accumulation – at the expense of cultural forces, such as the values of a religion, status group, or the family. Moreover, practitioners of the causal analytic and world systems approaches assume that a single societal domain or variable can be legitimately elevated *in general* to a position of causal priority.

Weber, on the other hand, asserts, for example, that the investigation of all enduring structures and economic relations must include consideration of the beliefs and values that legitimate and uphold them. He underscores as well that these values may originate in the universal organizations just as well as status groups or religious doctrines, and they may endure across millennia despite structural transformations. At the analytic level, he perceives values as driving forces, not to mention forces of stability and resistance, every bit the equal of economic forces. Furthermore, Weber, unlike adherents of the world systems and causal analytic approaches, charts a complex interaction between values, traditions, and practical interests. He affirms in addition, in explicit opposition to the world systems and causal analytic schools in particular though also to rational choice theorists, the central causal significance of variable subjective meanings and the variable intensity of social action.

In discussing causality, Weber allocates a major role to social *carriers*. To become sociologically significant, patterned action requires cohesive classes, strata, or organizations as its bearer. Indeed, carriers may themselves potentially influence regular action-orientations. This may occur in a decisive manner. However, and despite significant influences upon recurring action that can be charted analytically, carriers must never be examined in isolation. On the one hand they interact continuously with further causal forces (such as historical events, technological innovations, and geographical factors); on the other hand the extent to which carriers possess power must be taken into consideration. Moreover, to Weber, conflict, competition, and the tension that often exists across patterned action-orientations as well must be viewed as causally significant. Each of these factors is endowed, in his comparative-historical sociology, with the capacity to call forth regular action.

Weber's principled and radical multicausality pushes his substantive sociology in the direction of the interpretive historical school, which also acknowledges a full panorama of causal forces. Nonetheless, Weber's distinctiveness even here is soon unmistakable: this approach fails explicitly to argue in behalf of the centrality of carriers and the variable intensity of action.

Chapter 3 defined the basic purpose of Weber's sociology: the causal analysis of unique cases and developments. This aim allies him strongly with the interpretive historical and causal analytic schools. However, Weber's comparative-historical sociology breaks sharply from most of the proponents of these schools in regard to the major subject of this chapter: its level of analysis rooted in ideal types. This heuristic tool supplies the foundation for Weber's causal procedures and strategies. Its formation and basic features were addressed, as well as its most fundamental usage: to provide a means of orientation to amorphous social reality and assist the clear definition of cases. The question of why the unique empirical case or development occurred "historically so and not otherwise" can be asked only after the formulation of clear definitions. If these conceptual instruments, according to Weber, are not available to serve as "standards" against which single cases and developments can be "measured," the conduct of comparative "mental experiments" that seek rigorously to isolate significant causal action-orientations remains impossible. Furthermore, in offering means of orientation, these "yardsticks" distinguish Weber's comparative-historical sociology from the problem focus of the interpretive historical and causal analytic schools. They separate him as well from the pre-formulated theory of the world systems approach. All of these schools lack a comparable heuristic construct. This being said in behalf of the ideal type, it must also be noted that Weber's failure to specify more clearly procedures for its construction constitutes a severe problem. His references to "rules of experience" and "historical judgments" do not adequately, by contemporary standards, guard against subjective procedures.

The ideal type fulfills a further basic purpose in Weber's sociology of causality, as addressed in chapter 4: it constructs *hypothesis-forming mod-*

els. Nearly all models are constructed in Weber's analytic treatise, *E&S*. In formulating delineated, empirically-testable causal hypotheses, they assist the isolation of significant causal factors at the empirical level and oppose all narrative and problem-focussed approaches. Weber's dynamic, contextual, affinity, antagonism, and developmental models were examined.

His affinity and antagonism models, for example, chart analytic relationships, or "logical interactions." Rather than deriving from historical and changing factors, such as power, external constraint, rulership, or particular historical events, these interactions result from logical, or "internal," affinities and antagonisms across a *theoretical framework*, one provided by the societal domains (the universal organizations, classes, and status groups, and the religion, law, economy, and rulership life-spheres) and domain-specific ideal types of *E&S* (for example the charismatic, patriarchal, feudal, patrimonial, and bureaucratic types of rulership, and status groups such as intellectuals, feudal nobles, peasants, and civil servants). Thus, under no circumstances should analytic relationships be viewed as themselves constituting actual empirical causal relationships. They remain models alone, strictly separate from social reality where all logical relationships continuously intersect. Nonetheless, as heuristic relationships, they are endowed with great power: intra-domain and inter-domain antagonism and affinity hypotheses assist the isolation, identification, clear conceptualization, and analytic, location of empirical interactions of patterned action. Causal analysis is thereby facilitated. In-depth, historical investigation then serves to test each hypothesized relationship. Although the interpretive historical, causal analytic, and world systems schools all acknowledge the interactions of factors, none of these contemporary approaches provides either a theoretical framework comparable to Weber's or means of any sort to identify *typical* interactions.

Weber's hypothesis-forming *developmental models* as well contribute significantly to the capacity of his substantive sociology to draw the comparative-historical enterprise away from the problem focus of the causal analytic and interpretive historical schools and toward the theoretical framing of empirical developments. These limited analytic generalizations must be kept quite distinct from his other models. On the one hand, a *course* of action is hypothesized that implies ideal-typical stages through which action may proceed. At each stage, delimited and empirically-testable causal hypotheses are formulated regarding the further unfolding of regular action-orientations. On the other hand, these models are anchored in and set into motion by a driving force linked indigenously to the postulated course of action.

Such developmental constructs pushed forth by a single set of action-orientations are repeatedly formulated in the *E&S* analytic treatise. The postulated "developmental paths" are presented in a manner more internally consistent and systematically unified than any given empirical development. Weber emphasized, for this reason, that the stages of each developmental model never either capture "invariable stages" of history or themselves constitute "effective forces." Empirically, of course, his comparative-historical sociology remains radically multicausal. Thus, when discussing these models, he emphasizes repeatedly that they must not be "confused with reality." In every empirical case, *various* causal forces call forth new action-orientations and "intervene" to upset all postulated paths of action. Major developmental models in *E&S*, including their driving forces, were examined: the models anchored in and set into motion by interests (the closure model of social relationships and the routinization of charisma model) and formal (the market and the state) and theoretical (religion) rationalization processes.

These developmental models as well uproot all Weberian causal analysis from a reliance upon thick description to establish causality, as is characteristic of the interpretive historical approach. Least of all does Weber seek, as is also clear from the centrality of the dynamic, contextual, and affinity and antagonism models, to understand history in reference to a theoretical scheme, as does the world systems approach. Each of these delimited models serves indispensable purposes in his comparative-historical sociology: to facilitate the clear definition of the particular empirical case or development at hand and to provide a theoretical framework that enables a conceptual grasp upon and focussed investigation of empirical cases, relationships, and developments.

Model building remains pivotal throughout *E&S*. As organizing mechanisms that serve heuristic purposes only, hypothesis-forming models are useful to comparative-historical sociologists. Moreover, model building as such inserts a consistently theoretical dimension into the very core of Weber's sociology. For him, and regardless of the content of the particular model utilized at the moment, the comparative-historical enterprise emphatically involves, as a fundamental procedure, the theoretical framing of empirical action-orientations. Indeed, Weber's emphasis upon hypothesis-forming models on the one hand and societal domains and domain-specific ideal types on the other, as well as ideal types as such, serves an explicit purpose: he aims to draw comparative-historical research away from a sheer problem or case focus and the attempt to establish causality through a thick historical narrative (as does the interpretive historical school) or a research design methodology alone (as does the causal analytic approach). Concepts and procedures that assist the theoretical framing of problems and questions in a manner even remotely comparable to *E&S*'s models are never articulated by contemporary schools.

Of course, as noted (see chapter 4), model-building of the kind practiced by Weber is *intentionally* downplayed, even neglected, by contemporary schools. Practitioners of the causal analytic approach consider such models needlessly modest and instead proclaim, to them, a more ambitious goal, one rooted in a positivist epistemology: to construct *empirical* generalizations. Adherents of the interpretive historical school stand opposed to model-building as well in principle: they reject the possibility of formulating generalizations and remain convinced that causality can be established alone through richly detailed description. To world systems theorists model-building of this scale and centrality in the comparative-historical enterprise need not be carried out. Detailed empirical studies constitute an adequate means to demonstrate the correctness of the pre-formulated theory.

Finally, the examination of Weber's model- and domain-based theoretical framework in chapter 4 revealed again a further distinction vis-à-vis recent schools. Unlike the focus of these approaches upon the formation of the nation-state, Western modernization processes, and modern social movements, Weber's substantive texts range across a far broader historical panorama. They move freely from the classical civilizations of Antiquity to the present and from East to West.

Although it is at the core of his comparative–historical sociology, the model building of *E&S* should not be equated with Weber's *mode of causal analysis*. Chapter 5 addressed this theme. Systematic procedures and strategies designed to establish causality lie concealed in his substantive texts, even a causal methodology with distinct stages. This remains the case despite Weber's renunciation of the goal of discovering "general laws" in history and social life as well as his insistence that "fateful events play a tremendous role" (*E&S*, p. 1176/702). His aim to proceed, in behalf of causal explanations, by reference to rigorous procedures and strategies swings Weber away from the interpretive historical approach and toward the causal analytic school.

The interpretive historical school fails to articulate a mode of causal analysis. Because historical detail is assumed to convey causality, explicit causal procedures and strategies are deemed dispensable. Indeed, controlled comparisons are believed to be unobtainable. A central concept, combined with the formulation of a general question, alone suffices as theoretical guidelines for adherents of this school. On the other hand, proponents of the causal analytic approach explicitly and forcefully articulate a causal methodology. The construction and testing of causal hypotheses and the controlling of variables characterize their investigations. Pivotal is an experimental design methodology, as well as an entire terminology of causality. Weber would find precisely these features laudable. However, his mode of causal analysis overcomes the weaknesses of the causal analytic school – an elevation of single factors to positions of causal priority and a failure to uphold broadly multicausal procedures – and, moreover, *combines* a principled adherence to a radical multicausality with contextual–conjunctural procedures and strategies.

A distinction between "facilitating" and "necessary" regularities of action stands preliminary to the contextual–conjunctural stage of Weber's practiced causal methodology. This division also separates him from the

world systems, interpretive historical, and causal analytic schools. Furthermore, unlike contemporary approaches, Weber's mode of causal analysis
takes the major societal domains and domain-specific ideal types of *E&S* as
central. Now in conjunction with an explicit causal methodology, the *E&S*
theoretical framework is empowered to guide causal analysis.

It first assists the identification of necessary orientations of action and
synchronic and diachronic intra-domain and inter-domain interactions of
patterned action. Weber is particularly convinced that regular action-orientations established in the past may permeate deeply, often in unexpected
ways and with wide impact, into the present. Intra-domain and inter-domain diachronic interactions were discussed in chapter 5 as "legacies" and
"antecedent conditions." Synchronic interactions and the legacy diachronic
interactions illustrated the "penetration range" procedure common in
Weber's texts. Although practitioners of the world systems, interpretive
historical, and causal analytic schools regularly acknowledge synchronic
and diachronic interactions, none offers concepts and a theoretical framework that facilitate clear conceptualization.

The separation of facilitating from necessary action-orientations and the
evaluation of synchronic and diachronic interactions of patterned action
constitute, in Weber's practiced methodology, crucial stages preliminary to
the contextual–conjunctural stage. Only this latter stage is empowered to
establish "adequate causality." Rather than standing alone, regular action-
orientations, according to Weber's texts, exist in delineated contexts of
multiple patterns of action-orientations which interact in diverse ways,
indeed to such an extent that the creation of a single effect is extremely
unlikely. In effect, contexts of pluralistic action-orientations serve as constraining or conducive forces, thereby influencing the causal significance
and even substance of regular action-orientations. The same factor, depending upon its context, varies in its effect.

Moreover, Weber's causal methodology emphasizes that the interaction
of multiple action-orientations may itself become a causally significant
force. Qualitatively *new* patterned action may be called forth as a result of
interaction. New regularities of action may even reverberate widely, in the
process recasting entire arrays of action-orientations. Thus, not only the
contextual embeddedness of patterned action must be charted if adequate
causality is to be established; Weber asserts as well that regular action-
orientations interact *conjuncturally*: dynamic interactions occur such that
not only a strengthening or weakening of patterned action results, but also
qualitatively new regular action endowed with causal significance. Precisely
such dynamic effects, he insists, must be clearly and regularly acknowledged.

The pivotal conjunctural component in Weber's practiced causal methodology can be defined and evaluated as a causal element only by reference
to the critical level at which it occurs: the contextual level. Even patterned
action seemingly intimately bound into linear causal chains is, according to

Weber, in principle influenced dynamically by its social context. Although convinced that the *conceptualization* of regular action in isolation or as centered in hypothesis-forming models constitutes an indispensable heuristic operation, as does the ordering of action-orientations synchronically and diachronically in reference to an analytic framework of domains and domain-specific ideal types, Weber insists that these procedures alone cannot render even a modicum of justice to complex empirical reality. Single patterns of action-orientations always interweave empirically into contexts of social action, and *dynamic* interactions then occur. A viable causal methodology must articulate clear stages and procedures that capture the interaction of past and present, multiple regularities of action-orientations – or contexts – and the alteration of patterns of social action as a consequence of the ensuing dynamic interaction. To Weber, if the crystallization of sociologically-significant regular action is to be explained at the level of adequate causality, necessary synchronic and diachronic action-orientation must not only appear in the entire constellation, and appear simultaneously; they must also *interact* in a "correct" dynamic. Accordingly, the contextual–conjunctural stage of his causal methodology is designed to take cognizance of the empirical existence of pluralistic hosts of action-orientations, the influence of a social milieu upon them, and their dynamic interaction. Adequate causality can be established only in this manner. Although also contextual and even conjunctural, the world systems and causal analytic schools fail to ensure – through the postulation of a theoretical framework or any other heuristic construct – that synchronic, diachronic, and conjunctural interactions will be examined by reference to a full spectrum of causal forces.

The concluding section of chapter 5 illustrated Weber's mode of causal analysis. It reconstructed one of his own analyses: the rise to a position of preeminence of the caste system in India. This section sought in particular to demonstrate that the procedures and stages of his practiced causal methodology – the distinction between facilitating and necessary degrees of causal centrality, and synchronic, diachronic, and conjunctural interactions of regular action – can be utilized by comparative-historical sociologists today.

The major societal domains and domain-specific ideal types from *E&S* served as an heuristic construct throughout the analysis of the rise of the caste system. *E&S* articulates a theoretical framework that facilitated acquisition of a purchase upon diffuse realities, clear conceptualization and identification of potential causal forces, and delineation of the social context within which the case or development under investigation arose and spread. To the extent that comparative-historical sociologists allow their research to be guided by this construct and the central procedures and stages of Weber's causal methodology, the immediacy of the empirical reality and problem at hand is severed. Weber's mode of causal analysis constructs ideal types that ground investigations in empirical patterns of action and delimited problems, yet also firmly insists that the case or development under investigation must be rigorously framed. This remains the case even though he utilizes his theoretical framework – the societal domains and domain-specific ideal types of *E&S* – in a modest fashion: as an orientational mechanism only.

Setting the Agenda

The important achievements and contributions of Weber's comparative-historical sociology with respect to the central dilemmas and problems of comparative-historical sociology today have been examined throughout this study and summarized in the preceding section. His substantive texts have been seen to be unique in a number of specific ways. They are unusual in a more general sense as well: they address forcefully the range of issues and dilemmas confronted by the comparative-historical enterprise today.

Even while taking social action as his basic unit of analysis, Weber provides explicit and specific ways of linking agency and social structure: the order, legitimate order, and sociological loci modes of patterning action. In doing so, he charts the *diverse* ways in which subjective meaning orients action, demonstrates the sociological significance of the unequal *intensity* of action, and charts the contextual constraints and opportunities that surround regular action. Then, on behalf of his goal to offer causal analyses of cases and developments, he constructs a vital heuristic tool – the ideal type – and demonstrates its capacity to define discrete cases and developments and to formulate a variety of hypothesis-forming models that assist causal analysis.

Such ideal types contribute theoretical frameworks that uproot Weber's research from narrative procedures and a problem focus alone. This central accomplishment is sustained through the organization of his comparative-historical sociology around major societal domains, or a limited number of analytically independent realms within which patterned social action significantly occurs, and an array of domain-specific ideal types. Taken together, societal domains and domain-specific ideal types construct a further theoretical framework that assists the identification of causal forces at the origin of empirical cases and developments. Moreover, Weber's substantive texts affirm a broad multicausality that not only bestows analytically equal weight upon a wide spectrum of patterned action-orientations, including action oriented to values and traditions, but also asks the crucial question of whether new regularities of action acquire social carriers that are powerful. Finally, his comparative-historical sociology contains a unique and rigorous *causal methodology*, one that, in order to establish adequate causality, combines cognizance of varying degrees of causal centrality with an insistence upon the causal significance of synchronic, diachronic, and contextual–conjunctural interactions of patterned action-orientations. This causal methodology is juxtaposed, in his substantive texts, with the theoretical framework provided by *E&S*'s domains and domain-specific ideal types to articulate a powerful *mode of causal analysis*.

While addressing the broad variety of questions comparative-historical sociology must confront, Weber consistently abjures dogmatic and extreme positions. He repeatedly follows a middle course.

(*a*) His agency foundation – methodological individualism, *Verstehen*, the four types of social action, and a pluralism of motives – stresses the importance of the acting individual and subjective meaning, yet, in emphasizing the multiple ways in which action becomes *patterned* and occurs in cohesive groups, Weber explains as well, even while avoiding all diffuse concepts such as "society" and "social system," the origins of social structures.

(*b*) He constructs a comparative-historical sociology that moves beyond narrative procedures and a problem focus, yet, by formulating ideal types, retains the centrality of patterned action, the notion of *Verstehen*, and causal analysis as his overall goal and abstains from advocating an abstract, ahistorical level of analysis or the construction of general laws.

(*c*) Weber refuses, even while proposing that patterned action can be *conceptualized* as rooted contextually in the social conditions of existence, to postulate a rigid functional determinism.

(*d*) He insists repeatedly upon the sociological significance of values and the potentially binding character of action oriented to values, even in the face of economic interests, yet guards against idealism.

(*e*) Weber declares that the causal explanation of unique cases and developments must be the goal of sociology, yet asserts that, rather than strong causality, "adequate causality" can alone be attained.

(*f*) He formulates a comparative-historical sociology of universal range, even one that includes developmental models of long-term rationalization processes, yet rejects all evolutionary axioms, even to the extent of repudiating unequivocally the *Gemeinschaft/Gesellschaft*, particularism/universalism, and tradition/modernity dichotomies.

(*g*) Weber observes that patterns of social action repeatedly crystallize in bounded groupings, yet, on the one hand refuses to organize his substantive texts around the question of social order and the putative necessity of "adaptive upgrading," "value-generalization," and "inclusion" (see Parsons, 1966, 1971) and, on the other hand, asserts unequivocally that tension, conflict, rulership, and power are ubiquitous in social life.

(*h*) He discerns omnipresent conflict, yet also discovers constellations of regular action-orientations that arise repeatedly to formulate firm social contexts, which in turn circumscribe opposing patterns of action and render them devoid of sociological significance.

(*i*) Weber constructs various theoretical frameworks for comparative-historical investigations and insists upon their pivotal centrality, yet, in denouncing schemes that purport to encompass all empirical reality and aim to erect a closed system of laws, argues for their "modest" utilization as orientational analytics only.

Taken separately, and despite the particular strengths of each school, the world systems, causal analytic, and interpretive historical approaches fail to match Weber's sweeping treatment of the wide range of issues critical to the comparative-historical endeavor. In addition, contemporary schools often do not propose rigorous procedures and strategies for research. In some cases, extreme positions are offered.

The centrality in Weber's substantive texts of theoretical frameworks, which encompass not only societal domains and domain-specific ideal types but also diverse hypothesis-forming models, is not accidental. He argues repeatedly that the task of sociology must always include the construction of theories. He sees, however, a natural temptation to which sociologists are continuously exposed: to define their calling as involving, with the assistance alone of several key concepts and a concise definition of the research problem at hand, simply a deep immersion in empirical reality. In this sense, Weber opposes the interpretive historical school most vehemently. The first purpose of his theoretical frameworks, thus, is clear: to disentangle sociologists from the immediacy of the problem under investigation and to *constrain* engagement in a back and forth movement between (*a*) hypothesis-forming models and societal domains and domain-specific ideal types that assist the identification and conceptualization of empirical problems, cases, and developments in theoretical terms, and (*b*) the empirical reality under investigation.

However, these theoretical frameworks serve a further indispensable purpose. The very *pluralism* of hypothesis-forming models and societal domains in Weber's comparative-historical sociology precludes the one-sided and narrow consideration of causal questions. It *forces* contemporary sociologists to take cognizance of and explore the relevance, for the specific problem at hand, of an entire spectrum of causal forces. It prevents, for example, the elevation of a single causal force, such as the economy or the state, to the level of analytic priority. Values, in particular, must be incorporated into the research process in regard to both the theoretical framing of the case or development and its empirical exploration.

Weber is particularly concerned about the fate of cultural factors. Even in his day he saw the temptation for sociologists to focus, simply for reasons of practicality, exclusively upon structural, demographic, and economic forces. This temptation has today become even more difficult to resist, if only as a consequence of the ready availability of massive structural, demographic, and economic data and the ease of data manipulation through statistical methods and computer technology. Weber's entire sociology can be seen today as an attempt "to keep culture in," both at the analytical and empirical levels, and to acknowledge its interwovenness with, in particular, economic and rulership forces. Indeed, the urgency of this task becomes greater to the degree that, as a consequence of modern satellite technologies and continuous intercultural contact, the planet on which we live becomes smaller. Weber's comparative-historical sociology, especially in light of its universal range and emphasis upon the interpretive understanding of subjective meaning, offers the appropriate procedures and strategies to lead the way in the twenty-first century.

This remains the case even though many of the societal domains, domain-specific ideal types, and models defined and utilized by Weber may not be fully appropriate for contemporary research. The content, for example, of certain ideal types in *E&S* – such as the family, the neighborhood, the bureaucracy – will best be defined somewhat differently today. Yet the rigorous and coherent strategies and procedures of Weber's substantive texts should be retained and applied. In light of the new horizons it is now obliged to confront, sociology will benefit from doing so.

References

Abbott, Andrew. 1983. "Sequences of Social Events." *Historical Methods*, 16, 4: 129–47.
——. 1984. "Event Sequence and Event Duration: Colligation and Measurement." *Historical Methods*, 17, 4: 192–203.
——. 1988. "Transcending Linear Reality." *Sociological Theory*, 6, 2: 169–86.
——. 1989. "A Primer on Sequence Methods." *Organization Science*, 1, 4: 1–18.
—— and John Forrest. 1986. "Optimal Matching Methods for Historical Sequences." *Journal of Interdisciplinary History*, XVI, 3: 471–94.
Abramowski, Günter. 1966. *Das Geschichtsbild Max Webers*. Stuttgart: Klett Verlag.
Albrow, Martin. 1990. *Max Weber's Construction of Social Theory*. New York: St Martin's Press.
Alexander, Jeffrey. 1983. *The Classical Attempt at Theoretical Synthesis: Max Weber*. Berkeley: University of California Press.
—— Bernhard Giesen, Richard Münch and Neil J. Smelser, eds. 1987. *The Micro–Macro Link*. Berkeley: University of California Press.
Almond, Gabriel A. and James S. Coleman, eds. 1960. *The Politics of Developing Areas*. Princeton: Princeton University Press.
—— and Bingham Powell, Jr. 1966. *Comparative Politics: a Developmental Approach*. Boston: Little, Brown.
Aminzade, Ronald. 1981. *Class, Politics and Early Industrial Capitalism: a Study of Mid-Nineteenth Century Toulouse, France*. Albany: SUNY Press.
Antonio, Robert J. 1984. "Weber vs. Parsons: Domination or Technocratic Model of Social Organization." Pp. 155–74 in *Max Weber's Political Sociology*, ed. by Ronald M. Glassman and Vatro Murvar. New York: Greenwood Press.
Baier, Horst. 1969. *Von der Erkenntnistheorie zur Wirklichkeitswissenschaft*. Unpublished *Habilitation*: University of Münster.
Beetham, David. 1974. *Max Weber and the Theory of Modern Politics*. London: Allen & Unwin.
Bellah, Robert, Richard Marsden, William Sullivan, Ann Swidler, and Steven Tipton. 1985. *Habits of the Heart*. Berkeley: University of California Press.
Bendix, Reinhard. 1962. *Max Weber: an Intellectual Portrait*. New York: Doubleday Anchor.
——. 1965. "Max Weber's Sociology Today." *International Social Science Journal*, XVII, 1: 9–22.

——. 1968. "Introduction." Pp. 2–13 in *State and Society*, ed. Reinhard Bendix. Berkeley: University of California Press.

——. 1970. "Concepts and Generalizations in Comparative Sociological Studies." Pp. 175–87 in *Embattled Reason*. New York: Oxford University Press.

——. 1974. *Work and Authority in Industry*. Berkeley: University of California Press.

——. 1976. "The Mandate to Rule: an Introduction." *Social Forces*, 55, 2: 242–56.

——. 1977a. *Nation-Building and Citizenship*, enlarged ed. Berkeley: University of California Press.

——. 1977b. "Tradition and Modernity Reconsidered." Pp. 361–433 in *Nation-Building and Citizenship*, enlarged ed. Berkeley: University of California Press.

——. 1978. *Kings or Peoples*. Berkeley: University of California Press.

——. 1984. *Force, Fate, and Freedom*. Berkeley: University of California Press.

—— and Bennett Berger. 1970. "Images of Society and Problems of Concept Formation in Sociology." Pp. 116–38 in Bendix, *Embattled Reason*. New York: Oxford University Press.

—— and Guenther Roth. 1971. *Scholarship and Partisanship*. Berkeley: University of California Press.

Bergesen, Albert, ed. 1983. *Crises in the World System*. Beverly Hills: Sage.

Bonnell, Victoria E. 1980. "The Uses of Theory, Concepts & Comparison in Historical Sociology." *Comparative Studies in Society & History*, 22, 2: 156–173.

——. 1983. *Roots of Rebellion: Workers' Politics and Organizations in St Petersberg and Moscow, 1900–1914*. Berkeley: University of California Press.

Brenner, Robert. 1976. "Agrarian Class Structure and Economic Development in Pre-Industrial Europe." *Past and Present*, 70, 1: 30–75.

Brubaker, Rogers. 1984. *The Limits of Rationality*. London: Allen & Unwin.

Bruun, H. H. 1972. *Science, Values and Politics in Max Weber's Methodology*. Copenhagen: Munksgaard.

Bücher, Carl. 1894. *Die Entstehung der Volkswirtschaftlehre*. Tübingen: Mohr (translated in 1907 by S. M. Wickett as *Industrial Evolution*. New York: Holt).

Burawoy, Michael. 1989. "Two Methods in Search of Science: Skocpol versus Trotsky." *Theory and Society*, 18: 759–805.

Burger, Thomas. 1976. *Max Weber's Theory of Concept Formation*. Durham, NC: Duke University Press.

Buxton, William. 1985. *Talcott Parsons and the Capitalist Nation-State*. Toronto: University of Toronto Press.

Calhoun, Craig. 1982. *The Question of Class Struggle*. Chicago: University of Chicago Press.

Chase-Dunn, Christopher. 1989. *Global Formation: Structures of the World Economy*. Cambridge, MA: Blackwell.

Cohen, Jere, Lawrence E. Hazelrigg, and Whitney Pope. 1975. "De-Parsonizing Weber." *American Sociological Review*, 40, 2: 229–41.

Coleman, James. 1990. *Foundations of Social Theory*. Cambridge, MA: Harvard University Press.

Collins, Randall. 1968. "A Comparative Approach to Political Sociology." Pp. 42–68 in *State and Society*, ed. Reinhard Bendix. Berkeley: University of California Press.

——. 1975. *Conflict Sociology*. New York: Academic Press.

——. 1981. "Weber's Last Theory of Capitalism: a Systematization." *American Sociological Review*, 45, 6: 925–42.

——. 1986a. *Max Weber: a Skeleton Key*. Beverly Hills: Sage.

——. 1986b. *Weberian Sociological Theory*. London: Cambridge University Press.

Cook, Karen, ed. 1990. *The Limits of Rationality*. Chicago: University of Chicago Press.

Coser, Lewis A. 1971. *Masters of Sociological Thought*. New York: Harcourt Brace Jovanovich.

——. 1975. "Two Methods in Search of a Substance." *American Sociological Review*, 40, 6: 691–700.

Downing, Brian. 1988. "Constitutionalism, Warfare, and Political Change in Early Modern Europe." *Theory and Society*, 17, 7: 7–56.

Dumont, Louis. 1980. *Homo Hierarchicus*. Chicago: University of Chicago Press.

Eisenstadt, S. N. 1963. *The Political Systems of Empires*. New York: Free Press.

——. 1968a. "Introduction." Pp. ix–lvi in *Max Weber on Charisma and Institution Building*, ed. S. N. Eisenstadt. Chicago: University of Chicago Press.

——, ed. 1968b. *The Protestant Ethic and Modernization*. New York: Basic Books.

——. 1981. "The Format of Jewish History – Some Reflections on Weber's 'Ancient Judaism.'" *Modern Judaism*, 1, 1 (May): 54–73; 1, 2 (Sept.): 217–234.

Freund, Julien. 1969. *The Sociology of Max Weber*. New York: Vintage Books.

Friedman, Debra and Michael Hechter. 1988. "The Contribution of Rational Choice Theory to Macrosociological Research." *Sociological Theory*, 6, 2: 201–18.

——. 1990. "The Comparative Advantages of Rational Choice Theory." Pp. 214–29 in *Frontiers of Social Theory*, ed. George Ritzer. New York: Columbia University Press.

Fulbrook, Mary. 1978. "Max Weber's 'Interpretive Sociology': a Comparison of Conception and Practice." *British Journal of Sociology*, 29, 1: 71–82.

——. 1983. *Religion and the Rise of Absolutism in England, Württemberg, and Prussia*. New York: Cambridge University Press.

Geertz, Clifford. 1971. *Islam Observed*. Chicago: University of Chicago Press.

Gerth, H. H. 1946. "Introduction." Pp. 3–74 in *From Max Weber*, ed. H. H. Gerth and C. Wright Mills. New York: Oxford.

Girndt, Helmut. 1967. *Das soziale Handeln als Grundkategorie Erfahrungs-swissenschaftlicher Soziologie*. Tübingen: Mohr.

Glassman, Ronald and Vatro Murvar, eds. 1983. *Max Weber's Political Sociology: a Pessimistic Vision of a Rationalized World*. Westport, CT: Greenwood Press.

Goldfrank, Walter, ed. 1979. *The World-System of Capitalism: Past and Present*. Beverly Hills: Sage.

Goldman, Harvey. 1988. *Max Weber and Thomas Mann*. Berkeley: University of California Press.

Goldstone, Jack. 1983. "Capitalist Origins of the English Revolution: Chasing a Chimera." *Theory and Society*, 12: 143–80.

——. 1987. "Cultural Orthodoxy, Risk and Innovation: the Divergence of East and West in the Early Modern World." *Sociological Theory*, 5, 2: 119–35.

——. 1991. *Revolution and Rebellion in the Early Modern World*. Berkeley: University of California Press.

Green, Martin. 1974. *The von Richthofen Sisters*. New York: Basic Books.

Green, Robert W., ed. 1973. *Protestantism, Capitalism, and Social Science: the Weber Thesis Controversy*. Lexington, MA: D. C. Heath & Co.

Gurr, Ted Robert. 1970. *Why Men Rebel*. Princeton: Princeton University Press.

Habermas, Jürgen. 1979. "History and Evolution." *Telos*, 39: 5–44.

——. 1984. *The Theory of Communicative Action*, vol. I. Translated by Thomas McCarthy. Boston: Beacon Press. 1991, Cambridge, UK: Polity Press.

Hamilton, Gary G. 1977. "Chinese Consumption of Foreign Commodities: a Comparative Perspective." *American Sociological Review*, 42, 6: 877–91.

Hechter, Michael. 1987. *Principles of Group Solidarity*. Berkeley: University of California Press.

Hennis, Wilhelm. 1983. "Max Weber's 'Central Question.'" *Economy and Society*, 12, 2: 136–80.

——. 1987a. *Max Weber: Essays in Reconstruction*. London: Allen & Unwin.

——. 1987b. "Personality and Life Orders: Max Weber's Theme." Pp. 52–74 in *Max Weber, Rationality and Modernity*, ed. Sam Whimster and Scott Lash. London: Allen & Unwin.

Henrich, Dieter. 1952. *Die Einheit der Wissenschaftslehre Max Webers*. Tübingen: Mohr.

Holton, R. J. 1985. *The Transition from Feudalism to Capitalism*. New York: St Martin's Press.

Honigsheim, Paul. 1968. *On Max Weber*. Translated by Joan Rytina. New York: Free Press.

Hopkins, Terence K. and Immanuel Wallerstein. 1982. *World-Systems Analysis: Theory and Methodology*. Beverly Hills: Sage.

—— and Immanuel Wallerstein, eds. 1980. *Processes of the World System*. Beverly Hills, CA: Sage.

Hoselitz, Bert F. 1960. *Sociological Aspects of Economic Growth*. New York: Free Press.

—— and Wilbert E. Moore, eds. 1963. *Industrialization and Society*. The Hague: Mouton.

Huber, Joan, ed. 1991. *Micro-Macro Linkages in Sociology*. Newbury Park, CA: Sage.

Hughes, H. Stuart. 1958. *Consciousness and Society*. New York: Vintage Books.

Ibaraki, Takeji. 1982. "Die Bedeutung der Rationalisierungskonzeption Max Webers für die Gegenwart." Pp. 31–47 in *Jahrbuch für Anthropologie und Religionsgeschichte*, ed. Alfred Rupp. Saarbrücken: Homo et Religio.

Inkeles, Alex and David Smith. 1974. *Becoming Modern*. Cambridge, MA: Harvard University Press.

Janoska-Bendl, Judith. 1965. *Methodologische Aspekte des Idealtypus*. Berlin: Duncker & Humblot.

Kalberg, Stephen. 1979. "The Search for Thematic Orientations in a Fragmented Oeuvre: the Discussion of Max Weber in Recent German Sociological Literature." *Sociology*, 13, 1: 127–39.

——. 1980. "Max Weber's Types of Rationality: Cornerstones for the Analysis of Rationalization Processes in History." *American Journal of Sociology*, 85, 3: 1145–79.

——. 1983. "Max Weber's Universal-Historical Architectonic of Economically-Oriented Action: a Preliminary Reconstruction." Pp. 253–88 in *Current Perspectives in Social Theory*, ed. Scott G. McNall. Greenwich, CT: JAI Press.

——. 1985a. "The Role of Ideal Interests in Max Weber's Comparative Historical Sociology." Pp. 46–67 in *A Weber–Marx Dialogue*, ed. Robert J. Antonio and Ronald M. Glassman. Lawrence, KS: University Press of Kansas.

——. 1985b. "Max Weber." Pp. 892–6 in *The Social Science Encyclopedia*, ed. Adam Kuper and Jessica Kuper. London: Routledge & Kegan Paul.

——. 1987. "The Origin and Expansion of *Kulturpessimismus*: the Relationship Between Public and Private Spheres in Early Twentieth Century Germany." *Sociological Theory*, 5, 2: 150–64.

———. 1989. "Max Webers historisch-vergleichende Untersuchungen und das 'Webersche Bild der Neuzeit': eine Gegenüberstellung." Pp. 425–44 in *Max Weber heute*, ed. Johannes Weiss. Frankfurt: Suhrkamp.

———. 1990. "The Rationalization of Action in Max Weber's Sociology of Religion." *Sociological Theory*, 8, 1: 58–84.

———. 1991. "The Hidden Link Between Internal Political Culture and Cross-National Perceptions: Divergent Images of the Soviet Union in the United States and the FR of Germany." *Theory, Culture and Society*, 8 (May): 31–56.

———. 1992. "Culture and the Locus of Work in Contemporary Western Germany: A Weberian Configurational Analysis." Pp. 324–65 in *Theory of Culture*, ed. Neil J. Smelser and Richard Münch. Berkeley: University of California Press.

———. 1993a. "Cultural Foundations of Modern Citizenship." Pp. 91–114 in *Citizenship and Social Theory*, ed. Bryan S. Turner. London: Sage.

———. 1993b. "Saloman's Interpretation of Weber." *International Journal of Politics, Culture and Society*, 6, 4: 585–94.

———. Forthcoming a. "Max Weber's Comparative-historical Sociology: a Critique of Recent Approaches and a Reconstruction of His Analysis of the Rise of Confucianism in China.

———. Forthcoming b. "Max Weber's Analysis of the Rise of Monotheism." *British Journal of Sociology*.

———. Forthcoming c. *Max Weber's Sociology of Civilizations*.

Kantowsky, Detlev. 1986. "Die Fehlrezeption von Max Webers Studie über 'Hinduismus und Buddhismus' in Indien: Ursachen und Folgen." Pp. 121–36 in *Max Weber e l'India*. Torino: Pubblicazuioni del Cesmeo.

Käsler, Dirk. 1975. "Max-Weber-Bibliographie." *Kölner Zeitschrift für Soziologie und Sozialpsychologie*, 27, 4: 703–30.

———. 1988. *Max Weber: an Introduction to his Life and Work*. Translated by Philippa Hurd. Chicago: University of Chicago Press.

Kiser, Edgar and Michael Hechter. 1991. "The Role of General Theory in Comparative-historical Sociology." *American Journal of Sociology*, 97, 1: 1–30.

Kocka. Jürgen, ed. 1986. *Max Weber, der Historiker*. Göttingen: Vandenhoeck & Ruprecht.

Levine, Donald N. (1981) 1985. "Rationality and Freedom." Pp. 142–78 in *The Flight from Ambiguity*. Chicago: University of Chicago Press.

Levy, Marion J. 1966. *Modernization and the Structure of Societies*. Princeton: Princeton University Press.

Mann, Michael. 1986. *The Sources of Power*, vol. I. New York: Cambridge University Press.

Marshall, Gordon. 1980. *Presbyteries and Profits: Calvinism and the Development of Capitalism in Scotland*. Oxford: Clarendon Press.

Mill, John Stuart. (1843) 1950. *Philosophy of Scientific Method*, ed. Ernest Nadel. New York: Hafner.

Mitzman, Arthur. 1970. *The Iron Cage*. New York: Knopf.

Molloy, Stephen. 1980. "Max Weber and the Religions of China." *British Journal of Sociology*, XXXI, 3: 377–400.

Mommsen, Wolfgang J. 1974a. *The Age of Bureaucracy*. Oxford: Blackwell.

———. 1974b. *Max Weber: Gesellschaft, Politik und Geschichte*. Frankfurt: Suhrkamp.

———. 1985. *Max Weber and German Politics, 1890–1920*. Chicago: University of Chicago Press.

———. 1987. "Personal Conduct and Societal Change." Pp. 35–51 in *Max Weber, Rationality and Modernity*, ed. Sam Whimster and Scott Lash. London: Allen &

Unwin.

——. 1989. *The Political and Social Theory of Max Weber*. Chicago: University of Chicago Press, Cambridge, UK: Polity Press.

—— and Jürgen Osterhammel, eds. 1987. *Max Weber and his Contemporaries*. Boston: Unwin Hyman.

Moore, Barrington. 1966. *The Social Origins of Dictatorship and Democracy*. Boston: Beacon Press.

Münch, Richard. 1982. *Theorie des Handelns*. Frankfurt: Suhrkamp.

——. 1984. *Die Struktur der Moderne*. Frankfurt: Suhrkamp.

——. 1986. *Die Kultur der Moderne* (two vols). Frankfurt: Suhrkamp.

Murvar, Vatro. 1983. *Max Weber Today: Selected Bibliography*. Brookfield, WI: Max Weber Colloquia at the University of Wisconsin-Madison.

Nelson, Benjamin. 1949. *The Idea of Usury*. Chicago: University of Chicago Press.

——. (1965) 1970. "Weber's Legacy." Pp. 99–100 in *Max Weber*, ed. Dennis Wrong. Englewood Cliffs, NJ: Prentice-Hall.

——. 1974. "Max Weber's 'Author's Introduction' (1920): a Master Clue to His Main Aims." *Sociological Inquiry*, 44, 4: 269–78.

——. 1981. *On the Roads to Modernity*, ed. Toby E. Huff. Totowa, NJ: Rowman & Littlefield.

Nichols, Elizabeth. 1986. "Skocpol on Revolution: Comparative Analysis vs. Historical Conjuncture." *Comparative Social Research*, 9: 163–86.

Oakes, Guy. 1977. "The Verstehen Thesis and the Foundations of Max Weber's Methodology." *History and Theory*, XVI, 1: 11–29.

——. 1989. *Weber and Rickert*. Cambridge, MA: MIT Press.

Paige, Jeffery M. 1975. *Agrarian Revolution*. New York: Free Press.

Parsons, Talcott. (1937) 1949. *The Structure of Social Action*. New York: Free Press.

——. 1963. "Introduction." Pp. xix–lxvii in Max Weber, *The Sociology of Religion*. Translated by Ephraim Fischoff. Boston: Beacon Press.

——. 1966. *Societies: Evolutionary and Comparative Perspectives*. Englewood Cliffs, NJ: Prentice-Hall.

——. 1971. *The Evolution of Societies*, ed. and with an introduction by Jackson Toby. Englewood Cliffs, NJ: Prentice-Hall.

Poggi, Gianfranco. 1983. *Calvinism and the Capitalist Spirit: Max Weber's Protestant Ethic*. Amherst: University of Massachusetts Press.

Ragin, Charles. 1987. *The Comparative Method*. Berkeley: University of California Press.

—— and Daniel Chirot. 1984. "The World-System of Immanuel Wallerstein: Sociology and Politics as History." Pp. 276–312 in *Vision and Method in Historical Sociology*, ed. Theda Skocpol. New York: Cambridge University Press.

—— and David Zaret. 1983. "Theory and Method in Comparative Research: Two Strategies." *Social Forces*, 61, 3: 731–54.

Rex, John. 1971. "Typology and Objectivity: a Comment on Weber's Four Sociological Methods." Pp. 17–36 in *Max Weber and Modern Sociology*, ed. Arun Sahay. London: Routledge.

Rheinstein, Max. 1954. "Introduction." Pp. iii–xxv in *Max Weber on Law in Economy and Society*. Translated by Edward Shils and Max Rheinstein. Cambridge, MA: Harvard University Press.

Riesebrodt, Martin. 1980. "Ideen, Interessen, Rationalisierung." *Kölner Zeitschrift für Soziologie und Sozialpsychologie*, 32, 1: 111–29.

Ringer, Fritz. 1969. *The Decline of the German Mandarins*. Cambridge MA: Harvard University Press.

Rösel, Jakob. 1986. "The Link Between Rebirth and Caste Society: Some Questions on Weber's Model of Hinduism." Pp. 147–60 in *Max Weber e l'India*. Torino: Pubblicazuioni del Cesmeo.

Roth, Guenther, 1968. "Introduction." Pp. xxvii–ciii in Max Weber, *Economy and Society*, ed. and translated by Guenther Roth and Claus Wittich. New York: Bedminster Press.

——. 1971a. "The Genesis of the Typological Approach." Pp. 253–65 in Reinhard Bendix and Guenther Roth, *Scholarship and Partisanship*. Berkeley: University of California Press.

——. 1971b. "Sociological Typology and Historical Explanation." Pp. 109–28 in Reinhard Bendix and Guenther Roth, *Scholarship and Partisanship*. Berkeley: University of California Press.

——. 1971c. "Max Weber's Comparative Approach and Historical Typology." Pp. 75–93 in *Comparative Methods in Sociology*, ed. Ivan Vallier. Berkeley: University of California Press.

——. 1976. "History and Sociology in the Work of Max Weber." *British Journal of Sociology*, XXVII, 3: 306–18.

——. 1979. "Abschied oder Wiedersehen?" *Kölner Zeitschrift für Soziologie und Sozialpsychologie*, 31: 318–27.

——. 1981. "Introduction." Pp. xv–xxvii in Wolfgang Schluchter, *The Rise of Western Rationalism*. Berkeley: University of California Press.

——. 1987. "Rationalization in Max Weber's Developmental History." Pp. 75–91 in *Max Weber, Rationality and Modernity*, ed. Sam Whimster and Scott Lash. London: Allen & Unwin.

——. 1989. *Politische Herrschaft und persönliche Freiheit*. Frankfurt: Suhrkamp.

—— and Wolfgang Schluchter. 1979. *Max Weber's Vision of History*. Berkeley: University of California Press.

Rubinson, Richard, ed. 1981. *Dynamics of World Development*. Beverly Hills: Sage.

Salomon, Albert. 1934. "Max Weber's Methodology." *Social Research*, I, May: 147–68.

——. 1935a. "Max Weber's Sociology." *Social Research*, II, Feb.: 60–73.

——. 1935b. "Max Weber's Political Ideas." *Social Research*, II, Aug.: 368–84.

——. 1945. "German Sociology." Pp. 586–613 in *Twentieth Century Sociology*, ed. Aaron Gurvitch and Wilbert Moore. New York: The Philosophical Library.

Scaff, Lawrence. 1989. *Fleeing the Iron Cage: Culture, Politics and Modernity in the Thought of Max Weber*. Berkeley: University of California Press.

Schelting, Alexander von. 1922. "Die logische Theorie der historischen Kulturwissenschaft von Max Weber und im besonderen sein Begriff des Idealtypus." *Archiv für Sozialwissenschaft und Sozialpolitik*, 49: 623–752.

——. 1934. *Max Webers Wissenschaftslehre*. Tübingen: Mohr.

Schluchter, Wolfgang. 1979. "The Paradox of Rationalization." Pp. 11–64 in Guenther Roth and Schluchter, *Max Weber's Vision of History*. Berkeley: University of California Press.

——. 1981. *The Rise of Western Rationalism*. Berkeley: University of California Press.

——, ed. 1983. *Max Webers Studie über Konfuzianismus und Taoismus*. Frankfurt: Suhrkamp.

——, ed. 1984. *Max Webers Studie über Hinduismus und Buddhismus*. Frankfurt: Suhrkamp.

——. 1989. *Rationalism, Religion, and Domination: a Weberian Perspective*. Berkeley: University of California Press.

Schmoller, Gustav. 1900, 1904. *Grundriss der Volkswirtschaftslehre* (two vols). Leipzig: Duncker & Humblot.

Schönberg, Gustav, ed. 1882. *Handbuch der Politischen Ökonomie*. Tübingen: Laupp.

Schwartz, Michael. 1976. *Radical Protest and Social Structure*. New York: Academic Press.

Seidman, Steven. 1983. *Liberalism and the Origins of European Social Theory*. Berkeley: University of California Press.

Sewell, William H., Jr. 1985. "Ideologies and Social Revolutions: Reflections on the French Case." *Journal of Modern History*, 57, 1: 57–87.

Seyfarth, Constans and Walter M. Sprondel, eds. 1973. *Seminar: Religion und gesellschaftliche Entwicklung*. Frankfurt: Suhrkamp.

—— and Gert Schmidt. 1982. *Max Weber Bibliographie: eine Dokumentation der Sekundärliteratur*. Stuttgart: Enke Verlag.

Sica, Allen. 1988. *Weber, Irrationality, and Social Order*. Berkeley: University of California Press.

Silber, Ilana Friedrich. 1985. "'Opting Out' in Theravada Buddhism and Medieval Christianity." *Religion*, 15: 251–77.

Skocpol, Theda. 1979. *States and Social Revolutions*. New York: Cambridge University Press.

——. 1982. "Rentier State and Shi'a Islam in the Iranian Revolution." *Theory and Society*, 11: 265–83.

——. 1984a. "Emerging Agendas and Recurrent Strategies in Historical Sociology." Pp. 356–91 in *Vision and Method in Historical Sociology*, ed. Skocpol. Cambridge: Cambridge University Press.

——. 1984b. "Sociology's Historical Imagination." Pp. 1–21 in *Vision and Method in Historical Sociology*, ed. Skocpol. Cambridge: Cambridge University Press.

—— and Margaret Somers. 1980. "The Uses of Comparative History in Macrosociological Inquiry." *Comparative Studies in Society and History*, 22, 2: 174–97.

—— and Margaret Weir. 1984. "State Structures and the Possibilities for Keynesian Responses to the Great Depression in Sweden, Britain, and the United States." Pp. 107–68 in *Bringing the State Back In*, ed. Peter Evans, Theda Skocpol, and Dietrich Rueschemeyer. New York: Cambridge University Press.

Smelser, Neil J. 1959. *Social Change in the Industrial Revolution*. Chicago: University of Chicago Press.

——. 1976. *Comparative Methods in the Social Sciences*. Englewood Cliffs, NJ: Prentice-Hall.

Starr, Paul. 1982. *The Social Transformation of American Medicine*. New York: Basic Books.

Stephens, John D. 1979. *The Transition from Capitalism to Socialism*. Urbana, IL: University of Illinois Press.

Stinchcombe, Arthur. 1978. *Theoretical Methods in Social History*. New York: Academic Press.

Tenbruck, Friedrich. 1959. "Die Genesis der Methodologie Max Webers." *Kölner Zeitschrift für Soziologie und Sozialpsychologie*, 11: 573–630.

——. 1974. "Max Weber and the Sociology of Science: a Case Reopened." *Zeitschrift für Soziologie*, 3: 312–21.

——. 1975. "Wie gut kennen wir Max Weber?" *Zeitschrift für die gesamte Staatswissenschaft*, 131: 719–42.

——. 1977. "Abschied von 'Wirtschaft und Gesellschaft.'" *Zeitschrift für die gesamte*

Staatswissenschaft, 133: 703–36.

——. 1980. "The Problem of Thematic Unity in the Works of Max Weber." *British Journal of Sociology*, XXXI, 3: 316–51. (Originally published in 1975 in *Kölner Zeitschrift für Soziologie und Sozialpsychologie*, 27: 663–702.)

——. 1986. "Das Werk Max Webers: Methodologie und Sozialwissenschaften." *Kölner Zeitschrift für Soziologie und Sozialpsychologie*, 38: 13–31.

——. 1989. "Abschied von der 'Wissenschaftslehre?'" Pp. 90–115 in *Max Weber heute*, ed.Johannes Weiss. Frankfurt: Suhrkamp.

Thompson, E. P. 1966. *The Making of the English Working Class*. New York: Vintage Books.

Tilly, Charles. 1964. *The Vendee*. New York: John Wiley & Sons.

——. 1978. *From Mobilization to Revolution*. Reading, MA: Addison-Wesley.

——. 1981. *As Sociology Meets History*. New York: Academic Press.

——. 1984. *Big Structures, Large Processes, Huge Comparisons*. New York: Russell Sage.

—— and Edward Shorter. 1974. *Strikes in France, 1830–1968*. Cambridge: Cambridge University Press.

——, Louise A. Tilly, and Richard Tilly. 1975. *The Rebellious Century, 1830–1930*. Cambridge, MA: Harvard University Press.

Traugott, Mark. 1985. *Armies of the Poor*. Princeton: Princeton University Press.

Trimberger, Ellen Kay. 1978. *Revolution from Above: Military Bureaucrats and Development in Japan, Turkey, Egypt and Peru*. New Brunswick: Transaction Books.

Truzzi, Marcello. 1974. *Verstehen: Subjective Understanding in the Social Sciences*. Reading, MA: Addison-Wesley.

Turner, Bryan. 1981. *For Weber*. London: Routledge.

Wallerstein, Immanuel. 1974. *The Modern World-System*. New York: Academic Press.

——.1979. *The Capitalist World-Economy*. Cambridge: Cambridge University Press.

——. 1980. *The Modern World System II*. New York: Academic Press.

——. 1984. *The Politics of the World-Economy: the States, the Movements and the Civilizations*. Cambridge: Cambridge University Press.

——. 1989. *The Modern World System III*. New York: Academic Press.

Walliman, Isidor, Howard Rosenbaum, Nicholas Tatsis, and George Zito. 1980. "Misreading Weber: the Concept of 'Macht.'" *Sociology*, 14, 2: 261–75.

Walton, John. 1984. *Reluctant Rebels: Comparative Studies of Revolution and Underdevelopment*. New York: Columbia University Press.

Warner, R. Stephen. 1970. "The Role of Religious Ideas and the Use of Models in Max Weber's Comparative Studies of Non-Capitalist Societies." *Journal of Economic History*, 30: 74–99.

——. 1972. *The Methodology of Max Weber's Comparative Studies*. Unpublished Dissertation: University of California at Berkeley.

——. 1973. "Weber's Sociology of Nonwestern Religions." Pp. 32–52 in *Protestantism, Capitalism, and Social Science: the Weber Thesis Controversy*, ed. Robert W. Green. Lexington, MA: D. C. Heath & Co.

Watkins, J. W. N. 1953. "Ideal Types and Historical Explanation." Pp. 723–43 in *Readings in the Philosophy of Science*. New York: Appleton-Century-Crofts.

Weber, Marianne (1926) 1975. *Max Weber: a Biography*. Translated by Harry Zohn. New York: John Wiley & Sons, Inc.

Weber, Max [see "Abbreviations"]

——. (1889) 1970. *Handelsgesellschaften im Mittelalter.* Amsterdam: E. J. Bonset.

——. (1891) 1966. *Die Römische Agrargeschichte in Ihrer Bedeutung für das Staats- und Privatrecht.* Amsterdam: Verlag P. Schippers N.V.

——. (1905) 1978. "The Prospects for Liberal Democracy in Tsarist Democracy." Pp. 269–84 in *Weber: Selections in Translation*, ed. W. G. Runciman and translated by Eric Matthews. London: Cambridge University Press. (Originally published 1971. "Zur Lage der bürgerlichen Demokratie in Russland." Pp. 33–68 in *Gesammelte Politische Schriften*, ed. Johannes Winckelmann. Tübingen: Mohr.)

——. (1906) 1977. *Critique of Stammler.* Translated by Guy Oakes. New York: Free Press.

——. (1914) 1925. Letter of June 1914 to Georg von Below. Printed in the introduction to von Below, *Der deutsche Staat des Mittelalters*, 2nd ed. Leipzig: Quelle & Meyer.

——. 1917 (1921, 1946). "National Character and the Junkers." Pp. 387–95 in *From Max Weber*, ed. H. H. Gerth and C. Wright Mills. New York: Oxford.

——. 1924 (1988). *Gesammelte Aufsätze zur Soziologie und Sozialpolitik.* Tübingen: Mohr.

——. 1947. *The Theory of Social and Economic Organization*, ed. T. Parsons. Translated by A. M. Henderson and T. Parsons. New York: Free Press.

Wehler, Hans-Ulrich. 1986. "Max Webers Klassentheorie und die neuere Sozialgeschichte." Pp. 173–92 in *Max Weber, der Historiker*, ed. Jürgen Kocka. Göttingen: Vandenhoeck & Ruprecht.

Weiss, Johannes. 1975. *Max Webers Grundlegung der Soziologie.* München: UTB.

Whimster, Sam. 1980. "The Profession of History in the Work of Max Weber: its Origins and Limitations." *British Journal of Sociology*, XXXI, 3: 353–76.

—— and Scott Lash, eds. 1987. *Max Weber, Rationality and Modernity.* London: Allen & Unwin.

Wiley, Norbert, 1988. "The Micro–Macro Problem in Social Theory." *Sociological Theory*, 6: 254–61.

Winckelmann, Johannes. 1965. "Max Weber – das soziologische Werk." *Kölner Zeitschrift für Soziologie und Sozialpsychologie*, 17, 4: 743–90.

——. 1980. "Die Herkunft von Max Webers 'Entzauberungs-Konzeption.'" *Kölner Zeitschrift für Soziologie und Sozialpsychologie*, 32, 1: 12–53.

——. 1986. *Max Webers hinterlassenes Hauptwerk: die Wirtschaft und die gesellschaftlichen Ordnungen und Mächte.* Tübingen: Mohr.

Zaret, David. 1980. "From Weber to Parsons and Schutz: the Eclipse of History in Modern Social Theory." *American Journal of Sociology*, 85, 3: 1180–201.

Zingerle, Arnold. 1972. *Max Weber und China.* Berlin: Duncker & Humblot.

——. 1981. *Max Webers Historische Soziologie.* Darmstadt: Wissenschaftliche Buchgesellschaft.

Index

Abbott, A. 171
Abramowski, G. 17
adequate causality 145–6, 172, 191,
      200–1, 203
affinity models 93, 102–17, 197
   inter-domain 108–15
age, social prestige of 99
agency-structure linkage 9–10, 203
   modes of patterning action 30–46,
      194–5
   pluralism of motives 23–49
   summary 46–9
Albrow, M. 16
Alexander, J. 2
Almond, G. A. 3
American sociology 3
analogies, Weber's opposition to 83
analytic relationships 102–17, 197
   affinity and antagonism
      models 102–17
analytical level, *see* level of analysis
antagonism models 93, 102–17, 197
   inter-domain 108–15
   intra-domain 106–8
antecedent conditions
   diachronic interactions 163–8;
      inter-domain interactions 165–6;
      intra-domain interactions 164–5
Antonio, R. J. 16
autonomy 54–8, 135

Beetham, D. 16
behaviorism 26n
belief systems 54, 65–8, 195
Bendix, R. 1, 4, 5, 6, 7, 15, 16, 17, 126
Berger, B. 5
Bergesen, A. 4
Bonnell, V. E. 7
Brubaker, R. 17
Bücher, C. 118
Buddhism 60, 69, 72–3
bureaucracy 95–6
   relationship to democracy 95–6
bureaucratic rationalization 34–5
bureaucratic rulership, influence on
      capitalism 101
Burger, T. 16

Calvinism 36–7, 56
   and capitalism 52–3, 60, 63–4
capitalism
   and Calvinism 52–3, 60, 63–4
   influence of bureaucratic rulership
      on 101
caste system, dominance in India
      177–92
causal analysis
   aim of 81–4
   Weber's mode of 12–14, 193,
      199–202; overview and

comparison to recent schools
144–51; reconstructed   143–92
causal analytic school   7–9, 51, 81,
148–9, 191–2, 199–200
causal chain approach, weaknesses of
166–7
causal methodology   143–92, 145–9,
199–201, 202–3
and theoretical framework   151–77
causal sociology   77–8
strategies and procedures   79–192
causality
degrees of   152–5, 167, 171, 179–85
and subjective meaning   143–4
charisma, routinization of   124–6
charismatic rulership and the rational
economy: antagonism   112
Chirot, D.   4
civic strata   42–3
civil servants, relative prestige of
99–100
classes   57, 58, 61, 104, 150, 197
closure
economic relationships   121–2
religion   123–4
rulership organizations   122–3
of social relationships   120–4
Cohen, J.   16
Coleman, J. S.   3, 63
Collins, R.   4, 15, 16, 17
comparative analysis   152–5
comparative-historical sociology:
modern dilemmas and problems
3–9, 144–51, 193–205
competition   75–7
concept formation   85–7, 193
conflict   75–7, 203
Confucianism   56, 58, 65, 172
rise of   175–6
conjunctural interactions   13, 146–7,
168–77, 199–201
and context of patterned action   13,
168–77
example   189–91
context, of patterned action, and
conjunctural interaction   13,
168–77

contextual models, ideal types as   93,
98–102
contextual sociology   39–46, 45–6, 52,
146–7, 194
Cook, K.   63
Coser, L. A.   16, 171
cultural factors   10–11, 204–5

definitions, of empirical cases   87–91
democratization, passive   95–6
determinism   145, 203
developmental models   93, 117–42,
197–8
anchored in interests   120–7
formal, free market and the state
128–35
and rationalization processes
127–40
theoretical, religion   135–40
diachronic interactions of action   146,
147, 152, 158–68
example   187–9
legacies and antecedent conditions
158–68
penetration range   161–3, 200
"disjuncture thesis"   31n
domain-specific ideal types   149–51,
198
domains, see societal domains
Durkheim, E.   25, 171
dynamic models, ideal types as   93, 94,
95–8

economic availability   61–2
Economic Ethics of the World
Religions (Weber)   18, 53
economic interests   34n
economic relationships, closure   121–2
economics, and religion   50, 52
Economy and Society (Weber)   18,
53–5, 73–4, 92–142
Eisenstadt, S. N.   3, 17
elective affinity models   102–3,
109–10
empirical cases, definition of   87–91
ethical rationality   65–7
evolutionism   118–19, 203

external conditions   34–5, 37–8
external motivations   37–8

facilitating orientations of action   146,
   147, 151, 152–5, 199–200
   example   179–80
feudal rulership   44–5, 107
Forrest, J.   171
foundational strategies and procedures
   21–78
free market
   developmental model   128–32
   and the state   128–35
Freund, J.   15
Friedman, D.   63
Fulbrook, M.   16, 17

geography   68–71
Gerth, H. H.   16
Glassman, R.   17
Goldfrank, W.   4
Goldman, H.   16
Green, M.   16

Habermas, J.   17
Hazelrigg, L. E.   16
Hechter, M.   63
Hegel, G. W. F.   25
Hennis, W.   15, 17
Hinduism   56, 58, 60, 72, 180, 181,
   182–5, 190
historical events   68–71
historical individual   81–3
historical materialism   57
Hopkins, T. K.   4
Hoselitz, B. F.   3
households
   legacies   161
   universal organizations   43–4
Hughes, H. S.   16
hypothesis-forming models   91,
   92–142, 196–9

ideal types   30, 81–91, 196
   as contextual models   93, 98–102
   domain-specific   149–51, 198
   as dynamic models   93, 94, 95–8
   formation and major features   84–7

as hypothesis-forming models
   92–142, 196–9
   yardstick usage   87–91, 196
India
   dominance of caste system   177–92
   rise of impersonal view of
      supernatural   174
intellectuals, cognitive need of   127,
   135, 136–40
intensity of action, variable   51, 62–8,
   195, 202
interactive influences   13, 146–7,
   168–78, 200–1
interests   32–4, 199
   developmental models anchored in
      120–7
   economic   34n
   ideal and material   50
internal motivations   36–9
interpretive historical school   5–7,
   50–1, 81, 148, 191, 196, 199
Islam   60

Judaism   60

Kalberg, S.   18, 23, 27, 64, 67, 69, 112,
   130, 139, 157
Käsler, D.   15, 16
Kiser, E.   63

Lash, S.   2, 17
law
   antagonistic relationships   107
   antecedent conditions   165
   impact of   99
   legacies in   160–1
legacies
   diachronic interactions   159–64,
      200; inter-domain interactions
      161–2, 200; intra-domain
      interactions   160–1, 200; prevent
      action   163
legitimate orders   35–9, 194
level of analysis   11–12
   ideal types   81–91
Levine, D. N.   17
Levy, M. J.   3

logical interactions, *see* analytic
   relationships

Mann, M. 7
market economy 128–32
Marx, K. 25, 85
Marxism 1, 54, 57n, 66
Menschentyp 17, 37
methodological individualism 24–5,
   63, 194, 203
Mill, J. S. 7, 8, 148
Mitzman, A. 16
model building 12, 92–142, 198
modernization studies 3
Molloy, S. 16
Mommsen, W. J. 16, 17, 19, 85
monopolies 101
monopolization of opportunities
   120–4
monotheism, rise of 172–4
Moore, B. 1, 3, 7, 8, 9, 10, 51
motives, pluralism of 27–9
multicausality 10–11, 50–78, 191–2,
   195, 202
   principled commitment to 52–8,
     199–200
Münch, R. 17
Murvar, V. 17

necessary orientations of action 146,
   147, 151, 152–5, 200
   example 180–5
neighborhood, universal organization
   44
neighborhood ethic, legacies 162
Nelson, B. 17, 113

Oakes, G. 16
orders 32–5, 194
   upheld by custom 32
   upheld by self-interest 32–4
organizations, as social carriers 58
Osterhammel, J. 16

Parsons, T. 3–4, 85, 203
patrimonialism 96–8
pluralism 54, 62, 84–5, 204
   of motives 23–49, 27–9, 194

Pope, W. 16
positivism 82
Powell Jr., B. 3
power 71–4
   of command 73, 74
   from possession 73–4
*Protestant Ethic and the Spirit of
   Capitalism, The* (Weber) 52–3,
   143–4

Ragin, C. 2, 4
rational choice theory, opposition to
   62–8
rational economy, and charismatic
   rulership, antagonism 112
rational intellectualism, and religion
   136–40
rationalization models
   formal 127–35, 198
   theoretical 135–40, 198
rationalization processes 17
   developmental models anchored in
     127–40
reification 27, 38
religion
   antecedent conditions 164
   closure 123–4
   developmental model 135–40
   and economics 50, 52
   legacies in 160
   and rulership, synchronic
     interaction 155–6
   and status groups 108–12
   and universal organizations,
     synchronic interaction 155–6
religious ethic, and status ethic
   59–60, 87–8, 156
Ringer, F. 16
Roth, G. 2, 17, 90
routinization of charisma 124–7
Rubinson, R. 4
rulership 71–2
   antagonistic relationships 106–7
   antecedent conditions 165
   legitimization of 56
   and religion, synchronic interaction
     155–6

rulership (*cont'd*)
  types of 51
rulership organizations
  closure 122–3
  legacies 161

Salomon, A. 15, 19, 85, 93
Scaff, L. 16
Schluchter, W. 2, 17, 90
Schmoller, G. 118
Schönberg, G. 118
secondary literature 15–19
sects 59
Seidman, S. 16
Sica, A. 16
Skocpol, T. 1, 2, 4, 7, 7–9, 10, 51, 148
Smelser, N. J. 4, 17
social action 24
  affectual 26
  four types 26–7, 194, 203
  means-end rational 26
  traditional 26
  value-rational 26
social carriers 51–2, 57–8, 58–62,
    195–6, 202
social relationships, closure of 120–4
societal domains 53–4, 149–51, 199
  developmental aspects 75–7
  and relationships of affinity and
    antagonism 103–5
  and synchronic and diachronic
    interactions of action 155–68
sociological loci 39–46, 58–9, 194
sociology, Weber's goal for 145
Somers, M. 2
state
  developmental model 132–5
  and free market 128–35
status ethic, and religious ethic
    59–60, 156
status groups 58, 61
  and religion 108–12
  and status ethic 122
  warriors and civic strata 41–3
stratification principles, and social
    context 100
structural functionalism 3–4, 159

structuralism, Weber's 23–49, 149,
    194
structure, *see* agency-structure linkage
subjective meaning 24–5, 48–9,
    143–4, 145, 194, 205
  and variable intensity 63, 202
supernatural, in India, rise of
    impersonal view 174
Symbolic Interactionism 48n
synchronic interactions 146, 147, 152,
    155–9
  example 186–7
  penetration range 157–8, 200

technology 68–71
Tenbruck, F. 2, 15, 16, 17, 90
theoretical framework 13, 143–92,
    197, 198, 200, 204
  and causal methodology 151–77
  domains and domain-specific ideal
    types 149–51, 202
Tilly, C. 1, 4, 6, 7, 10, 50–1, 77
Tilly, L. A. 7
Tilly, R. T. 7

universal organizations
  antecedent conditions 165–6
  household and neighborhood 43–4
  relations to the economy and
    religion 112–14
  and religion, synchronic interaction
    155–6

value rationalization 64–7
value-relevance 10, 85, 195, 203,
    204–5
values, and antagonistic relationships
    107–8
Verstehen 24, 25, 48–9, 81, 143, 145,
    194, 203

Wallerstein, I. 1, 4
Warner, R. S. 17
warriors 41–2
ways of life 53, 56
Weber, Marianne 16

Weir, M.   7
Western rationalism   17
Whimster, S.   2, 17
Winckelmann, J.   2

world systems school   4–5, 51, 81, 147, 191, 200

Zaret, D.   2, 85